History's Vanquished Goddess
ASHERAH

History's Vanquished Goddess
ASHERAH

I. Primary Evidence. Archaeological & Historical Aspects of
Syro-Palestinian Pre-Biblical Religious Traditions,
Macrocosmically Examined

Darlene Kosnik

Emergent Press llc

History's Vanquished Goddess:
ASHERAH

www.GodsWifeAsherah.com
www.VanquishedGoddessAsherah.com

ISBN 978-0-9856095-7-3

Library of Congress Control Number: 2012948476
Library of Congress Subject Headings:
Religion/Antiquities & Archaeology
Religion/History
Religion/Sexuality & Gender Studies
Social Science/Women's Studies
Asherah (Semitic deity)
Mother Goddesses – Palestine/Israel
Excavations (Archaeology) – Palestine/Israel
I. Title

www.EmergentPressllc.com

to Truth Seekers

It's about
truth . . .

it's about
time.

Archaeology provides a historical bridge, enabling the past
to educate the present and empower the future.

"We will burn incense to the *Queen of Heaven* and will pour out drink offerings to her just as we and our fathers, our kings and our officials did in the towns of Judah and in the streets of Jerusalem. At that time we had plenty of food and were well off and suffered no harm. But ever since we stopped burning incense to the *Queen of Heaven* and pouring out drink offerings to her, we have had nothing and have been perishing by sword and famine."

Jeremiah 44:17-18, *NIV Topical Study Bible*
(Buursma 1989:861)

Although Israel's God was abstract, he may also have had a wife/consort.

Biblical Archaeology Review
(Taylor 1994:53)

Archaeologists, at some of the Holy Land's oldest shrines, are uncovering "tantalizing clues that God was not alone . . . that Yahweh may have had a companion . . . and her name was Asherah."

The Forbidden Goddess
(Rhys-Davies 1993)

Although "virtually expunged from the texts of the Hebrew Bible, and all but forgotten by rabbinical times," worship of the goddess Asherah "never died out, but enjoyed a vigorous life throughout the Monarchy."

What Did the Biblical Writers Know and When Did They Know It?
What Archaeology Can Tell Us about the Reality of Ancient Israel
(Dever 2001:97)

The Canaanites worshipped a goddess known as Asherah, Astarte, and Ashtoreth. Their condemnations throughout the bible attests "that these earlier gods were [worshipped as] queens of heaven."

In Search of the Lost Feminine
(Barnes 2006:187)

Although biblical evidence contends that ancient Israelite religion was essentially monotheistic, "critical discussions of the relevant biblical texts as well as extrabiblical evidence call this into question."

Religions of the Ancient World
(Johnston 2004:402)

CONTENTS

Content Formats

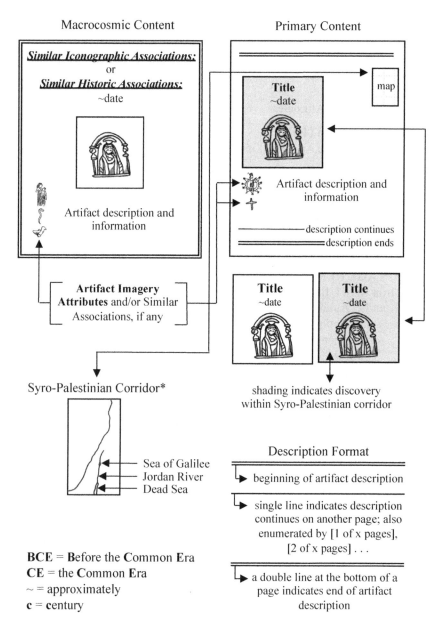

Macrocosmic Content

Primary Content

Similar Iconographic Associations:
or
Similar Historic Associations:
~date

Artifact description and information

Title
~date

map

Artifact description and information

description continues
description ends

Artifact Imagery Attributes and/or Similar Associations, if any

Title
~date

Title
~date

Syro-Palestinian Corridor*

shading indicates discovery within Syro-Palestinian corridor

Sea of Galilee
Jordan River
Dead Sea

Description Format

beginning of artifact description

single line indicates description continues on another page; also enumerated by [1 of x pages], [2 of x pages] . . .

BCE = **B**efore the **C**ommon **E**ra
CE = the **C**ommon **E**ra
~ = approximately
c = **c**entury

a double line at the bottom of a page indicates end of artifact description

Drawings by author unless otherwise noted.
*One sector of the Axis of Discovery resurrecting Women's History.

Artifact Imagery Attributes
[page 1 of 2 pages]

 Snake/ Serpent Goddess

 Tree Goddess

 Naked Female/ Goddess

 Nursing Mother/ Nutritive Life Force

 Water Goddess/ Sea Association

 Water of Life Goddess

 Goddess of the Staff or Mountain

 Goddess of the Steppe

 Sea Goddess

 Vegetative Earth Goddess

 Winged Goddess

 Mistress of Animals

 Queen of Heaven/ Stellar Association

 Prosperity/ Fecundity Goddess

 Hands Encircling/ Proffering Breasts

 Lion & Goddess Association

 Warrior Goddess

 Branch Goddess

 Goddess & King/God

 Breast Emphasis

 Emblematic Hairstyle of Goddess Hathor

 Qdš Stance on Lion

 Qdš Stance w/o Lion

 Pillar Figurine

 Animal Mother Goddess

 Symbol of Goddess Tanit

 Trinity

 Lunar Association

 Pubic Triangle

 Sacred Tree

 ~ Female Imagery and the Bountiful Earth ~

Artifact Imagery Attributes

Snake/ Serpent Association	Lion Association	Menorahic* Tree Association
Bovine & Female Association	Bovine Ears	Omega Symbol/ Womb Reference
Shrine/ Temple	Crown	Horned Crown
Sacred Tree Flanked by Animals	Astral Star of Venus	Cross Symbolism
Isis/ Minoan Knot	Goddess Inanna Temple Gatepost	Sistrum
Goddess & Dove/Bird Association	Egyptian Ankh	Horned Altar
Worshipper	Swastika	Ibex/Caprid
Pomegranate Association	Rosette of Goddess Inanna	Chalice
Shepherd	Fish/Sea Association	Scorpion

*According to the *Journal for the Study of the Old Testament,* recent archeological discoveries suggest the menorah may have been designed with the usual form of the cultic symbol of the goddess Asherah, an *asherah* – "firmly in mind" (Taylor 1995:29).

INTRODUCTION

In the past hundred years, Egyptian and Near Eastern archaeological discoveries have unveiled "a spiritual and cultural heritage undreamed of by earlier generations."

History Begins at Sumer: Thirty-Nine Firsts in Recorded History
(Kramer 1981:141)

In the beginning was the image . . .

Before the written word, and before the spoken word, the people of antiquity expressed themselves through their images.*

Thoughts frozen in time, ancient images are expressions of personal, social and religious history.

Windows into the past, images of antiquity disclose the divinities that inspired our ancestors and shaped our heritage; they are reflections of social and religious history, and, many are female.

The thousands of unearthed, Syro-Palestinian female images reveal a time of goddess worship, where Asherah, Anat, Astarte and Ashtaroth were the principal goddesses worshipped (James 1994:69).

The primary focus of this book is to chronicle the lost story of the Hebrew Mother Goddess Asherah.

Mentioned over 40 times in the Hebrew bible, Asherah is identified as Yahweh's primary** wife and is the only surviving goddess in Palestine by the end of the 7th and 6th centuries BCE (Keel 1998b:38).

Asherah's forgotten history unfolds on the following pages as the shovels of archaeology resurrect what the pens of history forgot.

---

*Similar images, as a universal form of socio-religious expression, are found in various cultures – at times, thousands of years and thousands of miles apart. Expanding upon this phenomenon, the secondary focus of this book is a macrocosmic introduction to some of these inclusive motifs elucidated by ***Similar Iconographic Associations*** and ***Similar Historic Associations***.

**Although a troubling notion to some, the archaeological evidence demonstrates that Asherah was but one of Yahweh's wives.

Ancient Asherah Representations

FIRST ASSOCIATIONS

I. Prehistory to Late Bronze Age   Pre-1550 BCE

From the time of their first settlements, the ancient Israelites worshipped the goddess Ashtaroth/Asherah (Judges 2:13; 10:6). Her worship was prevalent through the time of Samuel (1 Samuel 7:3-4; 12:10) and was royally sanctioned by King Solomon (1 Kings 11:5; 2 Kings 23:13). After the Philistines killed King Saul, his armor was placed in the Beth Shean temple of Ashtaroth/Asherah* (1 Samuel 31:10).

The Illustrated Bible Dictionary
(Douglas 1980:133) *referenced on pages 104-5

Asherah references in this section include:

"Lady of the Desert Plateau"
"Bride of the King of Heaven"
"Lady of Vigor and Joy"
"Lady of the Steppe"
"Mistress of Sexual Vigor and Rejoicing"

Hammurabi Dedication
to Ashratum/Asherah

"Asratum/Asherah
is my Mother"

"Ashtaroth-Karnaim,
Astarte/Asherah of the
Horns"

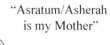

One of the first figurines experts identify as a possible representation of the goddess Ashtoreth/Asherah appears in the Chalcolithic Period:

Ashtoreth*/Asherah as Goddess of Flocks & Milk
~4500-4000 BCE

Seated upon a stool, this multitasking, naked female holds a vessel under her arm while balancing a cheese/butter urn atop her head. Understated legs support her rotund, decoratively painted, torso; indentations and a linear slit define her genitalia.

Discovered within an ancient temple at Gilat, Palestine, according to the *Biblical World in Pictures*, this figurine likely has some form of special symbolic significance. The figurine's discovery location, her exposed pubic area and her butter/cheese urn led the site excavator to conclude this figurine may represent ". . . a form of Ashtoreth[*/Asherah] as the goddess of flocks and milk[**]" (2002).

Extrapolating further, *The Oxford History of the Biblical World* states this figurine was likely used in socio-religious rituals to promote fecundity of flocks and life-sustaining milk production (Coogan 1998:19).

*The goddess Ashtoreth is identified with the goddess Asherah.

**The biblical phrase "*ashtoreth[/Asherah] of your flocks*" (Deuteronomy 7:13, 28:4, 18, 51), equates to "She of the Womb" (Patai 1990:302 n. 24).   Drawing after Epstein 1995:62.

Similar Historic Associations:
Goddess of Flocks & Milk
~1600 BCE

Throughout antiquity depictions of the nursing animal mother personified the fecundity of flocks and life-sustaining milk production of the Great Mother Goddess.

Discovered within Knossos, Crete's palace temple repositories, this ivory plaque depicts the Goddess as Animal Mother (Hawkes 1968:101).   Drawing after Ibid.

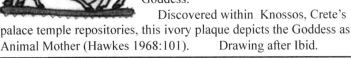

Bronze Age Shrine with Asherah-Image
~3200-2000 BCE

Excavations at an Early Bronze Age shrine at Ai uncovered a large post of carbonized wood, which

Post-like Tree

Goddess

may have represented an asherah, the religious symbol of the goddess Asherah.

Although originally identified as a "post," *The Illustrated Bible Dictionary* explains experts have reevaluated their initial interpretation of this wooden artifact and now identify it as an "Asherah-image" (Douglas 1980:131) after the goddess Asherah.

Similar Iconographic Associations:
Stylized Tree Goddess
~1400-1300 BCE

Discovered within a Mycenaean temple, this figurine depicts a "Goddess holding her breasts" (Taylor 1983:59). Stylized trees are painted on the sides and front of her garment; rosettes decorate her cheeks.

Some experts suggest the tubular shape and flanged base represents a tree trunk, an elemental iconography stylistically similar to Syro-Palestine's Iron Age pillar figurines.   Drawing after Ibid.

Sacred Tree

Goddess

Symbol of the Goddess Asherah is the Asherah/Sacred Tree

Over 70 years ago scholars identified sacred trees as a symbol of the goddess Asherah. Writing in a *Journal of the American Oriental Society* article entitled "The Sacred Tree on Palestine Painted Pottery," author Herbert G. May states "We need not stress the point that the Asherah was a sacred tree, symbol of the goddess, probably represented with the branches lopped off" (1939:251-9).

Tree Goddesses of Antiquity

**Receiving Goddess
Asherah
~2100-1800 BCE**

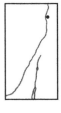

According to experts, this gold-plated, copper* figurine, discovered within a Ugarit palace, may represent the goddess Asherah (Cornelius 2004:32-3).

The goddess wears a crown and a long gown with serpentine, rolled edges; her breasts are bare. Her open right hand is in a receiving or holding position; her left hand once held a staff or scepter.

*This copper purity is 97.95% (Ibid. 109). Drawing after Ibid. Pl. 2.4.

**Goddess Asratum*/
Asherah on Ancient God
List, Temple List, Seal
and Hymn
~2112-2002 BCE**

Worship of the goddess Asratum*/ Asherah is attested to on an ancient Third Dynasty of Ur god-list from Nippur.

Further evidence of her worship is also found on a Babylonian text listing a temple dedicated to her, and on an Old Babylonian cylinder seal inscription bearing her name (Reed 1949:73).

During Grecian times, an Old Babylonian hymn was rewritten where Asratum* "appears as the consort of the god Amurru" and is identified as "the mistress of the plain"** (Ibid.).

*Identified by the Amorites as Asratum/Ashratum, this goddess is the ancestress of the Ugarit goddess Athirat/Atirat and the Canaanite/Hebrew goddess Asherah.

**with two other undeterminable epithets (Ibid.)

**Mother Goddess Asherah is
Primary Wife of Each Head God**

Although first identified as the Mother Goddess and wife of the head god Amurru, as the worship of Asratum/Athirat/Asherah assimilated into neighboring religious systems, Asherah retained her Mother Goddess title and her primary wife status with each subsequent chief male god.

Mother

Goddess

Similar Historic Associations:
Ancient Mother Goddess Nourishes Mankind on Her Breast
~3000 BCE

According to the *Bulletin of the American School of Oriental Research,* ancient Sumerian tablets identify a goddess who "nourish[es] mankind on her breast" (Schmandt-Besserat 1998:13).

Similar Historic Associations:
Quintessential Mother Goddess Isis
~850-650 BCE

Mother

Goddess

The consummate Mother Goddess Isis and her god-son Horus are depicted in a papyri swamp on this bronze, tomb bowl image discovered near Rome.
Drawing after Frankfort 1996:329 Il. 392.

Similar Historic Associations:
Quintessential Mother Goddess of the Universe

The "older, Neolithic and Bronze Age mythologies of the Goddess Mother of the Universe" personified the vital life forces "in whom all things have their being, gods and men, plants, animals and inanimate objects alike, and whose cosmic body itself is the enclosing sphere. . . within which all experience, all knowledge, is enclosed" (Campbell 1968:626).

Asratum/
Asherah
is My
Mother

Similar Historic Associations:
"Ishtar is My Mother"
~1570-1545 BCE

After the Hyksos were driven out of the area, Egyptian records identify one of the captured slaves as *"Ishtar-ummi,"* which translates as the goddess "Ishtar is My Mother" (Pritchard 1969: 233).

**Mother Goddess
Asherah**
~2000-1550 BCE

Dating to the Middle Bronze Age, this figurine was once part of an ancient incense stand discovered at Shechem.

This maternal figure holds a crowned child. The rolled ends of her hair are fashioned in the traditional style of the Egyptian goddess Hathor.

According to *Biblical Archaeologist* author William G. Dever, figurines of this type may be part of the veneration of Asherah, the principal "Mother Goddess," and possibly intended as talismans aiding in "conception, childbirth, and lactation" (1987).

Drawing after Ibid.

Mother

Goddess

**Ancient Titles of
Asratum/Asherah**
~1850-1531 BCE

Written references to the goddess Asratum/Ashratum/Asherah date back to the First Dynasty of Babylon.

Ancient Amorite* tablets indicate Asratum/Ashratum/Asherah was a prominent religious figure. Her titles include:

"Lady of the Desert Plateau" (Finegan 1979:366),

"Bride of the King of Heaven,"

"Lady of Vigor and Joy" (Reed 1949:20),

"Lady[/Mistress] of the Steppe[/Grassy Meadowland]" and

"Mistress of Sexual Vigor and Rejoicing" (Day 1986:386).

*The Amorites founded, and were the first kings of, the city of Urusalem/modern Jerusalem (more on this to follow).

Mistress
of the

Steppe

Ishtar is
My
Mother

**"Asratum[/Asherah] is
my mother"**
~1850-1531 BCE

During the First Dynasty of Babylon, the goddess Asratum/Ashratum/Asherah's name is found on a cuneiform tablet as a component in the personal name "*Asratum-ummi*," which translates as the goddess "Asratum[/Asherah] is my mother" (Day 1986:386).

Mother Goddesses of Antiquity

Ashtoreth/
Asherah

of Egypt

**Ashtaroth*/Asherah
of Gezer**
~1800-1550 BCE

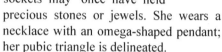

This bronze, naked, female figurine was discovered at Gezer within a special treasure repository (Keel 1998a:33).

Horns extend from her conical headdress; deep-set eye sockets may once have held precious stones or jewels. She wears a necklace with an omega-shaped pendant; her pubic triangle is delineated.

According to Rev. James Stewart in *The Story of the Bible,* this figurine is identified as the biblical "Ashtaroth[*]-Karnnaim, Astarte [/Asherah] of the Horns"** (1952:279).

*The goddess Ashtaroth/Ashtoreth is identified with the goddess Asherah.

**According to *Nelson's Illustrated Encyclopedia of Bible Facts,* "Ashtaroth-Karnaim" translates as "(the goddess) Ashtaroth [/Asherah] of the two horns," where Ashtaroth-Karnaim was "a town of Bashan, [and] the seat of the worship" of the goddess (Packer 1980:698). Drawing after Stewart 1952:279.

Ashtaroth/
Asherah

of Gezer

Similar Historic Associations:
Ashtoreth*/Asherah of Egypt
~1800 BCE

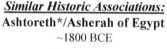

Driving a war chariot, this lion-headed goddess is identified as "Ashtoreth"* by *The Gods of the Egyptian, V. II* (Budge 1969:279).

Ashtoreth's* Egyptian titles include the "Mistress of Horses" and the "Lady of the Chariot" (Ibid. 278).

*At the time of Budge's initial research, it was not known Ashtoreth was actually a deliberate misvocalization of the goddess' name (more on this to follow).

Drawing after Ibid. 279 Fig. 10.

Celestial

Female

Queen of

Heaven

Celestial Queen of Heaven
~1800 BCE

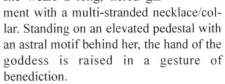

Discovered in Syro-Palestine, this partial cylinder seal impression depicts a Celestial Goddess as the Queen of Heaven.

Crowned with a headdress, she wears a long, tiered garment with a multi-stranded necklace/collar. Standing on an elevated pedestal with an astral motif behind her, the hand of the goddess is raised in a gesture of benediction.

This blessing goddess may depict Asherah, Ishtar and/or Astarte, all identified as Queens of Heaven in Syro-Palestine.

Drawing after Collon 1987:174 Fig. 814.

Celestial

Goddess

Queen of

Heaven

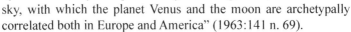

Similar Iconographic Associations:
Queen of Heaven Celestial Symbols
~1700 BCE

A female figure stands under a celestial canopy of stars and a rainbow on this fresco discovered at Akotiri.

According to Erich Neumann in *The Great Mother: An Analysis of the Archetype*, the "star, half-moon, and star-in-crescent are astral symbols referring to the Great Goddess as Queen of the Sky and particularly of the night sky, with which the planet Venus and the moon are archetypally correlated both in Europe and America" (1963:141 n. 69).

Drawing after photo by Diana Debra Oliver, Thera Museum.

Ancient Queens of Heaven

King
Hammurabi
Before

Goddess

**King Hammurabi
Asratum/Asherah
Dedicatory Inscription**
~1792-1750 BCE

A dedicatory inscription to the goddess Ashratum/Asherah, was discovered on a limestone plaque dating to ~1792-1750 BCE.

The inscription was provided by a provincial governor on behalf of King Hammurabi (Frankfort 1996:119).

Similar Historic Associations:
**King Hammurabi Before
Goddess Asratum/Asherah**
~1792-1750 BCE

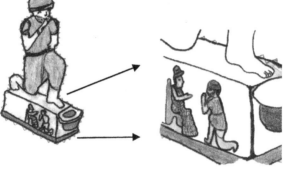

This bronze statuette depicts King Hammurabi kneeling before an offering basin. A relief incised on the side of the pedestal depicts Hammurabi kneeling before an enthroned goddess, likely Asratum/Ashratum/Asherah.

Hammurabi's face and hands were once covered with gold foil. The frontal, offering basin likely once held incense, grain and/or holy water.   Drawings after Frankfort 1996:122 Il. 135.

Kings Before Goddesses of Antiquity

Serpent

Goddess

"Serpent God" with Snake/Serpent
~1600 BCE

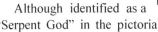

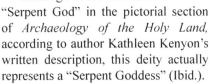

Discovered at Tel Beit Mirsim, Palestine, this stela depicts a "Serpent Goddess." Its rounded back indicates it likely once stood in a niche (Kenyon 1960:185).

Although identified as a "Serpent God" in the pictorial section of *Archaeology of the Holy Land,* according to author Kathleen Kenyon's written description, this deity actually represents a "Serpent Goddess" (Ibid.).

A Proto-Sinaitic epithet identifying Asherah as 'the one of the serpent,' suggests this may be a representation of the Canaanite and Hebrew goddess Asherah.

Excavators initially thought the snake was encompassing a tree, however, upon cleaning the stela "a large python coiled around the legs of a goddess" became visible notes William F. Albright in *Archaeology and the Religion of Israel* (1969:185 n. 51).

Drawing after Kenyon 1960 Pl. 34b.

Crowned

Goddess

Serpent

Goddess

Crowned

Goddesses

Similar Historic Associations:
Serpent Goddess with Snakes/Serpents
~1600-1400 BCE

A "Goddess Brandishing Snakes" is portrayed on this bronze, female figurine discovered on the island of Crete (Spycket 2000:115).

Depicted in traditional Minoan style, the goddess' breasts are bare above a flounced skirt.

Drawing after Ibid. Fig. 97.

Similar Historic Associations:
Female Menstruation Due to Eve Having Sex with the Serpent/Snake in the Garden of Eden

According to *The Mothers: Matriarchal Theory of Social Origins,* Jewish, Rabbinic tradition attributes female menstrual cycles to Eve having sex with the serpent. A common Rabbinical opinion among the Jews was "that menstruation owes its origin to the serpent having had sexual intercourse with Eve in the Garden of Eden" (Briffault 1963:315).

Lion & Prosperity Goddess of Plants & Animals Ashratum/Asherah
~1800-1550 BCE

Discovered at Tel el-Ajjul, this composition depicts a goddess with a lion and a vulture/bird, surrounded by small trees or branches, a personification of the Prosperity Goddess of Plants and Animals.

According to *Gods, Goddesses and Images of God In Ancient Israel,* this "constellation of figures matches favorably with the epithet 'Mistress [/Goddess] of the Steppe

Mistress of the

Steppe

[/Grassy Meadowland]' . . . a title assigned to the goddess Ashratum in Middle Bronze Age Akkadian texts. She is the precursor of the deity known as Atirat/Asherah in later times" (Keel 1998a:22). Drawing after Ibid. 21 Fig. 4.

Crowned

Goddesses

Crowned Goddess Asherah Figurines
~1800-1600 BCE

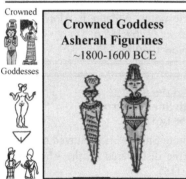

Created from gold-sheeting, these naked, female pendants were discovered at Gezer.

According to William G. Dever in *Biblical Archaeologist,* these figurines are likely representations of Asherah, the wife/consort of the Canaanite chief god El (1987).

Drawings after Mazar 1990:220.

Crowned

Goddesses

Similar Iconographic Associations:
Crowned Prosperity Goddess Figurine
~1750-1550 BCE

This lead figurine, discovered at Tel el-Ajjul, depicts a Naked Goddess wearing a horned crown. Bovine ears overlay the goddess' traditional Hathor hair style. Her pubic triangle is outlined and accentuated.

The hands of this Prosperity Goddess encircle her breasts, a gesture personifying nature's bounty, blessing, abundance and prosperity.

Drawing after Keel 1998a:34 Fig. 25b.

Goddess on

Lion-Throne

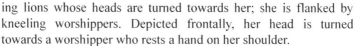

Enthroned Lion Goddess
Asherah
~1600-1500 BCE*

This seal impression, discovered within a Ugarit acropolis tomb, depicts a winged, crowned goddess holding the leash of a lion (whose paw rests upon her knee).

A second, naked goddess stands on the back of kneeling lions whose heads are turned towards her; she is flanked by kneeling worshippers. Depicted frontally, her head is turned towards a worshipper who rests a hand on her shoulder.

Support for the identification of the seated goddess as Asherah comes from her "Lion Lady" epithet (Dever 2001:178), coupled with the iconography of harmonious ascendancy (leashed lion). In addition, the primary goddess' enthronement (upon the back of a horned bull/cow**), also invokes her aspect as the Goddess/Mistress of Animals.

Although a likely Asherah depiction, due to the lack of an identifying inscription scholars remain uncertain whether this is a "'genuine' Asherah" representation (Cornelius 2004:100).

*dating of ~16-15th century BCE per Cornelius (Ibid. 108); ~14-13th century BCE per Collon (1987:71)

** Cow horns were intentionally eliminated through breeding.

Drawing after Ibid. Fig. 314.

Goddess on

Lion-Throne

Similar Historic Associations:
Enthroned Lion Goddess

Lions protect, and provide the throne for, the hierophant Syrian Goddess Cybele.

Resting upon a crown of rays, her pontifical miter depicts a crescent, a city gate, towers and walls. The twelve zodiac signs are pictured on the border of her Episcopal cape. Her right hand holds several instruments including a sistrum, a caduceus and a distaff. She holds a thunderbolt in her left hand with animals, fruit, flowers and a bow on her sleeve.   Drawing after Hall 1928.

LATE BRONZE AGE CONSIDERATIONS

Although not one goddess of "Ugarit, 'Israel' and the Old Testament," Asherah is the "number one goddess in the relevant cultures."

Asherah: Goddesses in Ugarit, Israel and the Old Testament
(Binger 1997:147-8)

II. Late Bronze Ages I & II   ~1550-1200 BCE

A preponderance of archaeological artifacts attests to various religious practices coexisting "in Judah alongside the official worship of Yahweh."

Biblical Archaeology Review
(Borowski 2005:30)

Asherah references in this section include:

"Mother of the Gods"
"Nursemaid of the Gods"
"Progenitress of the Gods"

Tanit/Tannit
"the One of the Serpent"

"Elat/Goddess"
"*Qdš*/Holiness"

"Wizard of Asherah"

"Servant of
Asirta/Asherah"

"Finger of Ashirat/
Asherah"

"Creatrix of the Gods"

"Lion-[Goddess/]Lady"

"Lady Asherah of the Sea"
"Lady who Traverses the Sea"
"Lady Who Treads on the Sea(dragon)"

Mother

Goddess

**Mother of the Gods,
Asherah**
~1550 BCE

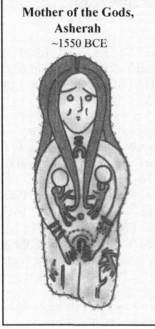

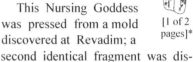

According to *Gods, Goddesses, and Images of Gods In Ancient Israel* this Naked Goddess figurine represents "the secret powers of mother earth, giving birth to humans and animals, nourishing them, and causing them to flourish" (Keel 1998a:74).

This Nursing Goddess was pressed from a mold discovered at Revadim; a second identical fragment was discovered at Aphek.

[1 of 2 pages]*

Several layers of symbolic expression are reflected in the iconography of this figurine.

The hair of this goddess is fashioned in an elongated Hathor style; her pendant depicts parallel lines above a semi-circular downward opening – an Ω-shape alluding to the womb. Bracelets encircle her arms which extend to, and expose, her genitalia. A child nurses at each breast. Caprids flank sacred trees on her thighs.

*This, and subsequent occurrences of this notation, are read as page 1 of 2 pages describing this artifact. Drawing after Ibid. 75 Fig. 82.

Mother

Goddess

Similar Iconographic Associations:
Golden Mother of the God
~1600 BCE

This gold figurine depicts a small child sitting on the lap of an enthroned Hittite Sun Goddess. The Mother Goddess wears earrings, a necklace and a large, circular solar headdress.

Embellishments on the throne arms are in the shape of lion paws.

Drawing after Canby 1986:56.

Creatrix

Goddess

Similar Historic Associations:
Mother Goddess and Pharaoh-God Child
~1318-1301 BCE

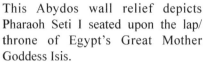

This Abydos wall relief depicts Pharaoh Seti I seated upon the lap/throne of Egypt's Great Mother Goddess Isis.

Isis was the maternal pathway to kingship and sovereignty. Every Pharaoh identified himself as the reincarnation of Isis' son-god Horus.

Epithets of Isis include: "She who Bore the Pharaoh" and "She who Gave him his Power with her Milk" (Witt 1971:15).

As the power behind the throne, Isis' hieroglyph was the image of a throne, 𐎆, and her lap was perceived as the throne of Egypt.

Drawing after Pritchard 1954:184 Fig. 545.

Nursing

Goddess

Similar Historic Associations:
Mother Goddess and Child
~4000 BCE

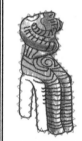

A painted spiral, triangles and linear striations decorate this enthroned Nursing Mother Goddess. Created by artists over 6,000 years ago, this clay figurine was discovered within a Grecian acropolis.

Drawing after author's photo, National Museum, Athens.

Mother

~ Female Imagery and the Bountiful Earth ~
Similar Historic Associations:
Mother and Child
~7,000-5,000 BCE

Carrying her child in a back sling, this African mother toils with a weighted digging stick.

Drawing after Hentum 1999. Thank you to Swedish researcher Bengt Hentum.

& Child

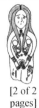

This figurine's symbolism correlates with contemporary Ugarit texts identifying Atirat/Asherah as the "Creatrix of the Gods" (Keel 1998a:74), an identification initially made 50 years ago by William F. Albright, the Father of Biblical Archaeology, writing in *The Biblical Period from Abraham to Ezra* (1963:17).

[2 of 2 pages]

Additionally, Genesis 49:25 equates Atirat/Asherah with the Ω-shape/womb symbolism identification of "womb" and "breasts and womb" (a literal translation of *Rahmay**) (Keel 1998a: 74) further affirming her epithet of the "Creatress of the Gods" on the Revadim and Aphek figurines.

Mother of

the Gods

Although the Revadim and Aphek figurines symbolically parallel biblical literature, their iconography is attested to much earlier in contemporary Ugarit tablets which identify Atirat/Asherah as the "Nursing Mother of the Gods, Shahar and Shalim"** (Ibid.).

*Ugarit tablets identify Asherah as Rahmay hundreds of years before biblical texts equate the two.

**The city of Jerusalem was actually founded for the god Shalim/ Shalem (see Jerusalem information box below), likely making Asherah the mother of Jerusalem.

Urusalem (Jerusalem) – Founded for the God, Shalem/Shalim

Although three patriarchal religions claim Jerusalem as their holy city, in actuality Urusalem was founded for none of their gods.

According to the *Anchor Bible Dictionary* and *The Interpreter's Dictionary of the Bible*, Jerusalem's original meaning is "Foundation of [the god] Shalem[/Shalim]"* (Buttrick 1962 II:843; Freedman 1992 III:751) and the deities originally worshipped there were S[h]alem[/Shalim]/El and Astarte[/Asherah]/Salmanitu (Langdon 1964:45- 6).

*After whom King David named his sons Absalom and Solomon (Freedman 1992 V:1153).

Mother Goddesses of Antiquity

Crowned

Goddess

Similar Iconographic Associations:
Crowned Goddesses
~1800-1550 BCE

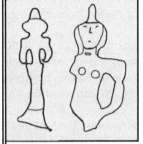

These bronze (left) and silver (right), naked, female figurines of Crowned Goddesses were discovered among the standing stones of Middle Bronze Age Hazor.
Drawing after Ben-ami 2006:40-1.

Crowned

Goddess

Similar Iconographic Associations:
Crowned Goddess
~1500-1200 BCE

Made of gold, this Crowned Goddess was discovered at Tel el-Ajjul.

The goddess wears a tall pointed headdress and a necklace enhanced with incised, circular indentations. Her genital area is accentuated by a loop superimposed within the dotted background of a heart-shaped outline. One bent arm crosses over her abdomen; the other rests upon her chest.   Drawing after Hall 1928.

Similar Historic Associations:
Maternal Divine Principle

According to *The Cult of the Mother-Goddess*, "While it is uncertain whether the earliest figurines represented the Mother-goddess as such, they were indicative of the recognition and veneration of maternity as a divine principle" (James 1994:257).

~ Female Imagery and the Bountiful Earth ~

The Masks of God: Primitive Mythology states that the early female figurines represent the same Mother Goddess who became "so conspicuous in the later agricultural civilizations of the Near East and has been everywhere celebrated as the Magna Mater and Mother Earth" (Campbell 1969:314).

Crowned

Goddess

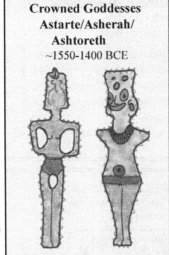

Crowned Goddesses
Astarte/Asherah/
Ashtoreth
~1550-1400 BCE

Unknown
Proveniences

Discovered at unknown proveniences in the "Holy Land," these female figurines are identified as the "fertility goddess" of the Canaanites, Sidonians and Philistines (Negev 2001:61).*

Made of silver, a pointed horn crowns the head of the left figurine. Her arms cascade to her waist, below her bare breasts. An incised undergarment is depicted above a circular incision.

Naked except for a crown, necklace, belt and a smile, the figurine on the right is made of clay.

According to the *Archaeological Encyclopedia of the Holy Land,* these figurines are representations of the goddess "Astarte," "Asherah" and/or "Ashtoreth" (Ibid.).

*Thousands of female figurines, similar to those depicted here, have been excavated at sites dating to the Canaanite and Israelite periods (Negev 2001:61). Drawings after Ibid. 62.

Crowned

Goddess

Similar Historic Associations:
Crowned Blessing Goddess
~1900 BCE

A goddess blesses a king and animals on this Babylonian seal impression. The emblematic rosette star of the Sumerian goddess Inanna is positioned between them.

Drawing after Collon 1987:56 Fig. 224.

Ancient Crowned Goddesses

Blessing

Goddess
Asherah

Similar Iconographic Associations:
Blessing Goddess
~1400-1200 BCE

Missing one gold earring, this bronze Syrian Goddess (Pritchard 1954:161) raises her hands in a posture of benediction. Her garment is embellished with decorative spirals.
Drawing after Ibid. Fig. 466.

Blessing

Goddess
Asherah

R
o
s
e
t
t
e

Rosette
Star of

Inanna/
Ishtar

Similar Historic Associations:
King Before Blessing Goddess
~2000-1550 BCE

A Blessing Goddess is approached by a suppliant goddess, the owner of the seal and a king (Collon 1987:128) on this Syro-Palestinian cylinder seal.

This ceremonial scene is performed under the emblematic rosette star of the goddess Inanna/Ishtar. At first glance its presence on this Syro-Palestinian configuration is puzzling; however, further investigation reveals the goddess Inanna/Ishtar "became popular in Syria where she was also variously equated with Astarte, Anath, Asherah and Ashtaroth" (Ibid. 167-70).
Drawing after Ibid. 127 Fig. 544.

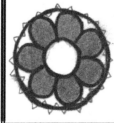

Similar Historic Associations:
Rosette of Wisdom and Sophia

Sophia/Wisdom (once a Gnostic Mother Goddess, now a Christian saint), was historically personified on this Landsberg, sevenfold rosette mandala. The central circle depicted Sophia as Wisdom/the Universal Mind (Walker 1988:220). Drawing after Ibid.

Blessing

Goddess

Blessing Goddess Asherah
~1550-1400 BCE

This gold-plated bronze figurine was discovered within a goldsmith's work-shop at Ugarit.

Wearing a long gown with rolled edges and ser-pentine cording, her arm is upraised in a gesture of benediction.

Although lacking an identifying inscription, according to *The Many Faces of the Goddess: The Icono-graphy of the Syro-Palestinian God-desses* this figurine is one of the "best candidates" for identification as the goddess Asherah (Cornelius 2004: 100). Drawing after Ibid. Pl. 3.9.

Blessing

Goddess

Blessing Goddess Asherah
~1550-1400 BCE

Discovered within a Ugarit acropolis, this Egyptian-ized, female figurine is likely also one of the "best candidates" for identifi-cation as the Canaanite and Hebrew goddess Asherah (Cornelius 2004:100).

This seated goddess wears an Egy-ptian crown and a multi-layered, ornate collar/necklace. Her right hand is upraised in a blessing posture.

An "Isis-knot" (Ibid. 110), depict-ed on the front of her gown, integrates the symbol of the goddess Tanit (Asherah's epithet in the first millennium (Olyan 1988:60)), assimilating the two goddesses. Drawing after Cornelius 2004:Pl. 2.5.

Blessing Goddesses of Antiquity

`the One
of the
Serpent'

Similar Iconographic Associations:
Serpent Goddess/'the One of the Serpent'
~1500 BCE

Discovered within a sealed vault at Crete's Knossos palace, this statue is identified as a "Serpent Goddess" (Campbell 1964:151), the Mediterranean version of 'the One of the Serpent.'

This is likely a representation of the protective goddess identified in Cretan Linear B tablets as *"Athenai Potniai:* 'the Lady of Athens'" (Ibid. 71).

Ancient texts reveal she was the king's "personal protectress" paralleling the attributes of Athena as protectress of Athens and "the guardian protectress of heroes" (Ibid. 149).

Drawing after photo by Liza Meyers, Heraklion Museum, Crete.

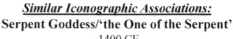

`the One
of the
Serpent'

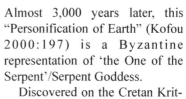

Similar Iconographic Associations:
Serpent Goddess/'the One of the Serpent'
~1400 CE

Almost 3,000 years later, this "Personification of Earth" (Kofou 2000:197) is a Byzantine representation of 'the One of the Serpent'/Serpent Goddess.

Discovered on the Cretan Kritsa plain at the Virgin of Kera church, this goddess holds the tail of a snake/serpent as she feeds him from a chalice.

Drawing after photo by Judith Meyers, Kritsa Crete.

'the One

of the
Serpent'

**Proto-Sinaitic Inscription:
'the One of the Serpent'**
~1540-1290* BCE

On the side of this Sinai temple sphinx figurine, scholars discovered a Proto-Sinaitic** inscription containing the name of the goddess Tanit[/Tannit].

According to *Canaanite Myth and Hebrew Epic* author Frank M. Cross, the inscription translates as "the One of the serpent or, possibly, the Dragon Lady" (1973:32).

'the One

of the
Lion'

Lady who

treads on
the Sea

Extrapolating further, Cross states that the term Tanit exactly parallels the "old epithet of Asherah . . . [as] the 'One of the Lion,' or the 'Lion Lady'," thus equating the two goddesses (Ibid. 33).

Further confirming the Asherah-Tanit identification, Cross cites another comparative association of the two goddesses: "Closely parallel also are the epithets . . . 'Lady of the Serpent,' identified in the Proto-Sinaitic texts by Albright, and . . . 'the Lady who treads on the Sea(-dragon),' both old epithets of Asherah/'Elat" (Ibid.).

The Story of the Semitic Alphabet proposes a date of ~1940-1760 BCE (Whitt 1995:2380-1).

**The Proto-Sinaitic inscriptions were an integral key in tracing the historical development of the Semitic alphabet.

Drawing after May 1984:20.

'the One

of the
Lion'

Similar Iconographic Associations:
Lion Goddess/'the One of the Lion'
~600-450 BCE

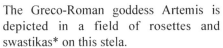

The Greco-Roman goddess Artemis is depicted in a field of rosettes and swastikas* on this stela.

The lioness looks over her shoulder toward the goddess, as Artemis holds her tail and pats her head. A cross is pictured on the earring of the goddess.

*Prior to their 20th century corruption, swastikas had a long history of positive symbolism.

Drawing after Frothingham 1911:361 Fig. 4a.

Kabi-
Dagan

Diviner/
Wizard

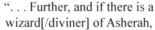

**Wizard of Asherah
at Taanach**
~1500 BCE

Fortunes were told and prophecies made by a renown Wizard/Diviner of Asherah at Taanach.

Egyptian correspondence addressed to Rewashsha, the Prince of Taanach, attests to the presence of an established oracle at Taanach with an acclaimed wizard of Asherah.

The communication reads, in part,

". . . Further, and if there is a
wizard[/diviner] of Asherah,
let him *tell our fortunes,* and let me hear *quickly* and
the omen and interpretation send to me"
(Pritchard 1973:277).

Diviner/
Wizard
Kabi-
Dagan

Similar Iconographic Associations:
Seal of Wizard
~1400-1300 BCE

This tablet impression depicts a god/king/wizard approaching a winged goddess. The goddess faces him with an upraised arm holding a sword/ritual object.

The figures wear tall, conical headdresses with horned protrusions above their foreheads. Their upturned footwear is indicative of Hittite style. Streamers flow from the goddess' arms and waist.

The inscribed Hittite hieroglyphics read "*Kabi-Dagan, the diviner[/wizard]*" (Collon 1987:70).
Drawing after Ibid. 71 Fig. 311.

Lion-Headed

Goddess

**Lion-Masked Goddess
Astarte/Asherah**
~1500-1300 BCE

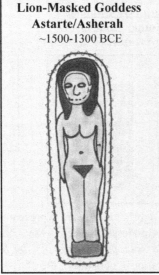

According to *The Hebrew Goddess,* this Beth Shean figurine is a representation of the Naked Goddess Astarte wearing a lioness-mask (Patai 1990 Pl. 17).

Throughout antiquity the fluidity of ancient religious traditions assimilated Astarte with the Asherah (Dever 2001:195) suggesting this may also be a representation of the goddess Asherah.

In addition, Asherah's epithet of "Lion Lady" (Cross 1973: 33) further affirms this figurine is likely identified with Asherah.

Drawing after Patai 1990 Pl. 17.

Lion-Masked

Goddess

Similar Iconographic Associations:
**Lion-Headed Healing Goddess
Sekhmet**
~712-525 BCE

The lion-headed, Egyptian Healing Goddess, Sekhmet, is depicted on this fragmented figurine. An inscription on its back identifies the goddess as "beloved of Ptah and [a] healer" (Freeman 1999:27).

Pharaoh Amenhotep III placed 730 images of Sekhmet in his temple, imploring the Healing Goddess' help with his illnesses (Ibid. 24).   Drawing after Ibid. 27.

Ancient Goddess and Lion Associations

Nursing Mother

Goddess

Similar Historic Associations:
Samarian Mother Goddesses
~720-587 BCE

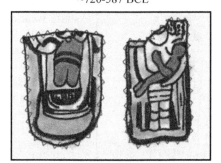

Discovered at Samaria, these figurine molds are representations of enthroned nursing "Mother Goddesses" (Keel 1998a:333).

According to *Gods, Goddesses, and Images of God In Ancient Israel,* these configurations personify the Isis-Horus mythology, locally adapted (Ibid.).

Drawings after Ibid. 334 Fig. 327a, b.

Nursing

Mother Goddess

Similar Historic Associations:
Cretan Mother Goddess
~1700-1400 BCE

An eternal, maternal motif – this bronze figurine of the Egyptian Mother Goddess Isis was discovered on the island of Crete.

Apuleius, writing ~150 CE, attributes Isis as saying:

". . . I, who am Nature,
the Parent of Things,
the Queen of All the Elements,
the primordial progeny of ages,
the supreme of Divinities,
the sovereign of the spirits of the dead,
the first of the celestials, and
the uniform resemblance of
Gods and Goddesses" (Hall 1928:45).
Drawing after Kofou 2000:230 Fig. 288.

Asherah is Prominent Goddess in Ancient Ugarit
~1440-1300 BCE

Initially many scholars rejected the existence of Asherah as a goddess, considering the notion untenable (Evans 1901:133 n. 4).

Ugarit Asherah [1 of 2 pages]

Even after the discovery of the first cuneiform tablets referencing her as a goddess, many scholars still refused to accept the possibility of her existence (Day 1986:386) and Asherah was still not universally acknowledged as a goddess (Freedman 1992:I.483).

Mother of the

Gods

Lady who

treads on the Sea

Everything changed in 1929 with the discovery of Ugarit's (modern Ras Shamra) ancient tablets* which rewrote history, reshaped scholarship** and attested to the worship of Athirat***/Asherah as a prominent goddess.

A primary goddess in Ugarit's religious pantheon, Asherah's titles include "Procreatress/Mother/Progenitress of the Gods," "Nursemaid of the Gods," "Lady Asherah of the Sea," "Lady who Traverses the Sea," "Lady who Treads on the Sea/Sea(dragon),"^ "Elat/Goddess" and "Qudsu/Holiness."^^ (Pritchard 1973:97-102; Day 1986:387-391; Patai 1990:37).

As the "Mother/Procreatress/Progenitress of the Gods," Asherah shares in creation with her husband god, El, and the gods are identified as the "seventy sons of Athirat[/Asherah]" (Day 1987:387). In addition, Asherah is identified as the mother of Yahweh (Smith 2001).

*These cuneiform tablets are written in a language consonantly similar to biblical Hebrew (Negev 2001:524).

**Although as late as 1954 *The Interpreter's Bible* stated, "the *asherah*, [was] perhaps the image of the god by that name" (Muilenburg 1954:297).

***Athirat's Ugarit -*th* is equivalent to Asherah's Hebrew -*sh* and Athirat's Ugarit -*t* (feminine ending) equates to Asherah's Hebrew -*h* (Lemaire 1984b:50), thus Athirat evolves into Asherah.

^See Cross 1973 and Day 1986 for more on these translations.

^^Discussion of Qudsu/*Qdš* follows.

Water/Sea Goddesses of Antiquity

Lady
Asherah

of the
Sea

Ugarit
Asherah
[2 of 2
pages]

As "Lady Asherah of the Sea," "Lady who Traverses the Sea," "Lady who Treads of the Sea/Sea(dragon)," Asherah was a prominent "Sea Goddess" with shrines at Tyre and Sidon. One of Asherah's servants was a "fisherman of the Lady Asherah of the Sea" (Patai 1990:37), who fished for her, saddled her donkey in silver and gold and placed her upon the donkey's saddle (Pritchard 1973:101).

Asherah's donkey ride, combined with her previous identification with Asratum as "Lady of the Steppe/Grassy Meadowland" (Day 1986:386) and "Mistress of the Plain" (Reed 1943:73) attests she was also an inland goddess.

D
o
n
k
e
y
Ride

S
e
a

G
o
d
d
e
s
s
e
s

✝

Sea
Goddess

Astarte/
Asherah

Similar Historic Associations:
Asherah, King David and Jesus of Nazareth

Asherah's donkey ride predates a mule ride by King David hundreds of years later (1 Kings 1:33, 38) and a donkey ride by Jesus of Nazareth thousands of years later.

Composite drawing after Serabit el Khadem painted relief (~1840-1792 BCE) (Keel 1978:270 Fig. 380) and a ~17th century BCE "Syrian goddess" (Collon 1987:127 Fig. 543) Syro-Palestinian seal.

Similar Historic Associations:
Sea Goddess Astarte/Asherah

The Sea Goddess Astarte stands on the prow of a galley holding a "cruciform standard" (Hill 1910:163) on this top coin image discovered at Sidon and dating to 98-10 BCE.

Recalling Asherah was identified as a Sea Goddess with a Sidonian shrine, who coalesced with the goddess Astarte, this configuration may represent Asherah or a synthesis of the goddesses.

Discovered at Berytus and dating to 218-222 CE, this bottom coin depicts the Sea Goddess Astarte enthroned on a galley/ancient ship with standards before her (Ibid. lviii).

Drawings after Ibid. XXII.9 (top); XL.5 (bottom).

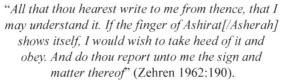

**Lunar Date of
Finger of Ashirat/
Asherah**
~1400 BCE

Lunar

Goddess

In correspondence discovered at Taanach, an Egyptian general mandates a report from Taanach's King Ishtarjashar.* The general informs the king:

*"All that thou hearest write to me from thence, that I
may understand it. If the finger of Ashirat[/Asherah]
shows itself, I would wish to take heed of it and
obey. And do thou report unto me the sign and
matter thereof"* (Zehren 1962:190).

The general is informing Taanach's king that his report is due at the "Finger of Ashirat/Asherah" (the end of the month when the crescent moon approaches Venus).

*Palestinian King Ishtarjashar's name includes the goddess Ishtar.

Lunar
Goddess
Reference

Similar Historic Associations:
Lunar Celestial Goddess Al-Uzza
~90-220 CE

This Nabataean limestone disc depicts the Celestial Lunar Goddess Al-Uzza framed by the zodiac, a crescent moon and a lunar staff.

Drawing after McKenzie 2003:189
Fig. 198.

Lunar

Goddess

Similar Historic Associations:
Astarte/Ashtoreth/Asherah Worshipped as Jewish Moon
~2000 BCE

According to *Moon Lore* by the Reverend Timothy Harley: "The question here is not whether the Jews worshipped Astarte, but whether Astarte was the moon. This we cannot hesitate to answer in the affirmative. . . . 'Ashtoreth[/Asherah] or Astarte[*] appears physically to represent the moon. She was the chief local deity of Sidon; but her worship must have been extensively diffused, not only in Palestine, but in the countries east of the Jordan, as we find Ashtaroth[/Asherah]-Karnaim (Ashtaroth[/Asherah] of two horns) mentioned in the book of Genesis (xiv.5)'" (1885:94).

*Identified with the Sumero-Babylonian Inanna/Ishtar and the North Arabian goddesses Ilat and Allat (Langdon 1964:381).

Blessing

Goddess

Blessing Goddess Asherah
~1400 BCE

Discovered near Tel Beit Mirsim, a Blessing Goddess extends her upraised right hand in a benediction posture on this Palestinian stela.

Crowned with a celestial, horned headdress, the goddess is encircled within a vegetative frame.

Although lacking an identifying inscription, "It is tempting, however, to suppose that the . . . stela might depict Asherah" (Cornelius 2004:36).

Drawing after Ibid. Pl. 3.8a.

Blessing Goddess

Asherah

Similar Iconographic Associations:
Blessing Goddess of Animals
~1550 BCE

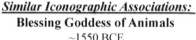

Standing on the back of a lion, a crowned goddess extends blessings toward a Naked Goddess and a stylized, sacred tree on this impression of a seal discovered at Megiddo. This is a representation of the Goddess of Animals/Mistress of Wild Beasts.
Drawing after Keel 1998a:55 Fig. 52.

Goddess
of

Animals

~ Female Imagery and the Bountiful Earth ~

Similar Iconographic Associations:
Goddess of Animals and the Bountiful Earth
~4000 BCE

Framed by animals, birds, mountains and religious motifs, this Egyptian configuration depicts a Prosperity Goddess of Animals and the Bountiful Earth.
Drawing after Neumann 1963:115 Fig. 12.

Goddess of Animals

Great Goddess

of the Aegean

Goddess of Animals, Asherah, Holiness, Aegean Great Goddess, Vital Force of Nature, Mother Goddess
~1400-1300 BCE

[1 of 2 pages]

Discovered at Minet el-Beida, this representation of a "Goddess" as the "Queen of the Wild Beasts"/"Goddess of Animals" depicts a bare-breasted goddess seated atop a mountain, flanked by, and feeding, nibbling ibexes (Lloyd 1961:150).

According to the *Encyclopedia Britannica* this depicts the goddess "Asherah," known in ancient literature as "the Goddess"/ "Elat" and her "Holiness"/ "Qdš" (www.britannica.com/38129/Asherah).

Extrapolating further, *The Art and Architecture of the Ancient Orient* identifies this ivory composition as a Creto-Mycenaean representation of "the Great Goddess of the Aegean" **(**Frankfort 1996:265-6).

The Cretan image (right) reflects stylistically similar traditional Creto-Mycenaean attributes – a bare-breasted Mother Goddess with flowing hair wearing a multi-layered skirt and flanked by animals.   Minet drawing after Lloyd 1961:150.

Goddess of

Animals

Similar Iconographic Associations:
Goddess of Animals/Queen of Wild Beasts
~1500 BCE

This cylinder seal impression, discovered at Cyprus, depicts a crowned, enthroned "Goddess" (Lloyd 1961:147) in her aspect as the Goddess of Animals/Queen of the Wild Beasts.

Drawing after Ibid. 146.

Throughout antiquity, the stylized sacred tree was a revered epiphany of the Great Mother Goddess.

Ancient Equivalent Symbology
Mother Goddesses and Sacred Trees

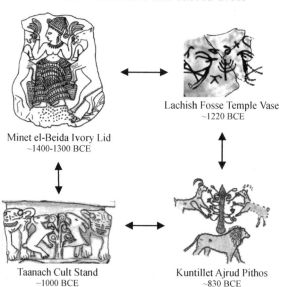

Minet el-Beida Ivory Lid
~1400-1300 BCE

Lachish Fosse Temple Vase
~1220 BCE

Taanach Cult Stand
~1000 BCE

Kuntillet Ajrud Pithos
~830 BCE

The ibex/goat-flanked, nurturing Mother Goddess configuration is an Asiatic-Ancient Near East adaptation understood to be "an explicit statement that the goddess is a personification of the vital force of nature" (Frankfort 1996:265-6), a concept exemplified on Palestinian-painted, pottery representations which substitute the ibex/goat-flanked sacred tree for the "Great Mother Goddess" (May 1939:252).

---

the Feminine as Revered Principle of Nature

 According to *The Great Mother: Analysis of the Archetype,* throughout antiquity "the Feminine, the giver of nourishment [was] everywhere a revered principle of nature" (Neumann 1963:131).

Similar Religious Expression in Syria, Israel and Judah

Experts now conclude the "complexity of religious expression . . . of Greater Palestine does not differ in form or content from practices known throughout Syria. It cannot be claimed that the religion of either Israel or Judah was in a substantive way different" (Thompson 1999:168-9).

However, Aegean Creto-Mycenaean configurations do not position a goddess between, or offering sustenance to, ibexes/quadrupeds. The artistic interjection of the "Great Goddess of the Aegean" between nibbling animals is an Asiatic adaptation from the Ancient Near East (Frankfort 1996:265).

[2 of 2 pages]

According to *The Art and Architecture of the Ancient Orient*, this deliberate and distinctive posturing explicitly personifies the goddess as a "vital force of nature" (Ibid.).

This elegant ivory configuration proved pivotal in deciphering the imagery of ancient, Palestinian-painted pottery.

Analyzing the positioning of sacred trees between nibbling ibexes/goats* in the *Journal of the American Oriental Society*, author Herbert G. May states the "key to the interpretation of the painted pottery tree design with a goat or goats on either side is that the sacred tree is the substitute for [the] mother goddess here depicted." May concludes that the goddess (flanked by goats) is iconograhically portrayed as a sacred tree (flanked by goats) on Palestinian painted pottery (1939:252). (See <u>*Ancient Equivalent Symbology*</u> information at left.)

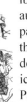

*This sacred-tree/goddess-between-ibex motif is discussed further in the Lachish Fosse Temple and Kuntillet Ajrud iconography.

Goddess

of Animals

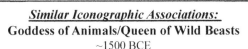

Similar Iconographic Associations:
Goddess of Animals/Queen of Wild Beasts
~1500 BCE

Worshippers approach an enthroned Goddess of Animals/ Queen of Wild Beasts whose feet rest upon a lion.

Unknown Provenience

A winged griffin/cherub stands protectively behind the goddess on an antlered ibex.

Although displaying Cypriote, Cretan and Syrian elements, this cylinder seal, and its resultant impression, actually originated in Syro-Palestine (Collon 1987:70). Drawing after Ibid. 71 Fig. 315.

Amorite King is "Servant of Goddess Ashirta/Asherah"
~1385-1344 BCE

According to the *Journal of Biblical Literature's* John Day, author of "Asherah in the Hebrew Bible and Northwest Semitic Literature," the name of King Abdi-Ashirta literally translates as "Servant of [the goddess] As[h]irta (Asherah)" (Day 1986:386).

Ruler of the Amorites, Abdi-Ashirta was eventually defeated by Pharoah Amenhotep III. A formidable ally, the Amorite king is mentioned 95 times in Egypt's el-Armana tablets (Hadley 2000: 45).

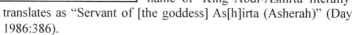

Similar Historic Associations:
King Before Goddess
~2000-1550 BCE

Kingly Servant of Goddess

Discovered in Syro-Palestine, this cylinder seal impression depicts a king and a priest approaching a primary goddess.

The tradition of a king portraying himself with, or before, a goddess has deep historical roots. Through the kings' association with the goddess, he gains theological sanction and interjects himself into the divine sphere, "beyond the realm of humanity [and] into the social world of the gods" (Frymer-Kensky 1992:61).

As ancient a tradition as one can be (over 4,000 years ago, King Eannatum declared himself to be the "beloved husband of Inanna"), the "relationship of [the goddess] Inanna to the *power* of kings goes back to the dawn of history." (Ibid. 61-2).

Drawing after Collon 1987:166 Fig. 770.

Ancient Kings Before Goddesses

Snake

Goddess

Palestinian Snake Goddess
~1300 BCE

Discovered at Hazor, this Palestinian, silver-plated, bronze standard is decorated with religious symbols (Pritchard 1975:Il. 65).

Describing the standard in *Archaeological Discoveries in the Holy Land,* Yigael Yadin states that it depicts "the snake goddess holding a snake in each hand" (1967:65).

Recalling that (1) snakes were identified with Asherah and (2) 'the one of the serpent' was one of her epithets, this representation likely depicts Asherah.

Drawing after Ibid.

Snake

Goddess

Goddess
of

Animals

Similar Iconographic Associations:
Sumerian Snake Goddess
~3000-2340 BCE

Dating back ~5,000 years, this Iraqi vase is a representation of the goddess in her dual aspects as the Snake/Serpent Goddess and Goddess of Animals/Queen of Wild Beasts.

Wearing a net skirt and a smile, the goddess stands between panthers/lionesses holding snakes/serpents in outstretched hands. The rosette star over her shoulder is "emblematic of the planet Venus, a manifestation of [the goddess] Inanna-Ishtar" (Frankfort 1996:40).   Drawing after Lloyd 1961:146 Fig. 109.

Goddess
Flanked

by
Animals

Similar Iconographic Associations:
Goddess as Stylized Tree/Generative Life Force
~1250-1000 BCE

These Taanach impressions depict caprids flanking sacred trees.

The sacred trees personify the Goddess with her vital, generative, life force and her ability to stimulate productivity in animals and plants (Keel 1998a:126).

Drawings after Ibid. 127 Fig. 154a, 154b.

~ The underlying mythological nucleus of the Vine/Vegetation Goddess, the Tree/Branch Goddess, the Naked Goddess and the Stylized Sacred Tree is the Great Mother Goddess of the Fruitful, Nourishing Earth. ~

Ancient Equivalent Symbology:
Middle Bronze Age to Late Bronze Age
Shifting Representations

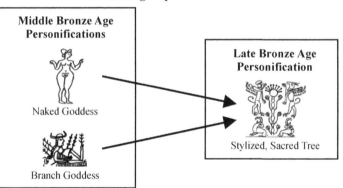

Middle Bronze Age Personifications

Naked Goddess

Branch Goddess

Late Bronze Age Personification

Stylized, Sacred Tree

Continuing an established symbolic representation, the Late Bronze Age's stylized, sacred tree configuration is personified by the Middle Bronze Age's Naked Goddess and/or Branch Goddess (Keel 1998a:72).

Stylized Tree

Goddess

Lachish Temple Vase
~1220 BCE

Discovered within a Lachish Temple, this dedicatory vase dates to a time when the Israelites were beginning to emerge in Canaan (Hestrin 1991: 52).

Most of the vase's re-covered fragments were discovered in a depository pit* outside the temple, except one fragment which was found on the temple sanctuary floor (Ibid.).

[1 of 3 pages]

An inscription, a lion, triangulated deer, a bird and two ibexes flanking a stylized, premenorahic tree encircle the shoulder of the vase (as depicted below left).

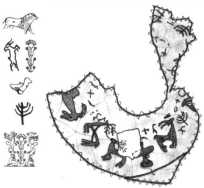

This iconography caught the attention of Ruth Hestrin, former curator of the Israelite and Persian Periods at the Israel Museum.

Extensively analyzing the vase, and a goblet also discovered at the site, Hestrin determined that the sacred tree motif was deeply embedded in ancient religious traditions as a personification of the source of life, growth and revival (1987:214). Her conclusions were published in the *Israel Exploration Journal* and *Biblical Archaeology Review.*

Gods, Goddesses and Images of God In Ancient Israel affirms the sacred trees' bountiful earth symbolism and add to it an aspect of nutritive blessing power, in that the stylized tree[**] "represents the fertile earth's procreative and nurturing power to bring blessing" (Keel 1998a:72).

*Religious objects were deliberately discarded in pits to prevent them from the profanity of everyday use (Dever 2005:160).

**The stylized sacred tree motif continues an established symbolism previously depicted (see left) by the Middle Bronze Age Naked Goddess and/or Branch Goddess (Keel 1998a:72).

Drawings after Hestrin 1991:51-52.

Stylized
Sacred

Tree
Goddess

Similar Iconographic Associations:
Tree Goddess Nursing Pharaoh
~1479 BCE

Pharaoh Tuthmosis III nurses from a tree on this burial chamber painting. An arm extends from the tree supporting the nutritive breast, upon which the Pharaoh rests his hands.

Historically, kings and priests substantiated their claim to power by claiming they nursed from the breast of the goddess (Neumann 1963:125). The Great Mother Goddess provided the kings' pathway to sovereignty. Drawing after Hestrin 1991:54.

Tree

Goddess

Similar Iconographic Associations:
Tree Goddess Presentation
~2000 BCE

Discovered in the Indus Valley, this seal impression depicts a Naked Goddess standing within the sacred tree from which Buddha gained enlightenment. A kneeling god presents a sphinx to the goddess (Campbell 1962:167). Drawing after Ibid. Fig. 17.

Goddess
of

Animals

Goddess
Flanked

by
Animals

Similar Historic Associations:
Mountain Herds of Astarte/Asherah
~2400 BCE

According to *Myths of Babylonia and Assyria*, configurations of the goddess, flanked by deer, ibex or one of her epiphanies, reflect the religious tradition of the "Mountain Herds of Astarte[/Asherah]" (Mackenzie 1915:120).

Inscribed above the vase's images is a dedication to the goddess worshipped in the temple. It is the longest known Proto-Canaanite inscription (Mazar 1990:276).

Painted in red, the dedication inscription translates as "Mattan. An offering to my Lady 'Elat[*]" (Hestrin 1991: 54). Experts contend 'Mattan' is likely the individual making the offering. Some experts, however, suggest [2 of 3 pages] 'Mattan' could be interpreted as 'gift,' rendering the possible translation, "A gift, an offering to my Lady 'Elat[*]" (Dever 2005: 226).

Although 'Mattan' or 'gift' may remain a question, 'Lady' and 'Elat' do not. Contemporary literature identifies these titles as epithets of the Canaanite and Hebrew Mother Goddess Asherah.

Concurring with this assessment and elaborating further in *Did God Have a Wife? Archaeology and Folk Religion in Ancient Israel*, William G. Dever states, "'Elat' is the feminine form of the name of the Canaanite male deity El, and it is one of the names of the great Mother Goddess of Canaan, used in *parallel* with 'Asherah'" (226).

Further substantiating an Asherah identification, Hestrin returned to the sacred tree symbolism and recognized the significance of the Proto-Canaanite term Elat/goddess (representing Asherah) inscribed directly above the stylized, premenorahic tree (an asherah**).

Proto-Canaanite Elat above premenorahic tree

"It is no accident," Hestrin stated, "that the word 'Elat[*] appears over the tree that represents 'Elat[*]/Asherah" (1991:54). This deliberate positioning correlates the relationship between the sacred tree/asherah** and Elat[*]/Asherah, thereby cementing the identification of the two.

Further supporting this parallel, symbolic representation, Hestrin references a multitude of stylistically similar artifacts from Egypt, Ugarit, Minet el-Beida, and Palestinian Taanach, Megiddo and Lachish.

*Early scholarship used the term 'Elat, 'Elat and/or Elath which later evolved into Elat.

**Stylized sacred trees were called asherahs throughout antiquity.

Triangular

Female
Imagery

Similar Iconographic Associations:
Triangular Working Women
~3200 BCE

Discovered on a bronze vessel, this flattened image depicts three triangular females weaving (center figure with a vertical loom), spinning (far left) and folding (right) textiles. Drawing after Quennell 1959:159.

Triangular

Goddess
Imagery

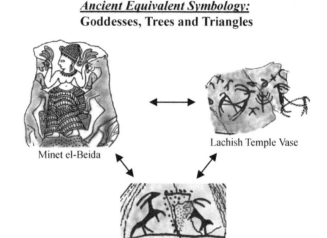

Ancient Equivalent Symbology:
Goddesses, Trees and Triangles

Minet el-Beida

Lachish Temple Vase

Lachish Temple Goblet

The above configurations demonstrate the association, exchange, and equivalent transference of attributes between the ancient Nurturing Mother Goddess, the pubic triangle and the sacred tree.

Reflections of social importance, these archaeological artifacts are thoughts frozen in time and unfiltered windows into the past.

Lachish Temple goblet

Triangular

Female

Hestrin next analyzed a goblet also discovered at the Lachish Temple site. The goblet depicts ibexes/goats flanking a stylized pubic triangle (rather than the vase's premenorahic tree). This motif is repeated four times around the goblet's exterior. [3 of 3 pages]

In an *Israel Exploration Journal* article, Hestrin states the "interchange of tree and pubic triangle proves . . . that the tree indeed symbolizes the fertility goddess, whom I believe to be Asherah" (1987:215).*

Extrapolating further in *Biblical Archaeology Review*, Hestrin equates the sacred tree and the pubic triangle as personifications of Asherah's generative force of nature, in that, both the tree and the pubic triangle symbolize life, growth and revival – attributes of the Great Mother Goddess Asherah (1991:52).*

Hestrin's analysis of Ancient Near East iconic attributes explains the sacred-tree/Asherah/pubic-triangle interchangeability and is confirmed by the *Journal of the American Oriental Society* stating, "Stylized trees and pubic triangles were used to represent a goddess, usually identified with Asherah, although other goddesses could also be candidates" (Lewis 1998:47).

*The sacred-tree/Asherah/pubic-triangle interchange is illustrated in the *Ancient Equivalent Symbology* information box at left.

Drawing after James 1998:14.

Fruitful Tree

Goddess

Similar Iconographic Associations:
Goddess with Tree in Triangle
~1550-1450 BCE

This gold pendant depicts a goddess head, breasts and a branch/tree sprouting from a pubic triangle. This is a personification of the prosperous Vegetative Goddess of the Fruitful, Nourishing Earth.

Although discovered at Ugarit, this pendant is stylistically similar to others unearthed at Megiddo, Tel el-Ajjul and Lachish (Keel 1998a:54). Drawing after Hestrin 1991:56.

III. Qdš Configurations ~1550-1200 BCE
Qdš Introduction
Asherah Egyptian Qdš Representations
Asherah Palestinian Qdš Representations

From the days of the first settlements in Israel, the Great Mother Goddess Asherah was worshiped by the Canaanites and then by the Hebrews.

The Hebrew Goddess
(Patai 1990:45)

In recent decades, thousands of female figurines and plaques have been unearthed at archaeological sites across the Syro-Palestinian corridor. As the artifacts surfaced, a recurring graphic configuration emerged.

The focal point, and central figure, of these stelae configurations is a Naked Goddess, identified as Qdš, who is variously depicted as:

–naked,
–with long legs,
–a shapely, slender silhouette,
–wearing a crown (or not),
–facing sideways or frontally,
–with her hair fashioned in the traditional style of the
        goddess Hathor,
–with other figures (flanked by gods or worshippers) or
        alone,
–holding objects (flower(s)/plant(s), snake(s)/serpent(s) or
        horned animals) and
–standing on the back of a striding lion, horse or neither.

The key to the identity of this goddess is provided by seven Egyptian stelae which depict the goddess and name her with inscriptions.

These inscribed stelae hieroglyphically identify the goddess as kdš, kšt, kdst and kdšt (Cornelius 2004:83-84), which has been variously translated as: Qdš, Qdšt, Qudsh, Qudšu,* Qadesh, Qadishtu, Qadosh, Quatesh, Qedesh, Qedeshet, Qetesh, Qodesh, Qudsha, Qudshu, Kadesh, Ke(d)eshet, and/or Kenet.**

Qdš = Asherah

In addition, the *Bulletin of the American Schools of Oriental Research* defines Qdš as an epithet of the goddess Asherah (Albright 1948:17) and adds Asherah's name to the goddess list.

Further endorsing Asherah's identification with Qdš are:

Qdš = Asherah

–*The Asherah in the Old Testament* equating Athirat of Ugarit and the Hebrew Old Testament Asherah with the "contemporary Egyptian nude goddess" (Reed 1949:78) Qdš,

Qdš = Asherah

–*Canaanite Myth and Hebrew Epic* affirming the "epithet of Asherah found in Ugarit and in Egypt is '*Qudšu*,[*]' 'Holiness'" (Cross 1973:33), and

Qdš = Asherah

–*Only One God? Monotheism in Ancient Israel and the Veneration of the Goddess Asherah* stating the etymological equivalent meanings of their names conclusively identifies the two goddesses with each other (Becking 2001:129).

*"*Qudšu*," literally meaning "Holiness" (Cross 1973:33), is in direct contradiction to the oft applied 'sacred prostitute' concept.

The 'sacred prostitute' label has been rendered a discredited notion by scholarship (Cornelius 2004:94).

A concept whose time has gone, and actually never was, the 'sacred prostitute' label is more reflective of myopic tunnel-vision than intellectual advancement.

**The translation of Kenet was due to a previous misreading of an obscure letter; correction confirmed by British Museum (Ibid. 83).

Qdš =
Asherah

Additionally, an amended biblical text further cements the equivalent identification of Asherah with Qdš/Qudshu.

Corrected after a scribal "error," the original Deuteronomy 33:2-3 reads:

"YHWH came from Sinai
and shone forth from his own Seir,
He showed himself from Mount Paran.
Yea, he came among the myriads of [Qdš/]Qudshu,
at his right hand his own Asherah"[*]
(Becking 2001:115).

Qdš =
Asherah

This biblical correction specifically names Asherah as YHWH's wife under both her name, and under her title of Qdš/Qudshu (Ibid.).

In addition to the above mentioned aspects, the Asherah-Qdš identification was previously discussed in the:
–literary Asherah-Qdš parallelism of Ugarit's cuneiform tablets equating Asherah with Qdš (~1400 BCE, pages 31-32),
and will be addressed further with the:
–Winchester triple goddess stela equating Asherah with Qdš (1198-1166 BCE, pages 69-71) and the
–Ekron inscription equating Asherah with Qdš (~700 BCE, page 222).

At this point in time, the balance of archaeological and historical evidence supports an Asherah-**Qdš** identification and outweighs arguments to the contrary.

*An article entitled "Feminine Features in the Imagery of God in Israel" published in *Vetus Testamentum* parallels Asherah at the right hand of Yahweh with the wife/consort or paredros (one who sits beside the king) in 1 Kings 22:19, Psalms 65:10, Nehemiah 2:6 and also Athena as paredros of Zeus (Weinfeld 2996:528).

III. Qdš Configurations

Qdš Introduction
Asherah Egyptian Qdš Representations
Asherah Palestinian Qdš Representations

Asherah references in this section include:

The following pages identify the hieroglyphic goddess kšt, kdš, kdst and/ or kdšt as Qdš* or defer to earlier scholarly designations.

*The Egyptian, hieroglyphic goddess identifications of kšt, kdš, kdst and kdšt (Cornelius 2004:83-84) have been variously translated as Qdš, Qdšt, Qudsh, Qudšu, Qadesh, Qadishtu, Qadosh, Qedesh, Qedeshet, Qetesh, Qodesh, Quatesh, Qudsha, Qudshu, Kadesh, Ke(d)eshet, Kenet and as an epithet of Asherah.

Queen of

Heaven

**Queen of Heaven,
Mistress of All the Gods,
Goddess Qdš**
~1550-1150 BCE

Standing on an elevated platform atop a striding lion, the Naked Goddess Qdš faces a worshipper whose arm is upraised in a posture of worship. A gift-laden offering table is depicted between them (Pritchard 1954:304).

Wearing a crown of feathers or vegetative stalks, the goddess holds a snake/serpent in one hand and a lotus bud in the other.

Vestiges of an unclear inscription on the stela may translate as "perhaps the typical 'lady[/queen] of heaven, mistress of all the gods'" (Cornelius 2004:128).

Although this inscription does not name the goddess, the elements of this configuration iconographically identify her as a Qdš representation (Ibid. 45-6, 50-2, 193).

Drawing after Pritchard 1954:163 Fig. 472.

Queen of

Heaven

Similar Historic Associations:
Queen of Heaven, Goddess Gula
~1000 BCE

Depicted as the Queen of Heaven, the Healing Goddess Gula stands on a throne-ledge with her symbolic dog before her on this Akkadian seal impression.

Standing in front of a sacred tree with a nibbling ibex, a king/priest/worshipper raises his hand in a gesture of adoration.

Drawing after Collon 1987:169 Fig. 793.

Ancient Queens of Heaven

Queen of

Heaven

**Queen of Heaven,
Qadesh/Kedeshet**
~1320-1200 BCE

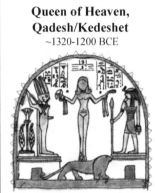

[Enlarged upper register]

The central figure in the upper register of this stela is the Naked Goddess "Qadesh" (Patai 1990 Pl. 25) standing on the back of a lion, holding snakes/serpents and lotus flowers, flanked by Reshep, the Syro-Palestinian god (right) and the Egyptian god Min (pointedly at left) (Cornelius 2004:49). The striding lion faces right.

The incised hieroglyphics translate as "Ke(d)eshet, lady[/queen] of heaven" (Ibid. 83).
Drawing after Pritchard 1954:163 Fig. 473.

Similar Historic Associations:
Warrior Goddess Anat
~1320-1200 BCE

[Enlarged bottom register]

The bottom register of this stela depicts three worshippers approaching the Warrior Goddess Anat.

Reflective of her warrior status, Anat holds a shield and lance in her right hand and an upraised club/battle-axe in her left hand.

Seated upon a throne, Anat wears an ankle-length gown with a necklace/collar. Her headdress is an Egyptian crown.

The first two worshippers approach the goddess with hands upraised in adoration. A striding boy, carrying a lotus stalk and fowl, follows the male and female adorants. Loaves of bread, incense and fowl are displayed on an offering table before Anat; lettuce is pictured below the table.
Drawing after Pritchard 1954:163 Fig. 473.

Queen of

Heaven

**Queen of Heaven,
Mistress of All the Gods,
Eye of Ra,
Without Her Equal,
Goddess Qedesh**
~1304-1237 BCE

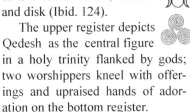

The inscription on this stela identifies the upper register goddess as "Qedesh" (Cornelius 2004:83).

Holding lotus flowers and a snake/serpent, Qedesh stands naked on the back of a striding lion. Her hair is styled in the goddess Hathor tradition; she wears a crown of a crescent moon, abacus and disk (Ibid. 124).

The upper register depicts Qedesh as the central figure in a holy trinity flanked by gods; two worshippers kneel with offerings and upraised hands of adoration on the bottom register.

In addition to identifying the goddess as Qedesh, this stela's inscription also enumerates her epithets as "lady[/queen] of heaven, mistress of all the gods, eye of Ra, without her equal" (Ibid. 83).

Drawing after Ibid. Pl. 5.3.

Queen of

Heaven

)O(

**Queen of Heaven is Goddess Epiphany and
Personification of Moon's Receptive Power of Nature**

According to *Easton's Bible Dictionary*, the Queen of Heaven referenced in Jeremiah 7:18, 44:17 and 44:25, represents "the moon, worshipped by the Assyrians as the receptive power in nature" (Hare 2006), which in turn is an epiphany of the goddess.

Queen of

Heaven

Similar Historic Associations:
Queen of Heaven
~900 BCE

Surrounded by a celestial nimbus, this Assyrian seal impression depicts a crowned goddess Inanna/Ishtar as the Queen of Heaven.

Drawing after Frankfort 1939 Pl.
XXXIIIi.

Naked Goddess Qdš
1304-1237 BCE*

Although previously identified as an "Astarte Plaque," a preponderance of archaeological iconography has shifted scholarly classification of this stela to a Qdš representation (Cornelius 2004: 45-6, 193).

The crowned Naked Goddess Qdš faces frontally holding snakes/serpents and long-stemmed lotus flowers. Hair clips adorn her Hathor goddess hairstyle.

Remnants of an ornate necklace are visible at her neckline; bracelets and armlets adorn her arms. Vestiges of her pubic triangle remain evident.

*This date is secured by an image of Ramesses II on the reverse side (Ibid. 132).   Drawing after Edwards 1955 Pl. 4.

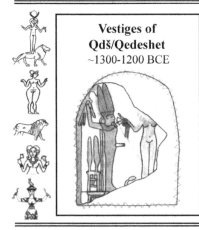

Vestiges of Qdš/Qedeshet
~1300-1200 BCE

The tip of a lion's tail and traces of a goddess' outstretched arm holding flowers remain visible on this Egyptian stela. Although damaged, enough of the iconography remains to identify it as a representation of the goddess "Qdš/Qedeshet" (Cornelius 2004:45-6, 193).

The Egyptian god Min (left) provides a poignant reminder of Qdš/Qedeshet's nakedness.

Drawing after Ibid. Pl. 5.6.

Qedeshet on Lion
~1300-1200 BCE

The inscription on this Egyptian stela identifies this Naked Goddess as "Qedeshet" (Cornelius 2004:84).

Standing on the back of a striding lion, Qdš/Qedeshet wears a disk crown of a crescent moon or horns. Her bovine ears are framed by elongated hair, with the ends curled in the traditional style of the goddess Hathor. Her pubic triangle is outlined.

The Egyptian god Min stands poignantly on an elevated platform at left. Although no god is portrayed on the right, an inscription references the Syro-Palestinian god Reshep (Ibid. 125). Drawing after Ibid. Pl. 5.5.

Goddess

on Lion

Similar Iconographic Associations:
Queen of Heaven Goddess on Lion
Before Worshipping King
~400 BCE

Standing on the back of a lion, the goddess Anahita faces a king (Boardman 2000:167) on this seal impression discovered at Anapa, Russia. The hands of the king are upraised in a posture of worship/adoration.

Depicted within a celestial orb, this is a representation of the goddess Anahita in her aspect as Queen of Heaven/ Celestial Goddess. Drawing after Ibid. 163.

Queen of

Heaven

**Lady of the Sky,
Mistress of All the Gods,
Lady of the Two Lands,
Beloved of Ra,
Eye of Atum,
Qadesh/Qedesh**

~1300-1200 BCE

Standing on the back of a striding lion, this Naked Goddess is flanked by the Syro-Palestinian god Reshep (right) and (left) the erect, Egyptian god Min (Cornelius 2004:124).

Crowned with a disk and crescent moon headdress, the goddess faces frontally. Her hair is depicted in the traditional, goddess Hathor style. She holds a snake/serpent in one hand and short stemmed lotus flower in the other. Her breasts and pubic triangle are outlined.

Curiously, although the Egyptian god Min stands at erect attention on a platform (left), it is the Syro-Palestinian god, Reshep, who holds an Egyptian ankh.

According to *The Ancient Near East in Pictures Relating to the Old Testament*, the front inscription translates as "Qadesh[/Qedesh (Ibid. 83)], lady of the sky[/queen of heaven] and mistress of all the gods" (Pritchard 1954:305).

The stela's reverse side reiterates these two titles, then also identifies the goddess with the additional epithets of "lady of the two lands," "child of Ra," "beloved of Ra" and "*udjat* eye of Atum" (Cornelius 2004:83).

Drawing after Pritchard 1954:164 Fig. 474.

Goddess

and Lion

Similar Iconographic Associations:
Goddess and Lions
~2004 BCE

Discovered within a palace structure at Ebla, Syria, this seal impression depicts a bare breasted goddess with a worshipper/priest. The arms of the goddess extend to the flanking lions, a harmonic representation of the goddess as Lion Lady and Goddess of Animals.

Drawing after Collon 1998:38 Fig. 127.

Queen of

Heaven

Ancient Holy Trinity with Qdš/Qedeshet as Queen of Heaven, Great of Magic, Mistress of the Stars
~1300-1200 BCE

Flanked by two gods, the Naked Goddess Qdš/"Qedeshet" (Cornelius 2004:45-6, 84) is pictured on the upper register of this stela flanked by two gods. She stands on the back of a striding lion holding long-stemmed flowers and snakes/serpents. Her hair is depicted in the traditional style of the goddess Hathor; her broken headdress may be a sistrum or a temple model (Ibid. 49, 125).

The bottom register depicts worshippers before an offering table.

According to *The Many Faces of the Goddess: The Iconography of the Syro-Palestinian Goddesses Anat, Astarte, Qedeshet, and Asherah*, the inscription on this stela identifies the depicted goddess as "Qedeshet, lady[/queen] of heaven, great of magic, mistress of the stars" (Ibid. 84).

Drawing after Ibid. Pl. 5.7.

Queen of

Heaven

Similar Historic Associations:
Queen of Heaven
~900 BCE

Surrounded by a celestial nimbus, a crowned goddess sits before an offering table and an approaching worshipper.

Sacred trees frame the ceremonial composition. Discovered at Neirab, Syria, this cornelian cylinder seal has gold caps and a bottom stamp seal.   Drawing after Collon 1987:84 Fig. 391.

Goddess

on Lion-
Griffin

Worshippers Flank Goddess Qdš/Qedeshet on Lion
1300-1200 BCE

Wearing a crown and a smile, the outstretched hands of this Naked Goddess holds flowers and snake(s)/serpent(s) as she stands on the back of a striding lion.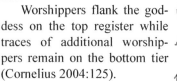

Worshippers flank the goddess on the top register while traces of additional worshippers remain on the bottom tier (Cornelius 2004:125).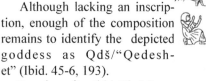

Although lacking an inscription, enough of the composition remains to identify the depicted goddess as Qdš/"Qedeshet" (Ibid. 45-6, 193).

Drawing after Ibid. Pl. 5.8.

Goddess

on Lion

Similar Iconographic Associations:
Goddess on Lion-Griffin
~2334-2193 BCE

Standing on the back of a winged, striding lion-griffin, the extended arms of this crowned goddess holds wriggling snakes/serpents. A masked and crowned worshipper/priest stands before her.

Although predating the Egyptian Qdš representations by almost 800 years, the stylistic similarities are readily apparent.

Drawing after Collon 1987:160 Fig. 726.

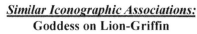

Ancient Goddess and Lion Associations

Worshippers Flank Qdš/Qedeshet
~1300-1200 BCE

Flanked by two "smaller male figures" (Cornelius 2004:126), the Naked Goddess on this damaged, limestone stela is iconographically identified as Qdš/"Qedeshet" (Ibid. 45, 193).

A headdress crowns her traditional Hathor hairstyle. The arms of the goddess extend outward toward the subordinate figures.

Drawing after Ibid. Pl. 5.10.

Socially Appropriate Qdš

This deliberately altered stela depicts the goddess Qdš clothed, less shapely (Cornelius 2004:10) and more socially appropriate.

Also, in response to objections of male anatomical representations making a poignant statement, only an obliterated smudge remains where an erection once existed.

Drawing after Ibid. Fig. B.

Similar Historic Associations:
Warrior Queen Kahena Leads 'Her Lions' Into Battle
~694 CE

At left, the African Berber Queen, *Dehiyya al-Kahina malkat Afriqah*, is depicted preparing to lead her army into battle.

The Jewish Queen, also known as Kahena, identified her fighting coalition as the "Lions of Africa and Judah" (HHF 2005).   Drawing after Ibid.

Ancient Goddess and Lion Associations

Goddess

on Lion-
Griffin

Similar Iconographic Associations:
Enshrined, Processional
Goddess on Lion
~3100 BCE

Elevating a chalice before her, this Sumerian goddess stands within a tripartite shrine on the back of a lion.

Leading a ceremonial procession, the goddess and lion are followed by a partial figure holding a ritual object. The tapered, reed-bundled gateposts with circular tops are emblematic of the Sumerian goddess Inanna.

From the dawn of writing in history's earliest texts, epithets of the goddess Inanna include:

Queen of all the Lands,
Queen of Heaven and Earth,
Mistress of all the Divine Laws and
the Holy Inanna
(Kramer 1981:25-28).

Etymologically, Inanna of Sumer translates into Ishtar of Babylonia. The two goddesses later assimilate into, and are identified with other goddesses including: Syria's Anat/Astarte, Hurrian's Shaushka, Iran's Anahita, Minoan's Rhea, Greece's Aphrodite and the Greco-Roman Kybele (James 1994:94, 147, 89, 94, 165, 147, 165). Drawing after Collon 1987:174 Fig. 808.

Goddess

on Lion

Similar Iconographic Associations:
Goddess on Lion-Griffin
~2334-2193 BCE

Wearing a horned crown, this Naked Goddess stands on the back of a winged lion-griffin, extending her arms outward in the typical posture of Qdš configurations.

A priest/worshipper stands before the goddess pouring libations over an altar shrine. A crowned, weather god rides in a chariot behind her. Drawing after Pritchard 1954:221 Fig. 689.

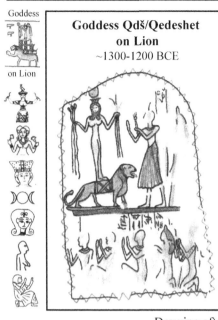

Goddess

on Lion

**Goddess Qdš/Qedeshet
on Lion**
~1300-1200 BCE

This stela depicts the Naked Goddess Qdš/ "Qedeshet" standing on the back of a lion (Cornelius 2004:45-6, 193).

Her extended hands hold snakes/serpents and lotus flowers. She wears a crown of an abacus, disk and crescent moon (Ibid. 127). Her goddess Hathor hairstyle frames her face.

The body of this goddess displays more exaggerated breasts than traditional depictions.

Two worshippers approach the goddess on the top register while five worshippers kneel below.

Drawing after Ibid. Pl. 5.14.

Qdš =
Asherah

Asherah as Qdš, Holiness and the Lion Lady

"Qdš" and "Holiness" were epithets of the goddess Asherah known in ancient texts ". . . as 'the Lion Lady,' [and] often depicted nude, riding on the back of a lion" (Dever 2001:178).

A Meandering, Serpentine History

Although much maligned in modern times, throughout antiquity the snake/serpent was revered for its healing powers (Numbers 21:9) and its wisdom (Genesis 3:1; Matthew 10:16).

Archaeological evidence attests to snake/serpent worship existent in the earliest religious traditions, dating back to ~70,000 BCE.

Scientific America reports an elongated serpentine rock which redefines "the earliest evidence for ritual behavior, or what could be called religion" (Minkel 2006; see page 248).

on Lion

**Goddess Qadesh
on Lion**
~1300-1200 BCE

This limestone stela depicts the Naked Goddess "Qadesh" standing on the back of a striding lion (Pritchard 1954:304).

The face of the goddess is framed by an elongated, Hathor hairstyle with curls cascading down her chest. She wears an elaborate unique crown of an abacus, a temple model and a crescent moon disk.

According to *The Ancient Near East in Pictures Relating to the Old Testament*, the inscribed hieroglyphics translate as "Qadesh, the beloved of Ptah" (Ibid.).

Drawing after Ibid. 163 Fig. 471.

Goddess

on Lion

Similar Historic Associations:
Palestinian Savior and Healing Goddess on Lion
~1500-1200 BCE

The "Savior" and "Healing Goddess Ishtar[/ Asherah] of Syria" (Keel 1978:83) is depicted on this Tel el-'Ajjul cylinder seal impression.

According to *The Symbolism of the Biblical World: Ancient Near Eastern Iconography and the Book of Psalms,* "the goddess on the lion is Ishtar/Astarte[/ Asherah] . . . who was celebrated in Egypt and Palestine as a savior-goddess" (Ibid.). Drawing after Ibid Fig. 96.

Goddess

& Lion

Similar Historic Associations:
Lion of Athena
~300 BCE

Inscribed with the name of the goddess Athena on its back, this limestone lion was discovered within an acropolis sanctuary dedicated to the goddess. A fragmentary female figurine, wearing Athena's emblematic snake-encircled aegis, was also discovered with the lion (Shone 2007:36). Drawing after Ibid. 37 Fig. 43.

Goddess

on Lion

**Goddess Qdš/
Qedeshet on Lion**
1300-1200 BCE

Holding a serpent and a flower, the Naked Goddess Qdš/ "Qedeshet" (Cornelius 2004: 45-6, 193) stands on the back of a striding lioness.

Crowned with a headdress of a disk and crescent moon or horns, the goddess' hair is fashioned in the trademark Hathor style.

This lioness is proportionally larger and more primitive than traditional depictions.

Drawing after Ibid. Pl. 5.18.

Goddess

on Lion

**Goddess Qdš/
Qedeshet on Lion**
~1300 BCE

This trinity depicts the Naked Goddess Qdš/"Qedeshet" (Cornelius 2004:45-8, 193) standing on her emblematic lion and flanked by male figures.

Facing frontally, Qdš/Qedeshet holds short-stemmed lotus flowers and a snake/serpent. Her hair is depicted in the traditional style of the goddess Hathor; her pubic triangle is defined.

The figure on the right, holding an Egyptian ankh, was initially identified as a woman; the phallic remnant was claimed to be "the remains of an earlier figure of [the Egyptian god] Min, or a later addition" (Pritchard 1954: 304).   Drawing after Ibid. 163 Fig. 470.

Goddess

on Lion

Similar Iconographic Associations:
Goddess on Lion
~2334-2154 BCE

This Mesopotamian seal impression depicts a parade/processional scene before a primary goddess. The goddess stands on a reclining lion with her arm upraised in a gesture of benediction.
Drawing after Wolkstein 1983:98.

Goddess

on Lion

Similar Iconographic Associations:
Measuring Goddess on Lion
~2300-1950 BCE

Discovered above an altar shrine, this Mesopotamian clay plaque depicts a winged Naked Goddess variously identified as Inanna/Ishtar and/or Lilith (Adam's first wife according to Kabbalahistic tradition).

Standing with taloned feet on the backs of lions, the Naked Goddess wears a tiered crown, bracelets and a multi-stranded necklace. Facing worshippers in a frontal posture enables the goddess to establish "a relation with all who approach" (Frankfort 1996:111).

The rods and measuring lines held by the goddess are used for utilitarian purposes, as well as to abstractly "indicate the limited span of man's life or his judgment at death" (Ibid.). The lions recline upon a mountain top – a venerated high place of antiquity later reflected in Golgotha.   Drawing after Ibid. Il. 119.

Female

Trinity

Similar Historic Associations:
Stone Age Female Trinity
~17,000-12/10,000 BCE

These three female images were discovered sculpted above a bovine on Paleolithic cave walls at Angles sur-l'Anglin, France.

This configuration may represent a "truly ancient version of the triple goddesses found in the much later religions of Europe and the Near East" (Camphausen1996:13).
Drawing after Ibid. Fig. 17.

Goddess

Trinity

Similar Historic Associations:
Mycenaean Goddess Trinity
~1400-1300 BCE

This Mycenaean seal impression depicts a Triple Goddess from the House of the Oil Merchant (Taylour 1983:119). The upraised arms of the female figures is a traditional Minoan religious motif.
Drawing after Ibid.

Goddess

on Lion

Holy Trinity Stela with Triple Goddess on Lion
1198-1166 BCE*

Standing on the back of a striding lion, this Naked Goddess holds a serpent in one hand and a long-stemmed lotus flower in the other.

[1 of 2 pages]

Wearing a horned crown, her hair is depicted in the traditional goddess Hathor hairstyle, which frames a partially damaged face. Her pubic triangle is outlined.

Although only a single figure is depicted, the hieroglyphic inscription identifies three goddesses: Qudshu, Astarte and Anat (Edwards 1955:50).

Addressing this triple-goddess fusion in the *Journal of Near Eastern Studies*, author I.E.S. Edwards states this inscription demonstrates the fluidity of ancient socio-religious beliefs by merging "into one deity three of the most important goddesses of western Asia" (Ibid. 50-1).

Goddess

Trinity

An article in *Biblical Archeologist* entitled the "Persistence of Canaanite Religion" further validates the triple-goddess, cultural-religio-historical fusion. Author R. A. Oden Jr. notes, "as early as the mid-second millennium B.C.[E.] the three goddesses [Qudshu/ Asherah, Astarte and Anat] share attributes, titles, and husbands" (1976:34).

This coalescence is attested to in the historical record as the three goddesses are worshipped separately and/or together throughout various historical periods, "It seems clear that at every period the three goddesses could be worshipped separately or together" (Ibid.).

*The date of 1198-1166 BCE per Cornelius (2004:128), previous dating of ~16-15th century BCE per Edwards (1955:49-51).

Drawing after Edwards 1955 Pl. III.

Ancient Trinities

Similar Historic Associations:
Jesus Describes the Defeat of Sophia
by Lion-Faced Power
~200 CE

Although existent for millennia, the lion's emblematic association with goddesses eventually undergoes a patriarchal transformation.

According to Jesus in the Gnostic Gospel of Sophia, *Pistis Sophia,* the lion-goddess relationship becomes adversarial when a lion-faced ruler assaults, then destroys, the goddess Sophia.

During conversations with his disciples, Jesus mentions Sophia who "saw the mystery of her name on my vesture and the whole glory of its mystery" (Mead 1955:34).

Hearing Sophia mentioned, Mary Magdalene asks about her. Jesus answers by describing the demise of Sophia/the feminine:

> "It came to pass . . . that all the rulers in the twelve aeons, who are below, hated her . . . It came to pass then, when the rulers of the twelve aeons were enraged against Pistis Sophia, who is above them, and hated her exceedingly . . . And he emanated out of himself a great lion-faced power . . . in order that they might there lie in wait for Pistis Sophia and take away her power out of her, because . . . the rulers who abide, or persist in performing the mystery, hated her, and all the guards who are at the gates of the aeons, hated her also" (Ibid. 35-36. Thank you to Maria Shaw Lawson.).

Female

Trinity

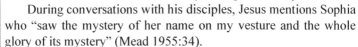

Similar Historic Associations:
Female Trinity is Vehicle of Holy Power
~30,000-4,000 BCE

Discovered on Castellon's Spanish cave walls, this female trinity is understood to represent "the vehicle of holy power" (Campbell 1969:381).

Drawing after Ibid. 380.

Qdš =
Asherah

In addition, over 60 years ago the *Bulletin of the American Schools of Oriental Research* identified the goddess Qudshu/Qdš with Asherah, incorporating Asherah in the goddess trinity.

[2 of 2 pages]

Writing in an article entitled "The Early Alphabetic Inscriptions from Sinai and Their Decipherment," author William F. Albright substantiates his equivalent identification of Qudshu with Asherah on the basis of both (1) ancient parallel Ugaritic epic epithets and (2) similar iconographic Egyptian Qudshu representations on Syro-Palestinian plaques which had previously been identified as Asherah (1948:17 n. 58).

Qdš =
Asherah

Over 40 years ago, Albright's conclusion is further endorsed by *Canaanite Myth and Hebrew Epic* affirming that Qudšu/Qudshu/ *Qdš* is to be understood as Asherah and the subsequent correlation and interchange of the goddesses identifies the two as equivalent (Cross 1973:50-51).

Qdš =
Asherah

This equivalent identification firmly establishes Asherah within the "Qudshu/Asherah-Astarte-Anat" trinity.

Asherah
in Tema
Trinity

Similar Historic Associations:
Asherah Worshipped in Nabataean Trinity
~549 BCE

A commemorative, Nabataean inscription reveals Asherah was worshipped as part of a holy trinity at Tema, North Arabia.

According to *The Asherah in the Old Testament*, Asherah is praised four times on an inscription commemorating the construction of a temple pillar by a priest (Reed 1949:79).

Female

Trinity

Similar Historic Associations:
Pompeiian Female Trinity
~100 BCE

Buried for ~1700 years, this fresco of the Three Graces was discovered under 60 feet of volcanic debris at Pompeii.
Drawing after Taylor 1891:168.

71

III. Qdš Configurations ~1550-1200 BCE
   Qdš Introduction
   Asherah Egyptian Qdš Representations
   Asherah Palestinian Qdš Representations

Asherah references in this section include:

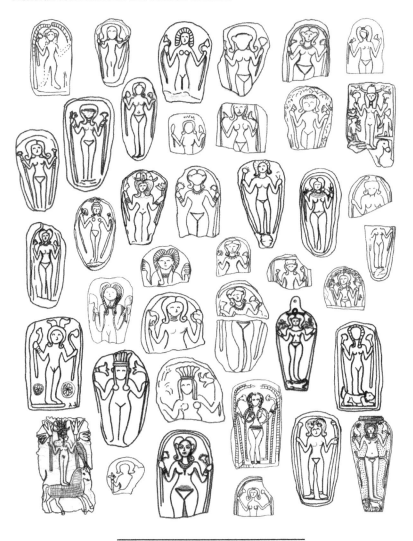

These Palestinian Qdš*-style representations have been identified as such by scholarship following previously established guidelines:**

> "The criteria that have been followed in identifying the figure on Palestinian terracottas are similar to those that apply to the inscribed stelae from Egypt, viz. the *pose* of the *naked goddess* and the *position of the arms* (i.e. extended in V-form) . . . although there are some exceptions" (Cornelius 2004:46-7).

*The Egyptian, hieroglyphic goddess identifications of kšt, kdš, kdst and kdšt (Ibid. 83-84) have been variously translated as Qdš, Qdšt, Qudsh, Qudšu, Qadesh, Qadishtu, Qadosh, Qedesh, Qedeshet, Qetesh, Qodesh, Quatesh, Qudsha, Qudshu, Kadesh, Ke(d)eshet, Kenet and as an epithet of Asherah.

**Pritchard in 1943, Schulman in 1984 and Cornelius in 2004.

Female
& Plants

Vegetation Goddesses
~1550-1150 BCE

Discovered at Gezer (top left and bottom right), an unknown provenience (top right) and Megiddo (bottom left), these Palestinian Vegetation Goddess plaques are stylistically similar to, and identified with, representations of the naked Egyptian goddess Qdš (Cornelius 2004:45-48). Drawings after Ibid. Pl. 5.32 (top left); 5.61 (top right); 5.55 (bottom left); 5.49 (bottom right).

Goddess
& Plants

Vegetative Vine Goddesses
~1550-1150 BCE

Stylistically similar to, and identified with, the Egyptian goddess Qdš representations, these Palestinian plaques of Vegetative Vine Goddesses holding plants were discovered at Tel el-Hesy (top left), an unknown provenience (top right) and Gezer (bottom left and right) (Cornelius 2004: 45-48). Drawings after Ibid. Pl. 5.39 (top left); 5.43 (top right); 5.51(bottom left); 5.48 (bottom right).

Goddess
& Plants

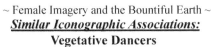

~ Female Imagery and the Bountiful Earth ~
Similar Iconographic Associations:
Vegetative Dancers
~800 BCE

This Mycenaean vase depicts a trinity of female dancers elevating plants/branches between them. Heart-shaped columns separate the figures.
Drawing after Iakovidis 2002:87
Fig. 53.

Vine

Goddess

~ Female Imagery and the Bountiful Earth ~
Similar Iconographic Associations:
Vine/Vegetation and Earth Goddess
~2400 BCE

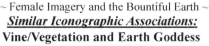

This vessel fragment, depicting a Vegetative Earth Goddess, is inscribed with the name of King Entemena of Lagash.

The enthroned goddess wears a vegetative, horned crown and has been variously identified as the "Lady of the Vine," Gesth-inanna, Inanna/Ishtar and/or Nin-hursag (Pritchard 1987:34).

Drawing after Ibid. Fig. 106.

V i n e

G o d d e s s

Vine

Goddess

~ Female Imagery and the Bountiful Earth ~
Similar Historic Associations:
Vine Goddess of Wisdom is the Light Goddess Sophia
~2000 BCE

The Mesopotamian "Vine Goddess of Wisdom, Siduri-Sabitu," assimilates into the "Light Goddess, Sophia,"* described by the Gnostics as "the virgin light [who] possesses the water of light, with which she baptizes the faithful" (Albright 1920:290).
*According to the *American Journal of Semitic Languages and Literatures,* the Light Goddess Sophia is also identified as Ishtar, the goddess of the plant Venus, as the virgin mother of the biblical Tammuz, and as the daughter-in-law of biblical Noah (Ibid. 294, 290, 288).

Vegetation

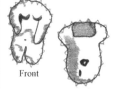

Goddess

~ Female Imagery and the Bountiful Earth ~
Similar Historic Associations:
Female Figurine with Embedded Seed
~7000-6000 BCE

A plant seed securely lodged in the back of this Catal Hoyuk female figurine affirms the universal symbolic association of female imagery with the bountiful earth.

Drawing after Hodder 2004:82.

Front

Back

Vegetation Goddesses
~1550-1150 BCE

Stylistically similar to, and identified with, the Egyptian goddess Qdš representations, these plaques of Vegetation Goddesses holding plants were discovered at Gezer (top left and bottom right), Beth Shemesh (top right) and an unknown provenience (bottom left) (Cornelius 2004:45-48).

Drawings after Ibid. Pl. 5.59 (top left); 5.36 (top right); 5.60 (bottom left); 5.46 (bottom right).

Vine/Vegetation and Earth Goddesses
~1550-1150 BCE

Discovered at Jericho (top left), an unknown provenience (top right, standing on the head of a lion?), Tel Harassim (bottom left), and Megiddo (bottom right), these Palestinian plaques of naked Vine/Vegetation and Earth Goddesses are stylistically similar to, and identified with, the Egyptian Qdš goddess representations (Ibid. 45-8).

Drawings after Ibid. Pl. 5.55a (top left); 5.42 (top right); 5.55b (bottom left); 5.44 (bottom right).

~ Female Imagery and the Bountiful Earth ~
Naked Goddess Represents the Bountiful Earth and Feminine Principle of Nature

First documented on ancient cuneiform tablets, the symbolic association of female imagery with vegetation (as a representation of universal life forces), transcends time and geography.

The cuneiform analogue is a precursor to, and an earlier personification of, the later Middle Bronze Age "Naked Goddess" as the "Feminine Principle of Nature," who "personifies the power of the earth to produce its fruits" (Keel 1998a:28).

Vegetation

Goddess

~ Female Imagery and the Bountiful Earth ~
__Similar Iconographic Associations:__
Vegetation Goddess
~2334-2193 BCE

Generated by a 4,000-year-old Akkadian cylinder seal, this seal impression depicts a ceremonial presentation scene before a mountain-enthroned crowned Vegetation Goddess.

The first deity approaching the enthroned goddess carries a branch/tree/bough. Two gods follow, balancing a ceremonial object/vase above a scorpion. The last of the processional figures is a smaller, female figure, likely a worshipper.

Drawing (reversed) after Collon 1987:34 Fig. 106.

Vegetation

Goddess

~ Female Imagery and the Bountiful Earth ~
__Similar Iconographic Associations:__
Vegetation Goddess is Mother Earth
~300 BCE

This relief depicts the Harvest Goddess of Agriculture. Known to the Greeks as Demeter and to the Romans as Ceres, she ritually presents vegetation/plants and snakes/serpents. Demeter gave grain, the first plough and farming knowledge to humans.

Describing Demeter's importance in the 5th century BCE, Euripides states "there are two principles[*] Supreme in human order: the first is Demeter, The Mother Earth; by whatever name you call her She stands for Bread, and feeds our mortal mouths with solid food" (Corrigan 1967:176-7).

*The second Grecian principle is that of the "son of God born of the virgin" (Ibid.).   Drawing after Neumann 1983:Pl. 60.

Vegetation

Goddess

Vegetation Goddesses
~1550-1150 BCE

Discovered at Gezer (top left and bottom right), Masmiyeh (top right) and Tel Zakhariya (bottom left), these Vegetation Goddess, Palestinian plaques are stylistically similar to, and identify the goddesses with, the Egyptian goddess Qdš (Cornelius 2004:45-48). Drawings after Ibid. Pl. 5.47 (top left); 5.61a (top right); 5.54 (bottom left); 5.50 (bottom right).

Vegetation

Goddess

Vegetative Vine Goddess
~1550-1200 BCE

A naked Vegetation Goddess wearing an ornate belt, ankle and arm bracelets is depicted on this plaque discovered at Beth Shemesh. Framed by a serpentine garland/vine arch, she holds a flower/plant in each hand; flowers adorn her shoulders. Her pubic triangle is defined.

According to *The Hebrew Goddess* author Raphael Patai, this is an "Astarte plaque," likely representing the goddess Astarte (1990:59 Pl. 12), analogous with Asherah and Anat (Oden 1976:34).

This plaque's stylistic similarities with inscribed Egyptian parallels also identify it as a representation of the goddess Qdš (Cornelius 2004:45-48). Drawing after Patai 1990:Pl. 12.

Ancient Palestinian Plaques

~ Female Imagery and the Bountiful Earth ~
__Similar Historic Associations:__
Vegetative Vine Goddess of Wisdom
~3000-2334 BCE

Vegetative
Vine

Goddess

Drinking through a tube, a crowned Vegetative Vine Goddess sits enthroned on the bottom register of this Iraqi seal impression. At top right a shepherd welcomes an approaching boat with dignitaries (Collon 1987:165).
Drawing after Ibid. 164 Fig. 756.

~ Female Imagery and the Bountiful Earth ~
__Similar Historic Associations:__
Vine Personifies the Goddess of Vine and Wisdom
~2000 BCE

Vegetative
Vine &

Wisdom
Goddess

According to the *American Journal of Semitic Languages and Literatures,* the "being who is symbolized as a vine [depicted next page] is a reflexion of the older goddess [depicted above] of the vine and of wisdom" (Albright 1920:286).

Vegetative
Vine

Goddess

Great
Earth

Mother

~ Female Imagery and the Bountiful Earth ~
__Similar Historic Associations:__
Great Earth Mother is
Mother of All Vegetation

The Great Mother: An Analysis of the Archetype defines the "Great Earth Mother who brings forth all life from herself" as "eminently the mother of all vegetation" (Neumann 1963:48).

Vegetative
Vine &

Wisdom
Goddess

**Vegetative Vine
Goddess**
~1550-1150 BCE

Discovered at an unknown provenience in Palestine, this terra cotta plaque depicts a naked "fertility goddess," likely identified as Astarte (Mazar 1990:273), who coalesced with Asherah (Oden 1976:34).

Unknown
Provenience

This plaque's stylistic similarities to Egyptian parallels also identifies her with the goddess Qdš (Cornelius 2004:45-8).

Commenting upon this iconography in *Archaeology and the Religion of Israel,* William F. Albright states this is a Palestinian configuration of "the goddess of fertility as a sacred harlot"* (Albright 1969:112). Drawing after Pritchard 1954:162 Fig. 469b.

---

*Sacred Harlot??!!
Who's Prostituting Who?

According to the original biblical text II Kings 23:7, King Josiah's (639-609 BCE) reform included the removal of "the sacred male prostitutes"* from the Jerusalem temple (Patai 1990:49).

The Hebrew Goddess states the function of the sacred male prostitutes was related to ". . . the fertility cult centering in the figure of the mother-goddess Asherah. Possibly, their services were made use of by childless women who visited the sanctuary in order to become pregnant. Such pilgrimages to holy places for the purpose of removing the curse of barrenness have remained an important feature of popular religion down to the present day among Moslems, Jews and Christians alike in all parts of the Middle East" (Ibid. 299 n. 59).

*The original Hebrew word used, *qedeshim,* is exclusively masculine, prohibiting female inclusion. To include female prostitutes, it would have been necessary to use both the masculine and feminine Hebrew plural terms, *qedeshim uqedeshot* (Ibid.).

Ancient Palestinian Plaques

Vegetative

Goddess

~ Female Imagery and the Bountiful Earth ~
Similar Historic Associations:
Vegetative Prosperity Goddess
~2500-2400 BCE

Seated upon a mountain throne, a "Vegetation Goddess" (Frankfort 1939:XXX) is approached by Akkadian deities and a worshipper.
Drawing after Ibid. Pl. XXj.

Vegetative

Goddess

~ Female Imagery and the Bountiful Earth ~
Similar Historic Associations:
Vegetative Traveling Goddess
~1600-1500 BCE

Discovered at Crete's Mochlos Island, a gold signet ring gold, generated this impression of a Vegetation Goddess traveling with a shrine and a sacred tree.   Drawing after photo by Elsa Beale, Heraklion Museum.

Vegetative

Goddess

~ Female Imagery and the Bountiful Earth ~
Similar Historic Associations:
Vegetative Resurrecting Goddess
~2334-2193 BCE

Standing on a mountain top, the Vegetation Goddess Inanna/Ishtar dispenses holy water over a resurrecting god on this Mesopotamian, cylinder seal impression. The goddess' wings symbolize victory (Collon 1987:165), an iconic tradition continued centuries later by Nike, the Victory Goddess.
Drawing after Ibid. 164 Fig. 761.

Females &

Vegetation

Vegetative Prosperity Goddess
~1550-1230 BCE

Wearing an ornate necklace, bracelets and her birthday suit, a Vegetation Goddess holding papyrus stalks/plants is depicted on this Tel Beit Mirsim plaque. Her face is framed by an elongated, Hathor goddess hairstyle.

This Palestinian plaque's stylistic similarities with inscribed, Egyptian, Qdš stelae identifies it as a Palestinian Qdš representation (Cornelius 2004:45-48).

Drawing after Pritchard 1954:162 Fig. 469l.

Vegetation

Goddess

Vegetation Goddess
~1400-1150 BCE

Purchased in the Hebron district of Jerusalem, this terra cotta plaque depicts a naked Vegetative Goddess holding long-stemmed plants. Her hair is shaped in the style of the goddess Hathor. She wears anklets above outward pointed feet; her pubic triangle is outlined.

The stance of the goddess and her attributes are stylistically similar to, and identify her with, inscribed Egyptian Qdš representations (Cornelius 2004:45-8). Drawing after Ibid. Pl. 5.41.

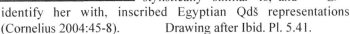

Vegetation

Goddess

~ Female Imagery and the Bountiful Earth ~
Similar Historic Associations:
Vulva/Seed Female Dancers
~4000-3800 BCE

At left, two fringe-skirted dancers are symbolically depicted "within a vulva/seed" (Gimbutas 1989:242).

Depicted within an elliptical cowrie shell, a symbol of the female reproductive system, the triangulated females represent fertility (Davis-Kimball 2002:163).

Drawing after Gimbutas 1998:242 Fig. 378.2.

Lady of
the

Vine

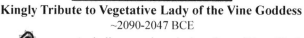

~ Female Imagery and the Bountiful Earth ~
Similar Historic Associations:
Kingly Tribute to Vegetative Lady of the Vine Goddess
~2090-2047 BCE

A dedicatory inscription from King Shulgi is inscribed on this 4,000-year-old gold earring.

Shulgi's dedication is to the "Vegetation Goddess" Geshtinanna, also identified as "The Lady of the Vine."

The earring's inscription reads:

"To Geshtinanna, his Lady,
Shulgi, the mighty young man,
King of Ur, King of Sumer and Akkade,
for his life, has dedicated [this earring]"
(Hurowitz 1994:32).
Drawing after Ibid.

Vegetation

Goddess

~ Female Imagery and the Bountiful Earth ~
Similar Historic Associations:
Listening Branch and Vegetation Goddess
~1800-1550 BCE

A Palestinian, Vegetative "Branch Goddess" is depicted at left (Keel 1998a:28).

The small trees/ branches flanking her indicate she personifies vegetative life forces.

Unknown
Provenience

Experts believe her oversized ears are "an expression of the willingness of the goddess to hear the worshippers who appeal to her" (Ibid.).
Drawing after Ibid. 27 Fig. 12a.

Vegetative
Prosperity

Syro-Pal.
Goddess

~ Female Imagery and the Bountiful Earth ~
Syro-Palestinian Prosperity Goddess
of Earth and Vegetation

Syro-Palestinian imagery depicts the "Prosperity Goddess" of the earth with plant elements, either growing out of the goddess or encircling her (Keel 1998b:47).

Vine

Goddess

Vegetation Goddesses
~1550-1230 BCE

These Naked Goddesses, discovered at Megiddo (left) and Beth Shemesh (right), hold plants and are reflective of the Vegetation and Vine Goddess tradition.

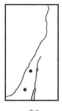

Their artistic, stylistic similarities with inscribed, Egyptian parallels –

their frontal stance, nakedness, goddess Hathor hairstyle and extended arms with hands holding plants – identify them as Qdš representations (Cornelius 2004:45-48). Drawings after Ibid. Pl. 5.45 (left); 5.53 (right).

Vegetation

Goddess

Vegetative Vine Prosperity Goddesses
~1550-1150 BCE

Discovered at Tell Beit Mirsim, these Palestinian plaques depict naked Vegetative Vine and Prosperity Goddesses.

Wearing feather-styled crowns, they face frontally with extended arms holding flowers/plants. Stylistically, their traditional Qdš presentation identify the goddesses as Qdš representations (Cornelius 2004:45-48). Drawings after Ibid. Pl. 5.40 (left); 5.57 (right).

Stylistically Similar

Ajrud Crowns

Vegetative Branch

Goddess

~ Female Imagery and the Bountiful Earth ~
Similar Historic Associations:

Great

Mother

The underlying mythological nucleus of the Vine/Vegetation Goddess, the Tree/Branch Goddess, the Naked Goddess and the Stylized Sacred Tree is the Great Mother Goddess as Nutritive Life Source.

Vegetation

Goddess

Palestinian Plaques of Antiquity

Vegetation

Goddess

~ Female Imagery and the Bountiful Earth ~
Similar Historic Associations:
Vegetation Goddess
~2004 BCE

Discovered in modern Iran, this cylinder seal impression pictures a seated goddess framed by vegetation symbols sprouting from her body. She faces, and offers benediction toward, a horn-crowned female.

A branch/small tree, animals and a crescent moon complete the configuration.   Drawing after Collon 1987:38 Fig. 135.

Vegetation

Goddess

~ Female Imagery and the Bountiful Earth ~
Similar Historic Associations:
Vegetation Goddess
~2500-2400 BCE

Four deities approach a goddess in this "Adoration of the Goddess of Vegetation" ceremonial presentation scene (Frankfort 1939:XXX).

Seated upon a mountain throne, the Vegetation Goddess holds branches/boughs; a stylized, sacred tree appears behind her.

Drawing after Ibid. Pl. XXk.

Goddess

of
Animals

Similar Historic Associations:
Qdš-Style Goddess of Animals
~1300 BCE

Displaying artistic elements stylistically similar to Egyptian *Qdš* representations, this Cyprus seal impression features a crowned Naked Goddess standing on the back of a striding lion – a representation of the goddess in her aspect of Goddess/Mistress of Animals (Cornelius 2004:98).   Drawing after Ibid. Pl. 5.11.

Goddess
on Horse

Vegetation

Goddess

Qdš-Style Goddess on Horseback
~1550-1150 BCE

Created from a pottery mold discovered at Tel Qarnayim, this terra cotta plaque depicts a naked Vegetation Goddess flanked by crowned, male gods (Keel 1998a:68).

Standing on the back of a horse, the goddess wears a crown with protruding horns. Birds (goddess symbols throughout antiquity) soar above the flowers she holds.

This configuration is stylistically similar to, and identified with Egyptian Qdš parallels (Cornelius 2004:45-48, 91).

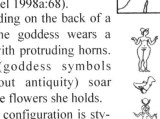

Drawing after Keel 1998a:67 Fig. 72; Cornelius 2004: Pl. 5.13 (where image is reversed with horse facing left).

Goddess

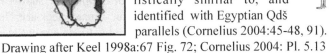

on Horse

Similar Iconographic Associations:
Syrian Goddess on Horseback
~1350-1200 BCE

Although discovered in Egypt, this configuration is likely a representation of a Syrian goddess (Pritchard 1954:305).

The charging goddess wears a large earring, a cross attached to a beaded necklace and her birthday suit. Her upraised arm brandishes a weapon overhead, while her horse traverses over an enemy combatant.

Drawing after Ibid. 165 Fig. 479.

Queen of

Heaven

Queen of Heaven, Asherah
~1450-1365 BCE

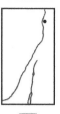

[1 of 2 pages]

Discovered in the tomb of a princess at the ancient port city of Minet el-Beida, Ugarit, this gold pendant depicts a crowned and Naked Goddess standing on the back of a striding lion.

Snakes/serpents cross behind her waist. Her hair is fashioned in the traditional Hathor goddess hairstyle. She wears an ornate necklace; her pubic triangle is outlined.

The elevated ibex and her stance upon a lion depict the goddess in her aspect as the Goddess/ Mistress of Animals.

In addition, the pendant's stylized, starry background identifies this goddess celestially as a Queen of Heaven.

According to *Biblical Archaeology Review*, this goddess is identified as Qudshu/Holiness by inscribed Egyptian parallels. Worshipped also as Ashtart/Astarte and Anat, it is likely this

Drawing by Jennifer Johnson after Patai 1990:Pl. 15.

Queen of

Heaven

Similar Historic Associations:
Queen of Heaven, Sophia
~1100 CE

This depiction of Sophia, the Goddess of Wisdom, as a celestial Queen of Heaven comes from a Medieval Spanish manuscript. Framed by an astral background, Sophia holds a starburst/ rosette* shield.

Drawing after Matthews 1992:70.

*An epiphany of the goddess throughout antiquity.

Queen of
Heaven,

Asherah

configuration represents "the principal goddess of the Canaanites, and probably of the Israelites as well"* (Coogan 1995:42).

Although historically several goddesses – Qdš**/Qudshu**/Holiness, Ishtar, Astarte, Anat and Asherah – have been identified as the Queen of Heaven, experts contend this gold pendant most specifically represents Asherah.

[2 of 2 pages]

Substantiating this conclusion, scholars state the religion of ancient Israel included the worship of the goddess Asherah during the first millennium. Known to us through archaeological discoveries and biblical references, experts extrapolate further on Asherah's significance, stating, "As with her manifestations elsewhere, she is the consort or wife of the chief deity – in Israel's case, Yahweh" (Ibid.).

**Recalling the hieroglyphic kšt, kdš, kdst and kdšt (Cornelius 2004, 83-84) have been variously translated as Qdš, Qdšt, Qudsh, Qudšu, Qadesh, Qadishtu, Qadosh, Qedesh, Qedeshet, Qetesh, Qodesh, Quatesh, Qudsha, Qudshu, Kadesh, Ke(d)eshet, Kenet and as an epithet of Asherah.

Israel
from
Canaan

*Israel from Canaan

According to *Biblical Archaeology Review,* "Discoveries such as this pendant remind us that Israel was very much a part of the Levant, rather than a separate entity. As Ezekiel put it 'By origin and birth you are of the land of the Canaanites' (Ezekiel 16:3)" (Coogan 1995:42).

Queen of
Heaven,

Asherah

Similar Historic Associations:
Queen of Heaven, Athena
~200-100 BCE

"*Then come, Athena, and hold your hand over the kiln . . .*" begins a prayer to Athena, "Goddess of Arts and Crafts," on a 2nd century BCE text (attributed to Homer in the 8th c BCE) (DeGrummond 2001:60).

This pottery fragment depicts the protectress goddess Menerva/Minerva (Latin)/ Athena (Greek) in her helmeted aspect as Warrior Goddess and celestially as a Queen of Heaven.

Drawing after Ibid.

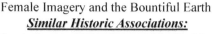

Female Imagery and the Bountiful Earth
Similar Historic Associations:
Vegetation and Vine Prosperity Goddess
~100 CE

Vegetation
& Vine

Goddess

Vulva

Seed

Standing upon a vulva seed, the Vegetation and Vine Goddess Tanit, dispenses the prosperity of nature. Wearing a lunar crown, she elevates bountiful chalices as an adorant stands below. A field of rosettes and rosette stars surround the goddess on this Carthaginian configuration. Drawing after Tubb 1998:145 Fig. 105.

Vine Association

Vine & Vegetation

Goddess

Similar Historic Associations:
Vine Personifies Light, Wisdom, Purity & Holy Water

According to the *American Journal of Semitic Languages and Literatures,* "In Mandaean [Gnostic] symbolism the vine . . . is the incorporation of light, wisdom, and purity; . . . From it flows the rivers, bearing holy water to provide sustenance for man" (Albright 1920:266).

Vine & Vegetation

Goddess

~ Female Imagery and the Bountiful Earth ~

Vegetation
& Vine

Goddess

**Vegetation and Vine
Goddesses**
~1400 BCE

These plaques depicting naked Qdš-style Vegetation Goddesses were discovered at Tel Batash (right) and Gezer (left).

Their hair is fashioned in the traditional style of the goddess Hathor. Bent at the elbows, their arms extend to the side and their hands hold long-stemmed flowers/plants. Their pubic triangles are delineated. The feet of the Tel Batash goddess point to the left; her face has been lost in time.

Drawings after Cornelius 2004:Pl. 5.33 (left); 5.34 (right).

Vegetation
& Vine

Goddess

**Vegetation and Vine
Goddesses**
~14000-1150 BCE

Discovered at Tel Harassim (left) and Aphek (right), the stylistic similarities of these terra cotta plaques – frontal stance, nakedness, goddess Hathor hairstyle, hands holding plants – identify them with representations of the Egyptian goddess Qdš (Cornelius 2004:45-48).

Although indiscernible, the first goddess (left) is standing on the back of a lion (Ibid. 132). The second goddess (right) is framed by a vine/rope-like garland. Her overlay ears are a bovine reference.

Drawings after Ibid. Pl. 5.25 (left); 5.31 (right).

Ancient Elevated Arm Iconography

Goddess

on Lion

Similar Iconographic Associations:
Goddesses on Lions
~3000-2334 BCE

Dating back almost five millennia, this partial composition is from the upper register of a cylinder seal discovered in modern Iran.

A crowned Warrior Goddess (left, with upraised bow) stands on the backs of striding lions. The second, Crowned Goddess kneels on the backs of reclining lions. Vegetative stalks sprout from her shoulders and her arms encircle her breasts. Astral symbols are depicted before her; an ibex stands on his hind legs behind her.
Drawing after Collon 1987:164 Fig. 758.

Goddess

with Lion

~ Female Imagery and the Bountiful Earth ~
Similar Historic Associations:
Princess-Priestess with Lion Griffin
~1300 BCE

This ceremonial, presentation scene depicts a Mycenaean princess-priestess (identified by her unique crown) ritually proffering wheat or barley. Beside her is a winged griffin, an epiphany of Minoan and Mycenaean goddesses.*

Drawing after photo by Lori North, Nauplia Museum.

*A stylistically similar ~1400 BCE Palestinian, cylinder seal (right and page 37) depicts a winged griffin behind an enthroned goddess.

Goddess ... on Lion

Qdš-Style Vegetation Goddess on Lion
~1400-1150 BCE

A naked Vegetation Goddess stands on the back of a reclining lion on this Tel Harassim plaque (Cornelius 2004:132).

Bent at the elbows, her arms extend outward and she holds a long-stemmed plant/flower in each hand. Her hair is shaped in an elongated style of the goddess Hathor.

Due to this plaque's stylistic similarities with inscribed Egyptian parallels, it is identified as a Qdš representation (Ibid. 45-48).

Drawing after Ibid. Pl. 5.24.

Goddess ... on Lion

Qdš-Style Vegetation Goddess on Lion
~1300 BCE

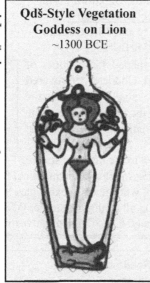

Standing on the back of a lion, this naked Vegetative, Prosperity Goddess wears a horned crown with a circular, center disc. Bovine-shaped ears overlay her hair which is shaped in the traditional style of the goddess Hathor. She holds long-stemmed flowers.

Cast from a mold discovered in an ancient Akko tomb, this bronze plaque-pendant is iconographically classified as a Qdš representation (Cornelius 2004: 45-48). Drawing after Keel 1998a:67 Fig. 70.

Goddess and Lion Associations of Antiquity

Vegetative Prosperity

Goddess

Vegetative Prosperity Goddess
~1200-1000 BCE

Discovered at Beth Shemesh, this plaque depicts a Vegetation Goddess with arms extended outward and hands holding plant(s)/flower(s). She wears a horned crown. Her pubic triangle is defined.

According to *The Hebrew Goddess*, this plaque depicts the goddess "Astarte[/Asherah] holding sacred flowers" (Patai 1990:Pl. 13).

In addition, due to this plaque's stylistic similarity with inscribed Egyptian parallels, it is identified as a representation of the goddess Qdš/Qedeshet (Cornelius 2004: 45-8).   Drawing after Patai 1990:Pl. 13.

Vegetative Prosperity

Goddess

Female Imagery and the Bountiful Earth
Similar Historic Associations:
Vegetative, Prosperity and Life Goddess
~1800-1550 BCE

The snail-shaped ram* horns of this Naked Goddess, discovered at Jericho, actually personifies the "source of the power of life in the plants and animals" (Keel 1998a: 20).

*In addition to the ram, the sphere of the goddess includes the maternal bovine, wild sheep, wild goats, ibexes, gazelles and deer (Ibid.), all analogous to the 'Mountain Herds of Astarte/Asherah' (see page 42).   Drawing after Ibid. 21.

Ancient Horned Goddesses

Vegetative
Prosperity

Goddess

**Vegetation Qdš-Style
Goddess**
~1400 BCE

The central figure of this terra cotta plaque, discovered at Tel Zafit, is a naked Vegetation Goddess holding long-stemmed flowers/plants. Facing frontally, her feet point to the right. She wears a unique, winged(?) crown. Her hairstyle is that of the goddess Hathor.

Unique double-encircled rosettes (symbol of the Sumerian goddess Inanna/Ishtar) add artistic embellishment.

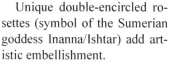

Due to stylistic similarities with inscribed Egyptian parallels, this Tel Zafit goddess is identified as a Qdš/ Qedeshet representation (Cornelius 2004:45-8).

Drawing after Ibid. Pl. 5.37.

Vegetative
Prosperity

Goddess

**Vegetation Qdš-Style
Goddess**
~1300-1050 BCE

A naked Vegetation Goddess holding long-stemmed flower(s)/plant(s) is depicted on this terra cotta plaque discovered at Lachish. Bovine shaped ears overlay her goddess Hathor hairstyle. She wears a necklace and bracelets. Her pubic triangle is accentuated.

With artistic elements stylistically similar to inscribed, Egyptian Qdš parallels, this Lachish configuration is identified as a representation of the goddess *Qdš* (Cornelius 2004:45-48).

Drawing after Ibid. Pl. 5.38.

Vegetative Prosperity Goddesses of Antiquity

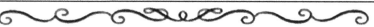

Equestrian

Goddess

Similar Iconographic Associations:
Equestrian Goddess
~1000-925 BCE

Discovered at Acre, this seal impression depicts a mounted goddess with a figure before her, his hand upon the horse's muzzle.

The goddess wears a conical headdress with a scarf flowing down her back. Her hand is raised in a gesture of benediction. A bird hovers behind her.

This horse-riding goddess composition is one of several depicted on Palestinian seals throughout Iron Age IIA (1000 BCE - 900 BCE) (Keel 1998a:141).

Drawing after Ibid.142 Fig. 163a.

Equestrian

Goddess

Similar Iconographic Associations:
Equestrian Divinity
~100 BCE

Holding a victory wreath and a shield, this Redonian female warrior is pictured on the back of a galloping/prancing horse.

Made of gold and minted by a Briton tribe, the Celts historically understood their female warrior figures to be divine (Green 1996:33).

Drawing after Ibid. 35.

Goddess

on Horse

Ancient Palestinian Warrior Goddesses

Equestrian

Goddess

Vegetation

Goddess

Equestrian Goddess
~12th c BCE

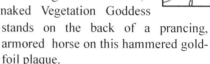

"Lady Godiva of the Bronze Age" reads the caption of this goddess depiction in a *Biblical Archaeology Review* article (King 2005:45).

Holding lotus blossoms, a naked Vegetation Goddess stands on the back of a prancing, armored horse on this hammered gold-foil plaque.

The headdress of the goddess is an elaborate, horned and feathered crown. Her eye was once inlaid with a precious stone/gem. A small triangle, cut from the gold-foil, denotes her pubic triangle.

Stylistically similar to inscribed, Egyptian goddess Qdš* stelae, this gold-foil, Palestinian plaque is identified as a Qdš*/Qedeshet* representation (Cornelius 2004:45-48, 91).

In addition to affirming her identification as Qdš,* the Lachish excavators also define this goddess as a local variation of the Egyptian Qudshu*/Qadesh* (King 2005:45), an epithet of Asherah.

Extrapolating further, the *Archaeological Encyclopedia of the Holy Land* states this may be a representation of the goddess "Ashtoreth[/Asherah]" (Negev 2001:290).

*Recalling the hieroglyphic kšt, kdš, kdst and kdšt (Cornelius 2004:83-84) have been variously translated as Qdš, Qdšt, Qudsh, Qudšu, Qadesh, Qadishtu, Qadosh, Qedesh, Qedeshet, Qetesh, Qodesh, Quatesh, Qudsha, Qudshu, Kadesh, Ke(d)eshet, Kenet and as an epithet of Asherah.   Drawing after King 2005:45.

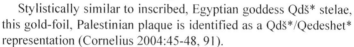

~ Female Imagery and the Bountiful Earth ~
**Palestinian Goddess is the
Creator of Vegetation and Life**

According to *Gods, Goddesses and Images of God In Ancient Israel,* ancient imagery depicted females with vegetation/water symbols as personifications of generative life forces and sustenance: "in Syria-Palestine . . . the image of a goddess served as an amulet which was venerated as a creator of vegetation, if not of life itself" (Keel 1998a:25).

IRON AGE REFERENCES

In ancient Palestine, Anat, Asherah, Astarte and Ashtaroth are the principal goddesses "whose names recur in the literary sources most frequently and continuously."

The Cult[*] of the Mother-Goddess
(James 1994:69)

*Historically, goddess religions have often been labeled as 'cults.' Consider the vastly different implications between the 'cult of Asherah' or the 'religion of Asherah,' and the 'cult of Jesus' or the 'religion of Jesus.'

IV. Iron Ages I, IIA & IIB   ~1200-800 BCE

During the first millennium, the goddess Asherah was worshipped in the popular religion of ancient Israel. "As with her manifestations elsewhere, she is the consort or wife of the chief deity – in Israel's case, Yahweh . . . Jeremiah (7:18 and 44:17-19) calls her the 'queen of heaven'."

Biblical Archaeology Review
(Coogan 1995:42)

Asherah references in this section include:

Asherah at Earliest
Israelite Worship Site

Temple of
Ashtaroth/Asherah

Temple of
Asherah

Arabian Asherah
Worship

Asherah is Eve

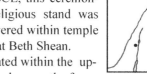

Goddess in Ceremonial Religious Shrine
~1200 BCE

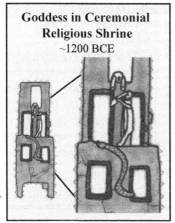

Dating to the 12th century BCE, this ceremonial, religious stand was discovered within temple ruins at Beth Shean.

Seated within the upper window are the fragmentary remnants of a naked female figure with her genitalia revealed. Below her is a standing figure and a meandering snake; the head of a striding lion peers out from the side.

According to *The Story of the Bible as Told by Living Writers of Authority,* this ceremonial stand is a small shrine "from [the goddess] Ashtaroth's[/Asherah's] house," as referenced in the biblical passage I Samuel 31:10 (Hollis 1952:373).

Goddess

in Shrine

Reconstructed Beth Shean temple shrine

The reconstructed shrine (at left) depicts a second figure in a window frame next to the fragmentary, first figure (also in a window frame). Their extended hands touch each others head.

Although damage to the existent, partial figure renders its sex undeterminable, site excavators originally believed both middle register figures were males and represented gods. However, recalling lions belong "exclusively to the sphere of the goddess," experts state it is far more likely females would be depicted with this symbol (Keel 1998a:86).*

The lion's presence may also indicate one of the female figures is representative of Asherah in her aspect as 'the Lion Lady.'

*This creates the possibility that three females/goddesses may be represented on this religious Beth Shean temple shrine.

Drawings after: Moorey 1991:45 (top); Hollis 1952:373 (bottom).

Ancient Goddess Temple Coins

Goddess

in Shrine

Similar Iconographic Associations:
Goddess in Ceremonial Religious Shrine
~2334-2000 BCE

This Uruk presentation scene depicts a goddess standing within a temple entrance as naked priests (Collon 1987: 172) approach with ritual, offerings. A stylized tree is pictured between the goddess and her priests.

Drawing after Ibid. 176 Fig. 826.

Goddess
Shrine

& Snake
/Serpent

Similar Iconographic Associations:
Goddess Before Shrine
~500 BCE

Poised within the entrance of a shrine, a snake/serpent protectively watches over the seated Harvest and Vegetation Goddess, Hera.

Drawing after Campbell 1964:15.

Ancient Goddess and Snake/Serpent Associations

Trophy
Present-
ation

Similar Historic Associations:
Shrine Presentation of Armor by
Goddess of Victory, Nike
~400 BCE

Nike, the Goddess of Victory, adjusts a trophy of armor on this seal presentation scene.

This scene is similar to the one described in 1 Samuel 31:10, where the armor of King Saul is placed in the temple of Ashtaroth/Asherah after his defeat and death (see Temple at right).

Drawing after Hornblower 1998:494.

Goddess

in Shrine

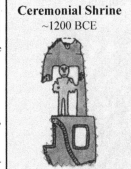

Goddess in Ceremonial Shrine

~1200 BCE

A goddess holds two birds/ doves in the doorway of this ceremonial religious stand discovered within a Beth Shean temple (Keel 1998a:84-86). A fragmented snake/serpent meanders below her.

Recalling birds and snakes are elements of the iconography of the goddess, and one of Asherah's epithets was 'the One of the Serpent,' this depicted goddess may represent Asherah.

Drawing after Ibid. 85 Fig. 104.

Goddess

Temple

Temple of Ashtaroth/ Asherah

~1200 BCE

A temple, over 3,000-years old and dedicated to the goddess Ashtaroth/Asherah, has been discovered at Tel el-Husn/Beth Shean. The temple is believed to have received the armor of Israel's King Saul as a gift to the goddess.

Ashtaroth

According to an article entitled "Mysteries of the Bible" in *U. S. News & World Report,* this temple is referenced in the bible, as "Archaeologists say this is almost certainly the temple referred to in 1 Samuel 31:10 where after [Israel's first] king Saul's death, soldiers 'put his armor in the temple of Ashtaroth[/ Asherah]'" (Sheler 1995:68).

Scholars in *Biblical Archaeology Review* affirm this suggestion, stating, "Two adjacent late 11th-century [BCE] temples at Beth-Shean have been associated with the two temples where Saul's armor and head were placed following his death on Mt. Gilboa (1 Samuel 31:10; 1 Chronicles 10:6-10)" (Shanks 1995:33).

Ashtaroth

Ashtaroth - Deliberately Corrupted Goddess Name

According to *The Interpreter's Dictionary of the Bible*, the term *Ashtaroth* is a deliberate Hebrew misvocalization interjecting *shame* into the name of the goddess (Buttrick 1962:255). In actuality, it is a "bastardized form" of the goddess' name (Dever 1984:21).

Nursing

Goddess

Similar Iconographic Associations:
Nursing Saint Sophia
~12th c CE

Two monks/nobles nurse from the breasts of "Sophia-Sapientia"/ Saint Sophia on this Vatican Library medieval manuscript image from the Vatican Library (Neumann 1963:329).

According to *The Great Mother: An Analysis of the Archetype*, the nursing men are receiving a "level of spiritual transformation" through the "'virgin's milk' of Sophia" (Ibid.).
Drawing after Ibid. Pl. 174.

Nursing

Goddess

Similar Iconographic Associations:
Nursing Goddess
~1300 BCE

This naked female torso, discovered at Beth Shean, embraces an infant in her arms. She wears bracelets and an ornately decorated necklace and belt. Her pubic triangle is outlined and emphasized.

Although stylistically similar to the Egyptian, Isis-and-Horus, mother-and-son representations, this is an indigenous Canaanite Nursing Goddess and not just an Egyptian theme local adaptation (Keel 1998a:84). Drawing after Ibid. 85 Fig. 103.

Nursing

Saint

Nursing Goddess
~1150 BCE

Discovered within Ugarit's royal palace, this ivory section was once the center inset of a large, backboard/royal couch panel (Cornelius 2004: 115-6).

Initially, this ivory centerpiece was first identified as a "Goddess Nursing Two Children" in *The Ancient Near East in Pictures Relating to the Old Testament* (Pritchard 1975 II:829).

Some scholars have more recently suggested the children most likely represent kings, (Cornelius 2004:39) although gods remain a possibility, as does one god and one king.

The combined consensus is that this palace, ivory centerpiece depicts a Nursing Goddess with two children, king(s) and/or god(s).

This four-winged, standing goddess wears an astral/solar disc in the center of her horned crown. Her long gown displays variegated, linear symmetrical designs. Her hair frames her face then cascades into the rolled ends of the goddess Hathor curls. Facing frontally, her feet point to the left.

The arms of the goddess protectively encircle the kilted children/king(s)/god(s) as she nurses them. One of the young figures holds an Egyptian ankh.

Although positive identification of the portrayed goddess remains elusive, experts suggest this may be a representation of the goddess Asherah* (Ibid. 38, 89).

*Other candidates include Anat and Astarte (Ibid.).

Drawing after Pritchard 1975:829 Pl. 60.

Winged Goddesses of Antiquity

Venus

Head

Pillar of Religion
Asherah Head
~1000-586 BCE

According to an article entitled "In the Path of Sennacherib" published in *Biblical Archaeology Review,* this "delicate face was the head of a typical 'pillar figurine'" (Borowski 2005:30).

Discovered at Tel Halif, this molded, female head was once attached to the top of a Judean pillar figurine identified as a "Pillar of Religion" (Ibid.).

Extrapolating further, the *Journal of Biblical Studies* identifies this head as representative of the goddess Asherah (Jacobs 2001: 4).   Drawing after Borowski 2005:30.

Religious

Head

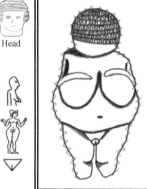

Similar Iconographic Associations:
Willendorf Venus
~30-26,000 BCE

Although created several thousand years earlier, this Paleolithic figurine displays a concentrically circular, spiraling hair design stylistically similar to the Judean pillar figurines.

Discovered at Willendorf, Austria, she was mockingly identified as a 'Venus' figurine. Her arms rest upon abundant breasts and a rotund body; her pubic triangle and vulva are delineated and defined.
Drawing after Putman 1988:459.

Ancient Israel and Judah Worshipped Asherah and Yahweh

According to a *Biblical Archaeology Review* article entitled "Idols of the People: Miniature Images of Clay in the Ancient Near East," "The Asherah cult thus came to be regarded as much a feature of popular religion in ancient Israel and Judah as the worship of Yahweh" (Hurowitz 2005:58).

Multiple Altars within Arad Temple's Holy of Holies
~1000-900 BCE

This "Holy of Holies of [an] Israelite sanctuary, with altars at each side of [its] entrance" (Aharoni 1967:98) was discovered at Arad.

Of the two horned altars and two sacred standing stones within the Holy of Holies sacred space, "one [is] conspicuously smaller than the other" (Dever 2001:181).

This, coupled with the bronze lion discovered at the site (see page 111),

verify "that Asherah, the 'Lion Lady' was worshipped *alongside* Yahweh at Arad" (Ibid. 183).
Drawing after Aharoni 1967:98.

Asherah at Earliest Israelite Worship Site
~1000-900 BCE

The "earliest Israelite remains" (Negev 2001:289) may have been discovered within an ancient religious worship site at Lachish.

According to the *Archaeological Encyclopedia of the Holy Land,* several cultic/religious artifacts were unearthed at this worship site including "the remains of the trunk of an olive tree which had been intentionally buried (an *asherah?*)" (Ibid. 290), which means there can be no denying, that one of Israel's earliest religious artifacts is likely a sacred tree/an asherah – the very symbol of the goddess Asherah.

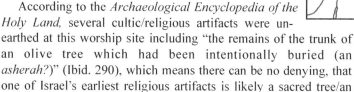

Asherah =
Sacred
Tree of
Asherah

~ Female Imagery and the Bountiful Earth ~
Similar Historic Associations:
Sacred Tree is an Asherah/ Symbol of the Goddess Asherah

Over 70 years ago experts identified sacred trees as a symbol of the goddess Asherah. An article entitled "The Sacred Tree on Palestine Painted Pottery" published in the *Journal of the American Oriental Society* stated, "We need not stress the point that the Asherah was a sacred tree, symbol of the goddess" (May 1939:251-9).

Goddess
&

Lion(s)

Similar Historic Associations:
Goddess and Lion
~2360-2180 BCE

Holding its leash and resting her foot upon the back of her signature lion, the winged Warrior Goddess Inanna/Ishtar holds a lion-scimitar (Pritchard 1954:377), as wings and weapons sprout from her shoulders. A minor goddess stands before Inanna/Ishtar with her hands upraised in worship.
Drawing after Ibid. 177 Fig. 526.

Lion of

Goddess
Asherah

Similar Historic Associations:
Goddess and Lion
~720 BCE

This Mesopotamian cylinder seal impression depicts a worshiper approaching the Warrior Goddess Inanna/Ishtar. Astrally crowned, the goddess stands on the back of a reclining lion before a sacred tree.
Drawing after Collon 1987:166 Fig. 773.

Goddess
&

Lion(s)

Similar Historic Associations:
Goddess and Lion
~224 CE

The Crowned Goddess Astarte/Asherah is depicted on the back of a striding lion on this Phoenician coin. Minted at Sidon, this configuration continues an iconic leonine-goddess tradition established thousands of years earlier.
Drawing after Hill 1910: Pl. XXV8.

Ancient Goddess and Lion Associations

Asherah is Eve
~1000 BCE

In a publication entitled *Asherah and the Cult of Yahweh in Israel,* author Saul M. Olyan states Eve "is an attested epithet of Tannit/[Tanit/]Asherah" during the first millennium BCE (1988:71).

Extrapolating further upon the Eve-Asherah identification, Olyan suggests Asherah's historical, serpent associations may reference a previous myth embedded within the Adam and Eve, Garden of Eden narrative: "One suspects that an early myth associating the serpent/sea dragon and Asherah has been lost. Perhaps a reflex of this myth is preserved in the Eden story in Genesis" (Ibid. 70-1).

Asherah Worship in Arabia
~1000 BCE

Three dedicatory texts attest to the worship of the goddess Asherah/Athirat in South Arabia, where she was the wife/consort of the moon-god Wadd (Reed 1949:75).

Goddess

& Lion

Lion of Goddess Asherah at Arad Temple Altar
~1000-950 BCE

According to the Biblical Archaeological Society's *Aspects of Monotheism,* this "small bronze lion, often associated with the Canaanite goddess Asherah was found near the altar of the temple to Yahweh at Arad" (*The Biblical World in Pictures* 2002).

Emblematic of Asherah, this bronze lion attests to her worship at Arad's Israelite religious site. Drawing after Ibid.

Goddess and Lion Associations of Antiquity

Breasted

Goddess

~ Female Imagery and the Bountiful Earth ~
Similar Iconographic Associations:
Baring a Religious Breast
~500 CE

This church floor mosaic represents the "Personification of Summer" according to "The Byzantine Church at Petra" (Fiema 2003: 245).

Wearing earrings, a crown/hat and half of a dress, 'Summer' holds vegetative symbols with one breast exposed.

Drawing after Ibid. 244 Fig. 270.

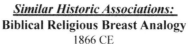

Similar Historic Associations:
Biblical Religious Breast Analogy
1866 CE

According to the 1866 *Comprehensive Bible Containing the Old and New Testaments According to The Authorized Version*, it is less cruel for mothers to kill their children as soon as they are born than for parents to not support the church.

Church ministers conveyed this message to parishioners through the use of a female breast analogy:

> "that the Church be sufficiently provided for is so agreeable to good reason and conscience, that those mothers are holden to be less cruel, that kill their children as soon as they are born, than those nursing fathers and mothers, (wheresoever they be,) that withdraw from them who hang upon their breasts (and upon whose breasts again themselves do hang to receive the spiritual and sincere milk of the word) livelihood and support fit for their estates" (1866:7).

Breasted

Church
Mosaic

Breasted Goddess Asherah
~1000 BCE

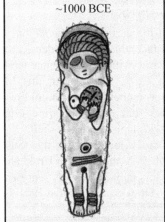

Used to mass produce similar figurines, the mold forming this figurine was discovered within an Israelite religious installation and is "one of the earliest Israelite figurines/molds found in an unambiguous context" (Nakhai 1994:22).

The Naked Goddess holds a tambourine or a circular loaf of bread. A series of bracelets adorn her wrists and ankles. One of her arms encircles an exposed breast. Circular incisions denote her nipple, navel and genital areas.

According to the *Biblical Archaeology Review,* this figurine likely represents the goddess Asherah (Ibid.). Drawing after Ibid.

Ancient Goddesses with Tambourines

Similar Historic Associations:
Colonial Religious Breast Analogy
1619-1769 CE

Reading was initially taught through religion in colonial America and America's first schoolbook, *The New England Primer*, consisted almost exclusively of religious selections.

One of its sections was entitled "Spiritual Milk for American Babes, Drawn Out of the Breasts of Both Testaments, for Their Souls' Nourishment" (Dostal 1990:7).

First published in Boston in 1619, *The New England Primer* remained in use in American classrooms for over 150 years.

Goddess

Heads

Similar Iconographic Associations:
Sumerian Goddess Head
~3300-3100 BCE

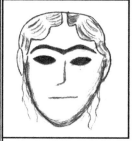

One of the earliest representations of the human face, this marble goddess head was discovered within the Inanna temple of ancient Uruk. The hair of this life-size head was embellished with gold overleaf; her eyes and eyebrows were originally inlaid with lapis lazuli and shell.

Variously identified as the 'Sumerian Mona Lisa,' 'the Lady of Uruk' and 'the Mask of Warka,' some believe this may be an early representation of the goddess Inanna.   Drawing after Lloyd 1961:43.

Goddess

Head

Similar Iconographic Associations:
Judean Goddess Head
~900-850 BCE

Made of ivory, this goddess head was discovered in southern Judah. She wears an elaborate necklace and head-dress/crown. Her recessed eyes were likely once inlaid with precious stones, shells or jewels.
Drawing after Hurowitz 1994:29.

Goddess

Head

Similar Iconographic Associations:
Religious Goddess Head
~900 BCE

Discovered at a high place of worship at Dan, according to the *Archaeological Encyclopedia of the Holy Land,* this female head may represent the goddess Astarte (Negev 2001: 132)/Asherah.
Drawing after Ibid.

Goddess

Head

Rehov Goddess Courtyard Head
~1000 BCE

By the 10th century BCE, the ancient, urban center of Rehov had been destroyed three times. It emerged from the ashes as an Israelite city.

Excavations at the Israelite site uncovered a courtyard goddess head and a religious area with a goddess figurine and two additional goddess heads.

The crowned female head (at left) was discovered within an open courtyard area and was identified by excavator Amihai Mazar as "The Goddess of Rehov" (1998:48).

Asherah/Astarte Goddess Figurine

The naked female figurine (at left) was mass-produced from a mold discovered at Rehov. She wears an elaborate headdress and a beaded necklace. A serpentine image is incised on her chest. Her pubic triangle is outlined; her stance may be that of a birthing posture (Mazar 2000:2).

Experts state this Rehov figurine may represent "the Canaanite goddess Asherah or Astarte" (Ibid.).

The Rehov "Israelite cult[/religious] installation" (Mazar 2000:45) consisted of an open-air, high place with a ten foot, raised platform, a standing stone and a podium. Discovered artifacts included chalices, cult stands, storage jars, a bronze bull, seals, animals' bones and two clay figurine heads. Both female, the figurine heads likely also represent "the Canaanite goddess Asherah or Astarte" (Ibid. 44).

Goddess

Heads

Additional Asherah/Astarte Goddess Heads from Ancient Rehov's Israelite, Religious Area

Drawings after: Mazar 1998:48 (top); Mazar 2000:2 (center); Ibid. 39, 45 (bottom) by Crissa Edwards.

Sacred
Tree of

Life

Similar Iconographic Associations:
Warrior-Priestess' Tree of Life
~500 BCE

A golden ram sits atop this reconstructed, 25 inch headdress discovered within a tomb chamber at Issyk, southern Kazakstan. The headdress had been buried within the grave of a 5' 3" individual wearing leather trousers.

The tomb chamber also contained a dagger, a sword, a whip, 4,000 small gold ornaments and 2,400 gold arrow ornaments. Excavators of the site identified this personage as the "Gold Man" and a chieftain (Davis-Kimball 2002:100-7).

Wool stretched across a wooden frame provided the backdrop for the headdress' gold foil birds perched atop mountains on Trees of Life. Trees in a meadow, mountain goats, snow leopards and other decorative icons are also depicted

Although high-status nomads of both sexes wore pointed head-dresses, archaeologist Jeannine Davis-Kimball noted the preponderance of fertility icons on the headdress, as well as its similarity with ones worn by Kazak brides.

Investigating further, Davis-Kimball discovered the tomb also contained a bronze mirror, a silver bird-headed spoon, a liquid beater and gold lion heads encircling a jacket – elements of female and priestess burials.

These additional factors, in conjunction with the "Gold Man's" height, led Davis-Kimball to conclude it was far more likely the deceased was a female Warrior-Priestess (Ibid.).

Drawings after Ibid. 103.

Similar Historic Associations:
Great Earth Mother is Mother of Vegetation/
Vegetative Tree of Life

Sacred
Vegetative

Tree of
Life

According to *The Great Mother: An Analysis of the Archetype,* the "Great Earth Mother who brings forth all life from herself is eminently the mother of all vegetation . . . [and] The center of this vegetative symbolism is the tree" (Neumann 1963:48).

Sacred
Vegetative

Tree of
Life

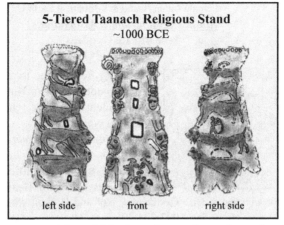

5-Tiered Taanach Religious Stand
~1000 BCE

left side   front   right side

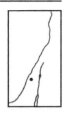

Sacred
Tree of

Life

Reconstructed from 36 broken pieces, alternating pairs of lions and winged sphinxes/cherubs are depicted on the sides of this rudimentary, clay, 5-tiered, religious/ceremonial stand discovered at Taanach.

A ring of superimposed circles decorate the top tapered edge, providing support for a statue or an offering bowl.

Sacred Tree of Life

At the base of the stand, two horned ibexes flank a stylized Tree of Life. The animals' heads turn towards the spiral leaves of the Sacred Tree of Life.

Analysis of "The Cult-Stands from Taanach: Aspects of the Iconographic Tradition of Early Iron Age Cult Objects in Palestine" led scholars to conclude this religious stand likely "served in the worship of a statue of the Great Goddess or perhaps her shrine" (Beck 1994: 381).

Affirming the stand's goddess association and extrapolating further in identifying the referenced goddess as Asherah, *Gods, Goddess and Images of God In Ancient Israel* states, "We have already seen examples of this constellation of [sacred tree] figures that function as substitute symbols for the goddess Asherah . . . [Subsequently, the] . . . house cult in which this stand was used might thus have been dedicated to the worship of the goddess (Asherah)" (Keel 1998a:155).

Drawings after Beck 1994:353 Fig. 1.

Tree of

Life

~ Female Imagery and the Bountiful Earth ~
Similar Iconographic Associations:
Tree of Life Goddess
~1550-1306 BCE

Emerging from a tree trunk, the Egyptian goddess Hathor/Nut dispenses nourishment into the chalice of a kneeling worshipper.

According to *The Great Mother: An Analysis of the Archetype,* the sycamore tree is identified with the goddess as Queen of Heaven and the Egyptian Tree of Life Goddesses, Nut and Hathor, who give birth to the sun (Neumann 1983:241-2).

Drawing after Boulanger 1965:25.

Goddess
Flanked

by Lions

Similar Iconographic Associations:
Great Goddess Flanked by Lions
~1550-1400 BCE

Discovered within the labyrinthine ruins of Crete's Knossos palace, this configuration represents the

Great Goddess of the Mountain,
Earth Mother Goddess,
Goddess of Animals,
Goddess of War,
Goddess of the Seas and the
Patroness of Fertility/Vegetation and the Underworld
(James 1994:250).

Crete's traditional horns of consecration are depicted on a Minoan shrine behind the goddess.

Drawing after author's photo, Herakleion Museum.

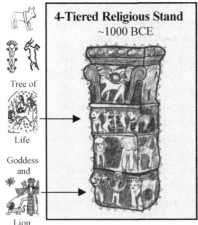

4-Tiered Religious Stand
~1000 BCE

[1 of 4 pages]

Tree of

Life

Goddess and

Lion

This 4-tiered, religious ceremonial stand was also discovered at Taanach.

The stand consists of four differing tiers/registers of images. Below a decorative edge, tier 1 depicts a circular disc above a bull calf/horse flanked by stylized trees.

"The next register [tier 2] should be familiar to us," states Ruth Hestrin in an article entitled "Understanding Asherah: Exploring Semitic Iconography" published in *Biblical Archaeology Review*. It is a "sacred tree sprouting three pairs of curling branches flanked by two clumsily shaped ibexes nibbling at the upper branches, symbolizing the chief goddess Asherah . . . the source of fertility. Flanking this group are two lionesses. Again we have the association of lions with the symbol of Asherah" (1991:58).

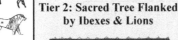
Tier 2: Sacred Tree Flanked by Ibexes & Lions

Tree of

Life

Tier 3 depicts sphinxes or cherubs flanking an empty space; tier 4 displays a naked female flanked by lions, a configuration once again representative of "Asherah, the mother goddess" (Ibid.).

Noting the symmetry of the lions on tiers 2 and 4, Hestrin states this deliberate positioning suggests they identify and belong to the same deity, the goddess Asherah.

Tier 4: Naked Female Flanked by Lions

Goddess Flanked

by Lions

Hestrin concludes, "Thus we find Asherah on this cult stand, once as a sacred tree [tier 2] and a second time as a nude woman [on tier 4]" (Ibid).

Drawings after: Coogan 1998: Pl. 12 (top); Taylor 1994:56 (center); Scham 2005:38 (bottom).

~ Female Imagery and the Bountiful Earth ~
Similar Historic Associations:
Wisdom as Asherah and Tree of Life

Wisdom =
Asherah =
Tree of
Life

A chapter entitled "Myth and Mythmaking in Canaan and Ancient Israel" published in *Civilizations of the Ancient Near East,* states in Hebrew tradition, Wisdom was

"a figure who has been compared to the Canaanite
goddess Asherah.
The symbolic tree of the goddess . . .
was a model for the figure of Wisdom.
The 'tree of life'. . . appears in Israelite tradition
as a metaphorical expression for Wisdom . . .
Wisdom is a female figure, providing life and nurturing"
(Smith 1995:2034).

Lion of

Asherah

Goddess
Flanked

by Lions

Similar Iconographic Associations:
Goddess Flanked by Lions
~1600 BCE

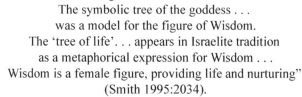

A bare-breasted female divinity stands between a lion and a lioness on this agate, seal impression (Evans 1901:164).

According to *The Journal of Hellenic Studies,* this is a representation of a Mycenaean "Lion Goddess" (Ibid. 166).
Drawing after Ibid. 164 Fig. 44.

~ Female Imagery and the Bountiful Earth ~
The Great Mother, the Feminine, as a Revered Principle of Nature – Personifies Nourishment & Life

According to *The Great Mother: Analysis of the Archetype,* throughout antiquity, "the Feminine, the giver of nourishment [was] everywhere a revered principle of nature" (Neumann 1963: 131).

This assessment is confirmed in *Biblical Archaeology Review* by J. Glen Taylor in an article entitled "Was Yahweh Worshiped As The Sun?" Taylor states, "Examination of the Taanach cult stand . . . [demonstrates] that the asherah as a cult symbol occurs right alongside a portrait of the goddess herself" (1994:53).

[2 of 4 pages]

Extrapolating further on the parallel symbolism of Asherah (the goddess) depicted with asherah (the sacred tree), Taylor observes, "The stand has an overall structure. Tiers 2 and 4 represent 'Asherah' – her symbol, the tree of life, flanked by ibex on tier 2. . . and the goddess herself, nude, on tier 4. These two tiers are united visually by the lions flanking the center figure on both tiers. With the two sets of lions, we should expect the same deity, once her representation and the second time her symbol" (Ibid. 58).

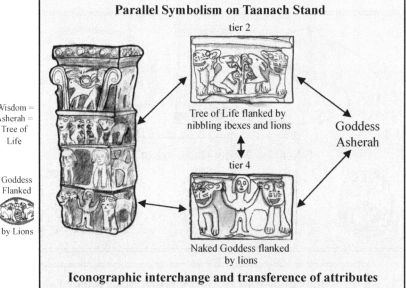

Parallel Symbolism on Taanach Stand

tier 2

Wisdom = Asherah = Tree of Life

Tree of Life flanked by nibbling ibexes and lions

Goddess Asherah

Goddess Flanked by Lions

tier 4

Naked Goddess flanked by lions

Iconographic interchange and transference of attributes

Additional confirmation of this interpretation comes from the *Journal of the American Oriental Society* in an article entitled "Divine Images and Aniconism in Ancient Israel" by author Theodore J. Lewis.

Lewis affirms the dual representation of the goddess stating, "the presence of a goddess (the nude female holding the lions' ears in tier four and the tree symbol flanked by two ibex in tier two) on this cultic incense stand is not disputed" (1998:59).

Horse

of Anat

Similar Iconographic Associations:
Jerusalem Warrior Goddess on Horse
~1550-1250 BCE

Discovered at Jerusalem, this configuration depicts the goddess Anat as a "warrior deity" (Keel 1998a:88).

The crowned goddess holds a weapon in her upraised arm while her horse steps over an enemy combatant.

A guiding dove is in flight before the goddess; a stylized ankh and an umbrellic image are depicted behind her.

Drawing after Ibid. 87 Fig. 110.

Palestinian Warrior Goddesses of Antiquity

Mythology of Warrior Goddess Anat Absorbed by Yahweh

According to *The Early History of God: Yahweh and the Other Deities in Ancient Israel*, the divine warrior mythology of the Canaanite goddess Anat eventually assimilates into Yahwehistic tradition.

Citing several examples of conflation, author Mark S. Smith demonstrates how the Canaanite divine "Warrior Goddess" language for Anat "was mediated to Israelite tradition for Yahweh" (1990:64).

Elaborating further Lewis states, "The nude female represented on the bottom tier of the tenth century Taanach cult stand represents the strongest evidence of an anthropomorphic representation of a goddess, probably Asherah due to the iconographic motifs of lions and a pair of ibex" (Ibid. 58).

[3 of 4 pages]

Lion

Goddess

Tree of

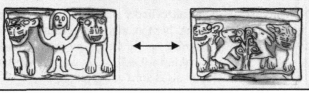

The Mother Goddess Asherah is likely the naked female (tier 4) projecting her nutritive attributes onto the (tier 2) sacred Tree of Life

Life

Although scholarship acknowledges goddess representations on tiers 2 and 4, the remaining tiers continue to generate controversy, as "scholars debate the presence of a male deity" in the stand's tiers 1 and 3 (Ibid. 59).

Historically, the quadruped on tier 1 has been variously identified as the symbolic calf or horse of the gods El, Baal and/or Yahweh.

Extrapolating further upon these traditional identifications in *Gods, Goddesses and Images of God In Ancient Israel,* authors Keel and Uehlinger state the quadruped is not a calf, nor is it a representation of the gods El, Baal or Yahweh (1998a:160).

Recalling that Late Bronze and early Iron Age configurations place the striding horse within the sphere of the warrior goddess Anat/Astarte, Keel and Uehlinger suggest it is far more likely that Anat/Astarte is to be understood as the deity symbolized on tier 1 (Ibid.).

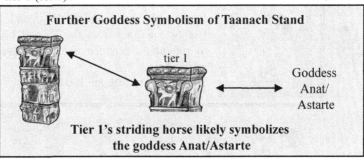

Further Goddess Symbolism of Taanach Stand

tier 1

Goddess Anat/ Astarte

Tier 1's striding horse likely symbolizes the goddess Anat/Astarte

Goddess
and

Lion(s)

Similar Iconographic Associations:
Lion Goddess Ishtar
~850 BCE

This Neo-Babylonian cylinder seal depicts the crowned goddess Inanna/Ishtar resting her foot atop her signature lion. The goddess holds a bow, lightning and a scepter mounted with her star, the planet Venus (Frankfurt 1939:218). A worshipper, king or priest approaches with upraised arms of adoration.
Drawing after Ibid. Pl. XXXVIi.

Prosperity
Goddess
from Tree
Trunks of
Life

~ Female Imagery and the Bountiful Earth ~
Similar Historic Associations:
Grecian Goddesses of Abundance
Fashioned from Tree Trunks of Earth's Fertility
~780 BCE

Believing tree trunks represented the fertility of the earth, the Greeks deliberately created "the divine statues" of their Goddesses of Abundance "from the trunk of a tree which eminently represents the earth's fertility" (Bachofen 1967:167).

Tree of
Life

~ Female Imagery and the Bountiful Earth ~
Similar Iconographic Associations:
Tree of Life Goddess
~1250-1240 BCE

This configuration, from the Egyptian Papyrus of Ani, depicts the goddess Hathor emerging from the Tree of Life to provide sustenance to the deceased scribe Ani.
Drawing after Budge 1901:Pl. 16.

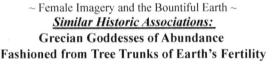
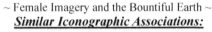

The introduction of tier 1's Anat/Astarte personification interjects a second goddess into the stand's symbolic interpretation, as pictorially summarized below:

Goddess Symbolism on Taanach's 4-tiered Stand

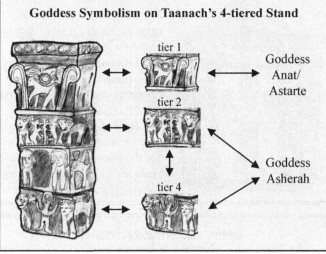

tier 1 ◄──► Goddess Anat/ Astarte

tier 2

Goddess Asherah

tier 4

 Most of Taanach's 4-tiered stand depictions are rendered from a side angle (depicted left), avoiding a frontal view of Asherah's vulvic circle (depicted right), an expression of generative life forces.

Drawing sources per previous citations.

Sacred

Tree of Life

Similar Historic Associations:
Goddess Protecting Tree of Life/Tree of the World
~1800-1650 BCE

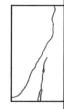

This Syrian cylinder seal impression depicts "the Tree of Life, simultaneously the Tree of the World, supporting the constellations. A female deity, related to Ishtar by the eight-pointed star, holds her hand protectively over the tree" (Keel 1978:51).

Drawing after Ibid. Fig. 46.

Goddess
Temple

Model
Shrine

Similar Iconographic Associations:
Goddess in Temple Shrine
~1800-1600 BCE

Discovered near Crete's Archanes Minoan palace, this temple shrine may be history's first documented case of window peekers.

From their rooftop view, two male figures (with a reclining dog) eavesdrop on a blessing goddess within a temple model shrine.

Bent at the elbows, the arms of the crowned goddess are upraised in the traditional Minoan religious posture. Drawing after author's photo, Herakleion Museum.

Goddess
Temple

Model
Shrine

Kubaba/
Kybele/
Cybele

Similar Iconographic Associations:
Goddess in Temple Shrine
~700-550 BCE

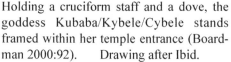

Holding a cruciform staff and a dove, the goddess Kubaba/Kybele/Cybele stands framed within her temple entrance (Boardman 2000:92). Drawing after Ibid.

Kubaba/
Kybele/
Cybele

Similar Historic Associations:
Servant-Girl of Kubaba/Kybele/Cybele
~2000-1550 BCE

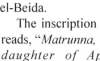

A king faces a goddess on this cylinder seal discovered at Minet el-Beida.

The inscription reads, "*Matrunna, daughter of Aplahanda [king of Carchemish], servant-girl of the goddess Kubaba[/Kybele/Cybele]*" (Collon 1987:50). Drawing after Ibid. 49 Fig. 189.

Goddess
Temple

Model
Shrine

Goddess Temple Model Shrine
~1000-850 BCE

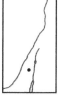

This temple model shrine was discovered at the early northern Israelite capital, North Tel el-Far'ah (Dever 2008: 62).

Comparative temple models indicate a deity, or a pair of deities, would typically stand in the shrine's doorway, as depicted on this Cyprus temple model shrine (right and next page).

According to *What Did the Biblical Writers Know and When Did They Know It? What Archaeology Can Tell Us About the Reality of Ancient Israel*, the deity standing in the entrance of the Israelite temple model shrine was "certainly Asherah, the old Canaanite Mother Goddess" (Dever 2001:152).

Drawing after Ibid. 154.

Goddess
Temple

Model
Shrine

Similar Iconographic Associations:
Palestinian Temple Model Shrines
~1000-850 BCE

Naked females, doves, asherah pillars and guardian lions are depicted on these Palestinian temple model shrines of unknown discovery provenience.

Drawings after Shanks 2005a:25.

Ancient Goddess and Lion Associations

Goddess
Temple

Model
Shrine

Similar Iconographic Associations:
Goddess Temple Model Shrine
~600 BCE

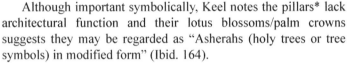

Discovered at Cyprus, this temple model shrine provides clues to understanding the function of the two frontal, free-standing, Asherah pillars.

According to Othmar Keel, author of *The Symbolism of the Biblical World: Ancient Near Eastern Iconography and the Book of Psalms*, "The two pillars before this model of an Astarte temple may have been understood as Asherahs" (1978:165).

Although important symbolically, Keel notes the pillars* lack architectural function and their lotus blossoms/palm crowns suggests they may be regarded as "Asherahs (holy trees or tree symbols) in modified form" (Ibid. 164).

Elaborating further, Keel states the Asherah pillars are symbolically used "to characterize the temple once more as a sphere of life" (Ibid.).

*Keel compares the sacred trees/asherah pillars to the Jachin and Boaz pillars of Solomon's temple which flank the High Priestess on a 1910 Tarot deck card (right). This is discussed further with Jerusalem's ivory pomegranate (pages 203-5).

Cyprus drawing after Dever 2008:58.

Goddess
Temple

Model
Shrine

Similar Iconographic Associations:
Priest/King Before Goddess Temple Shrine
~3000 BCE

A ceremonial barge with a priest/ king standing before a temple shrine of the goddess Inanna is depicted on this cylinder seal impression. Resting on a bovine pedestal, this tri-level shrine is stylistically similar to one previously depicted on the back of a lion also (at right and page 64).

Drawing after Woolley 1961:174 Fig. 808.

Goddess
Temple

Model
Shrine

**Goddess Temple
Model Shrine**
~1000-850 BCE

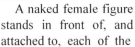

This elaborate temple model shrine was discovered in northern Palestine.

A naked female figure stands in front of, and attached to, each of the two free-standing columns. Partial female figures, some framed between spirals, are depicted above the columns and doorway.

Another female is positioned at the top of the temple, with four more naked female figures below her (although one may be a bird/dove) (Shanks 2005a:22).

According to *Biblical Archaeology Review,* "The figurines on the shrine are almost surely deities – or multiple copies of a single deity" (Ibid.).

Symbolic

Lion

Due to the inclusion of symbolic Asherah attributes in the shrine's composition: (1) naked females, (2) capitals/asherah pillars (as depicted on the Cyprus Temple Shrine at left) and (3) a recumbent lion, experts conclude that the "most likely candidate represented on this temple shrine is the Canaanite goddess Asherah" (Ibid.).

Drawing after Ibid. 21.

Goddess Temple Shrines of Antiquity

Symbolic

Lion

Similar Historic Associations:
Goddess and Lion Association
~200 BCE

Incised upon a Roman lamp, this representation depicts the Phrygian goddess Kybele seated upon a lion-throne.

Drawing after Strong 1913:72 Fig. 8.

Dove & Goddess

Temple Shrine

Similar Iconographic Associations:
Goddess Manifestation of Love
~1800-1550 BCE

Almost four millennia ago, this flying dove personified, and accentuated (Keel 1998a:31), the love of the Mother Goddess.

Historically, dove representations, including this one discovered at Megiddo, are attribute manifestations of the goddess and sometimes appear as her substitute (Ibid. 325).

Drawing after Ibid. 32 Fig. 19.

Dove &

Goddess

Similar Iconographic Associations:
Goddess Messenger of Blessing and Love
~700 BCE

This Lachish dove on a pedestal attests to Syro-Palestine bird iconography over a thousand years after the (above) Megiddo flying dove.

The dove/bird conveyed messages of blessing and love on behalf of the goddess (Keel 1998a:325).

Drawing after Ibid. 324 Fig. 320.

Dove &

Temple

Similar Historic Associations:
Priestess Before Temple Shrine
~3100 BCE

This cylinder seal impression depicts a priestess kneeling on a pedestal while holding an elevated chalice. A dove/bird in flight appears between her and an Iraqi reed temple. The temple is depicted with a vaulted, cathedral interior (Collon 1987:172).

Drawing after Ibid. 173 Fig. 801.

Dove of
Goddess

Symbolic
Lion

Temple Shrine with Double Throne
~1000-850 BCE

The inner sanctuary of this temple model shrine, which may have come from biblical Moab/southern Jordan (Dever 2008:56), contains a double throne.

Tree-like, frontal, asherah pillars, with lions at their bases, flank the shrine's entrance. A bird/dove sits atop the temple roof. These attributes are all "connected with well-known female deities, particularly Canaanite/Israelite Asherah and [her later aspect as the] Phoenician [goddess] Tanit" (Ibid. 59), suggesting this temple shrine was created to venerate the goddess Asherah/Tanit.

This double-throned temple shrine attests to the worship of Asherah with a companion god or goddess. Drawing after Ibid. 54.

Goddess

Temple

Temple of Asherah?
~900 BCE

According to the University of London's Professor Emeritus of the History of Religion E. O. James, temples of Asherah and Yahweh may have stood next to each other at Mizpeh (Tel en-Nasbeh).

According to *The Cult of the Mother-Goddess,* "On the the wall at Mizpeh (Tel en-Nasbeh) temples of Asherah and Yahweh appear to have stood side by side [during the 9th century] . . . and to have survived until the city was destroyed" (1994:80).

Goddess

Temple

Similar Historic Associations:
Temple of Astarte
~217 CE

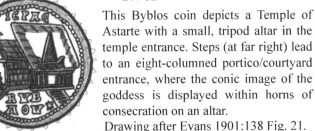

This Byblos coin depicts a Temple of Astarte with a small, tripod altar in the temple entrance. Steps (at far right) lead to an eight-columned portico/courtyard entrance, where the conic image of the goddess is displayed within horns of consecration on an altar.

Drawing after Evans 1901:138 Fig. 21.

Goddess as

Tree of Life

Cosmetic Palette with Asherah, Tree of Life and Doves
~925-720 BCE

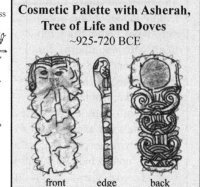

front   edge   back

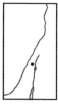

Discovered at Hazor, this ivory, cosmetic palette displays the head of a goddess on the back, doves on the sides and a "stylized *Tree of Life*" on the front (Yadin 1967:60).

According to *Gods, Goddesses, and Images of God In Ancient Israel*, this is a traditional configuration of historical, Bronze Age associative features which link the goddess and the dove (Keel 1998a:199).

This goddess likely has a name, "Since the goddess shown . . . can be interpreted as a late manifestation of the Late Bronze Age Tree Goddess, it is possible to identify the figure as Asherah" (Ibid.).   Drawing after Yadin 1967:60.

Goddess as

Tree of Life

Similar Iconographic Associations:
Tree of Life Goddess
~1600 BCE

The Egyptian goddess Nut emerges from the trunk of a tree, bestowing water and bread to a worshipper. A prayer to her from the *Book of the Dead* begins,

"Hail, thou sycamore of the goddess Nut! Grant thou to me of the water and of the air which dwell in thee"
(Budge 1969:107).
Drawing after Ibid. 106 Pl. 24.

Tree of Life

Goddess Asherah

Similar Historic Associations:
Kabbalah's Asherah is the Sacred Tree/Tree of Life

According to *Vestus Testamentum,* one of the primary components at the core of Jewish mysticism, the Kabbalah, is "the sacred tree (= the Asherah) or the tree of life"* (Weinfeld 1996:515).
*The Kabbalistic Asherah/Sacred Tree of Life parallels, and is strikingly similar to, the earlier Mesopotamian Sacred Tree of Life (Parpola 1996:515-6).

Figurine

Protective Goddess
Asherah
~900-750 BCE

Offerings of oil and incense were dedicated to a family's pillar figurine of an Israelite "goddess" discovered at Beer-sheba (Willet 2000).

According to *Women and Israelite House Religion*, the location of these figurines "indicates women [1] positioned images of the family's protective goddess near vulnerable entrances to their dwellings, [2] provided her with votive offerings, and [3] burned incense and oil to invoke her aid" (Ibid.).

Scholars identify the pillar figurines as "Asherah the mother goddess who gives life and nourishment" (Hestrin 1991).

Drawing after Willet 2000.

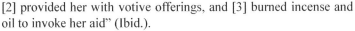

Goddess

Figurine

Similar Iconographic Associations:
Goddess Astarte Mold and Figurine
~732-604 BCE

A clay mold, discovered at Dor, cast this naked female figurine of the goddess Astarte (Stern 2001a: 79). The goddess' posture is that of the "traditional fertility goddess . . . [that is] a naked woman supporting her breasts with her hands" (Stern 1989:28-9). Drawing after Stern 2001a:79.

Similar Historic Associations:
Maternal Nature Principle is Grecian Feminine Godhead

In *Myth, Religion & Mother Right,* Plutarch states the Grecian festival, Bona Dea, celebrated the "feminine godhead . . . [as] the maternal nature principle that generates and nourishes all material life and promotes the material well-being of the people" (Bachofen 1967:191-2).

'Fertility Figures'

Goddess

Figurines

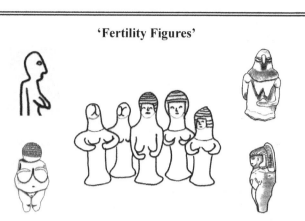

Numerous female figurines, including those depicted above, have historically been identified as 'fertility figures.'

This is a curious label considering the emphasized breasts.

Medically, there are no known cases of pregnancy through the breasts. Mammary glands are unable to reproduce and do not render females 'fertile.'

Similar Historical Associations
Pillar Figurines Represent
Yahweh's Wife the Goddess Asherah

Goddess

Asherah

According to Othmar Keel in *Biblical Archaeology Review,* "It is . . . inappropriate to sever the cult symbol [asherah/sacred tree] and deity [Asherah/goddess] in the interpretation of pillar figurines . . . The pillar figurines are clearly brought from the temple to private houses.

The pillar figurines thus represent a goddess. . . . If the figurines represent a goddess, the most likely candidate is Asherah.

Yahweh, officially worshiped in the temple of Jerusalem, had a wife until the religious reform of King Josiah in 622 B.C.E. (2 Kings 23:1-27), although it appears she had a rather modest or minor position" (Keel 2007:10).

Palestinian Plaques of Antiquity

Asherah Pillar Figurines
~900-750 BCE

Due to their tubular bases, these naked, buxom ladies have become known as 'pillar figurines.'

Their handmade flat, flanged bases allow for upright positioning.

Their heads are [1 of 3 pages]

fundamentally shaped, with either bird-beaked/pinched noses, or formed in a mold and then attached. The molded heads often display intricate hair and facial detail. Their arms and breasts are independently shaped then attached to their torsos. Their exaggerated breasts are encircled by their arms.

Due to the figurines' ample cleavage, they were labeled as 'fertility figures' (see information box at left).

By 1998, over 3,000 (Lewis 1998:36-54) of these figurines had been discovered "at all towns from all parts of Judah" (Stern 2001a:205).

In an article entitled "Another Temple to the Israelite God" published in *Biblical Archaeology Review*, author Andre Lemaire confirms the discovery of the pillar figurines at all Judaean excavation sites stating, they are "a common find from ancient Israel" (2004:43).

Goddess

Elaborating on the significance of the pillar figurines, Lemaire states, "Although their exact identity and function are unknown, they are thought to be fertility goddesses or perhaps representations of the goddess Asherah" (Ibid.).

Asherah

Prior to Lemaire's conclusion, Ruth Hestrin identified the pillar figurines as representations of the goddess Asherah, in an article entitled "The Lachish Ewer and the Asherah" published in the *Israel Exploration Journal*.

Goddess

Hestrin also believed the pillar figurines' tubular bases were deliberately formed to resemble a tree trunk, "the pillar represents the trunk of a tree – the Asherah" (1987:222). [An epiphany of the goddess Asherah, sacred trees were actually named asherahs after her (Albright 1957:310).]

Asherah

Drawing after Mazar 1990:501.

Ancient Palestinian Plaques

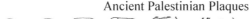

Tree
Goddess

of
Vegetative
Prosperity

~ Female Imagery and the Bountiful Earth ~
Similar Iconographic Associations:
Tree Goddesses of Vegetative Prosperity
~2350-2150 BCE

This Mesopotamian cylinder seal impression depicts Tree Goddesses emerging from tree trunks and the primordial holy water of creation.

The foliage projecting from the shoulders of the two goddesses depict them as "embodiments of vegetation" (Keel 1978:48). Their tree-crowns also identify them as Tree Goddesses of Vegetative Prosperity. The seated, mountain god may represent the Mesopotamian god, An, or the Syro-Palestinian god, El (Ibid.).   Drawing after Ibid. 47 Fig. 42.

H
o
l
y

W
a
t
e
r

Similar Historic Associations:
Primordial Holy Water Represents
Goddess of Life, Wisdom and All
~2000 BCE

According to the *American Journal of Semitic Languages and Literatures,* holy water "was associated both with the mother of all, the aqueous first principle. . . and with the goddess of life and wisdom, who held the spring of the water of life under her charge" (Albright 1920:266).

Water/Sea Goddesses of Antiquity

Goddess

Asherah

[2 of 3 pages]

In a *Biblical Archaeology Review* article entitled "Understanding Semitic Iconography," Hestrin further states, "It is now suggested that these pillar figurines . . . can be identified as Asherah, the mother goddess who gives life and nourishment" (1991:51).

The Cambridge Companion to the Bible also acknowledges a goddess association stating the exaggerated breasts may be suggestive of a "role in procreation" (Kee 1997:137).

Goddess

Astarte

The goddess identification they make, however, is that of Astarte: "Iron Age Astarte figurines . . . with enlarged breasts, possibly emphasizing her role in procreation . . . may represent the deity or simply be votive statues" (Ibid.).

Goddess

Astarte
Ashtoreth
Asherah

Confirming the Astarte identification, *Archaeology of the Land of the Bible Vol. II* states, "In Judah, unlike other kingdoms of the period, most of the figurines represent females and are of the type known as 'pillar figurines'. . . . This deity is usually identified with 'Astarte, the fertility goddess." (Stern 2001a:205-206).

Archaeology of the Land of the Bible suggests the pillar figurines were prominent in daily Israelite religious practice and depict Ashtoret/Ashtoreth[/Asherah] (Mazar 1990:51).

Gods, Goddesses and Images of God In Ancient Israel affirms an Asherah identification stating, "This motherly goddess, whose image emphasizes especially the face (accessibility) and full breasts (blessing), appears to be none other than the (repersonalized) Asherah" (Keel 1998a:369).

Archaeology of the Land of the Bible Vol. II encapsulates the debate asking: "Who were the deities represented by these Judaean clay figurines? We can only guess. . . But, more plausibly, they represent the national Judaean god, Yahweh, and his consort, 'Astarte, for all these figurines . . . are Judaean and only Judaean" (Stern 2001a:208).

The above expert testimony has variously identified the same pillar figurines as the goddesses Asherah, Astarte and Ashtoreth. What can be made of these seeming contradictions?

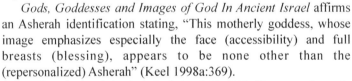

Asherah, Astarte or Ashtoreth?

In actuality, the differing names are not as contradictory as they initially appear.

According to a *Scandinavian Journal of the Old Testament* article entitled "The Divorce of Yahweh and Asherah in Hos 2,4-7.12 FF," the fluid, syncretistic nature of ancient religious beliefs

Holy
Sacred

Tree

Similar Historic Associations:
Tree of Egyptian Goddess Nut
in Legend of Virgin Mary

According to Coptic legend in *The Gods of the Egyptians or Studies in Egyptian Mythology,* Mary, the mother of Jesus of Nazareth, once hid herself and her infant son, Jesus, in the trunk of a Heliopolis sycamore tree – the holy tree of the Egyptian goddess Nut (Budge 1969:108).

Tree

Goddess

~ Female Imagery and the Bountiful Earth ~
Similar Iconographic Associations:
Veneration of the Tree Goddess
~1552-1306 BCE

Kneeling before the "Tree Goddess" (Neumann 1983:241 Pl. 102), two worshippers receive sustenance and nourishment.

The Tree Goddess holds a platter of breads and food while dispensing drink from a pitcher. An elongated breast is depicted between her arms.

Drawing after Ibid.

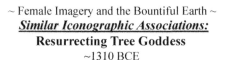

Tree of
Life

Goddess

~ Female Imagery and the Bountiful Earth ~
Similar Iconographic Associations:
Resurrecting Tree Goddess
~1310 BCE

Emerging from the trunk of a sacred tree, the Egyptian Tree Goddess Nut offers bread and water to a kneeling devotee.

Egyptians believed the Tree Goddess provided nourishment and protection to the deserving and righteous in the afterlife.

Drawing after Weeks 2001:361.

"in iron age Palestine Asherah gradually fuses with Anat and Ashtarte[/Astarte], but retains her same functions as mother goddess and fertility goddess" (Whitt 1992:51).

Commenting upon this phenomena in a *Biblical Archaeologist* article entitled "The Persistence of Canaanite Religion," author R. A. Oden Jr. explains the interchangeability of the goddesses' names and features. Oden states the "overlap of name, function, and consort is true of the three major goddesses of Canaanite religion. . . as early as the mid-second millennium B.C. [E.] the three goddesses share attributes, titles, and husbands" (1976:36). [3 of 3 pages]

Elaborating further Oden notes, "It seems clear that at every period the three goddesses could be worshipped separately or together" (Ibid. 34).

In summary, regardless of which goddess the pillar figurines* represent, the evidentiary, archaeological presence of over 3,000 pillar figurines suggests a reassessment of previous, antiquated, just-a-'fertility-figurine' labeling.

Israelite Goddess

*According to *The Cult of Asherah in Ancient Israel and Judah*, in addition to personifying the Great Mother Goddess Asherah/Ashtoreth/Astarte, the pillar figurines also represent a very distinctive "typically Israelite way of portraying the goddess" (Hadley 2000:196).

Astarte
Ashtoreth
Asherah

Underrated Asherah Pillar Figurines

Goddess

Asherah

The *Journal of Biblical Studies*, states that "Archaeology (while contributing significantly to the understanding of the 'Asherah/heterodox religions) has, nonetheless, also consistently continued to err in this evaluation by categorizing and, in effect, dismissing as non-consequential finds of pillar/Asherah figurines either as indicators of apostasy from true Yahwism . . . or as attempts at syncretism with Yahwism, both of which are imprecise and pejorative reductionisms to aberrant activities of otherwise positive human exercises" (Jacobs 2001:1).

Other Trinity Goddesses of Ancient Times

IRON AGE REFERENCES

V. Kuntillet Ajrud ~830-760 BCE
Introduction
Inscriptions
Drawings
Conclusion

In the official cults of ancient Israel and Judah, the evidence suggests "that among the large majority of the population . . . Asherah was worshipped as Yahweh's wife/consort."

Scandinavian Journal of the Old Testament
(Whitt 1992:65)

Asherah references in this section include:

"I have blessed you by Yahweh of Samaria and his Asherah"

"I bless you by Yahweh of Teman and by his Asherah"

". . . give YHWH of Teman and his ASHERAH
. . .YHWH of Teman and his ASHERAH . . ."

Prayer to Asherah/Asherata/Ashirta

Introduction

During 1975-76 archaeological excavations in the Sinai desert, startling artifacts were unearthed at an Israelite-Judean way-station, with an attached shrine and "religious center" (Meshel 1979:27).

According to a *Biblical Origins* article entitled "Official Religion and Popular Religions in Pre-Exilic Ancient Israel," the provocative nature of the Kuntillet Ajrud discoveries made them perhaps "the most widely discussed and controversial find in the history of Israelite archaeology" (Berlinerblau 2000), challenging previous convictions of Yahwehistic monotheism (Dever 1995b: 50):

1. **"I have blessed you by Yahweh of Samaria and his Asherah"**
2. **"I bless you by Yahweh of Teman and by his Asherah"**
3. **". . . give YHWH of Teman and his ASHERAH . . . YHWH of Teman and his ASHERAH . . ."**
4. **Prayer to Asherah/Asherata/Ashirta**

Concurring with this assessment, *Gods, Goddesses, and Images of God In Ancient Israel* states Kuntillet Ajrud's inscriptions and drawings "have created a sensation in the scholarly world and have dominated the discussion" (Keel 1998a:210).

Academic debate and the following discussion focus upon:
Kuntillet Ajrud's Inscriptions and
Kuntillet Ajrud's Drawings.

IRON AGE REFERENCES

Introduction to Kuntillet Ajrud's Inscriptions

According to *Bible Review,* the Hebrew blessing inscriptions discovered at Kuntillet Ajrud are the "oldest known Hebrew dedicatory inscriptions" discovered to date (King 1989:33).

Ajrud Inscrip. [1 of 9 pages]

Thoughts frozen in time, these inscriptions are unfiltered windows into the past. Uncensored vestiges of forgotten truths, these historical proclamations pair the Israelite god Yahweh with the goddess Asherah:

> 1. **"I have blessed you by Yahweh of Samaria and his Asherah"**
> 2. **"I bless you by Yahweh of Teman and by his Asherah"**
> 3. **"... give YHWH of Teman and his ASHERAH ... YHWH of Teman and his ASHERAH ..."**
> 4. **Prayer to Asherah/Asherata/Ashirta**

The goddess Asherah should not have been there. She should not be present in Hebrew dedicatory blessing inscriptions, but there she was. And, incredulously, Asherah is paired with Israel's god – a disconcerting, blasphemous notion to some, yet evident to all.

A *Biblical Archaeology Review* article entitled "Was Yahweh Worshiped as the Sun?" encapsulates the controversy stating, "The Kuntillet Ajrud pithoi[/storage jars] were especially shocking when discovered because they seemed to suggest quite explicitly that Yahweh did have a [wife/]consort" (Taylor 1994:53).

These profound implications were elaborated upon further in *Biblical Archaeology Review*: "For the first time contemporary texts revealed the God of Israel, long believed to be a recluse bachelor, as sharing His life with a female partner" (Hurowitz 2005:58).

Although Ajrud's discoveries were made over 35 years ago, they continue to generate controversy and debate. Analysis of the controversial nature of Ajrud's inscriptions follows . . .

1. Kuntillet Ajrud Inscription 1:
"I have blessed you by Yahweh of Samaria
and his Asherah"

The first Hebrew inscription discovered was inscribed on one of Ajrud's 3-foot pithoi/storage jars and reads:

> "I have blessed you by
> Yahweh *shmrn* and his Asherah"
> (Freedman 1992:I.484).

Experts debated three controversial areas within this inscription:

> ▷ Is *shmrn* translated as *our guardian* or *of Samaria*?
> ▷ Is a Hebrew pronominal suffix translated as *his* or *its*?
> ▷ Is *a/Asherah* translated as *asherah* or *Asherah*?

Interjecting these interpretations within the translation generates the possibilities of:

> "I have blessed you by
> Yahweh *our guardian* or *of Samaria* and
> *his* or *its asherah* or *Asherah.*"

The specifics of each of these controversies are reviewed below.

▷ Is *shmrn* translated as *our guardian* or *of Samaria*?

The first area of contention is the interpretation of the Hebrew term *shmrn.*

According to the editors of the *Anchor Bible Dictionary*, the original Hebrew *shmrn* could be translated as *our guardian* or *of Samaria* (Ibid.) rendering either:

> "I have blessed you by
> Yahweh, *our guardian*, and his or its asherah or Asherah," or
> "I have blessed you by
> Yahweh *of Samaria* and his or its asherah or Asherah."

Elaborating further, however, the *Anchor Bible Dictionary* favors the translation *of Samaria* (capital of the northern kingdom of Israel), considering this to be the "more likely" (Ibid.) translation:

> "I have blessed you by
> Yahweh *of Samaria* and his or its asherah or Asherah."

▷ Is a Hebrew pronominal suffix translated as *his* or *its*?

The next contentious area is a Hebrew pronominal suffix, bringing into question the interpretation of either *his* or *its* (Olyan 1988:33) directly before the last word, generating the possible translations of:

"I have blessed you by
Yahweh of Samaria and *his** asherah or Asherah," or
"I have blessed you by
Yahweh of Samaria and *its* asherah or Asherah."

Ajrud
Inscrip.
[3 of 9
pages]

This term choice directly impacts the meaning of the inscription by ascribing the association of a/Asherah to the city of Samaria (*its* Asherah) or to Yahweh (*his** Asherah).

Addressing the differing inferences, *Asherah and the Cult of Yahweh in Israel* dismisses the relevance of the distinction between the translation of *his* versus *its*, stating that the direct association of a/Asherah with Yahweh is far more significant (Ibid.).

Only One God? Monotheism in Ancient Israel and the Veneration of the Goddess Asherah, validates this conclusion and expands upon it noting the opposition of the pronoun usage of '*his** Asherah' is actually "increasingly proved to be unfounded by a great deal of comparative material" (Becking 2001:117).

Fundamentally, due to numerous archaeological discoveries,** the initial objections of a Hebrew pronominal suffix expressed as '*his** Asherah' becomes increasingly untenable under the weight of comparative material.

Upon removal of the pronominal suffix issues, the translation is more likely interpreted as

"I have blessed you by Yahweh of Samaria and
his asherah or Asherah."

▷ **Is *a/Asherah* translated as *asherah* or *Asherah*?**

Herein lies the primary source of controversy for this inscription and similar Hebrew inscriptions containing references to a/Asherah.

Sacred

Tree

The use of a lower case *a* in *asherah* generates a variety of translation possibilities including a sacred tree, a wooden pole, a grove of trees or a holy place.

A capital *A*, however, renders the translation as *Asherah*, the goddess, and pairs Israel's god Yahweh with the goddess Asherah.

*The objection to the Hebrew interpretation of '*his* Asherah' hinges upon a grammatical pronominal suffix issue using a possessive pronoun with a proper name. The following pages review this further.

**Including the forthcoming Iron Age IIC discussion of Khirbet el-Qom's blessing inscription (pages 207-209).

~ Female Imagery and the Bountiful Earth ~
Similar Historic Associations:
Life-Giving Tree Goddess
~1600-1300 BCE

Emerging from a sacred tree, an Egyptian Tree Goddess dispenses the "Fruit and Drink of Life" (Yarden 1971:38) to the deserving.
Drawing after Ibid. Fig. 216.

Similar Historic Associations:
Sacred Tree Symbolizes Source of Life,
Growth and Regeneration

Sacred

Tree

According to the *Israel Exploration Journal*, "The sacred tree symbol was embedded in the traditions of the cultures of the ancient Near East, and goes back to the very early periods . . . The tree symbolized the source of life and represented growth and regeneration" (Hestrin 1987:214).

Sacred

Tree

Sacred Trees Represent Life-Giving Goddess(es)

Goddesses and Trees, New Moon and Yahweh: Ancient Near Eastern Art and the Hebrew Bible, states "both real and artificial trees were objects of worship in Syria and Palestine for centuries because they were seen as manifestations of a single female deity or of a number of different ones" (Keel 1998b:16).

More explicitly, the tree veneration "was actually intended for the life-giving goddess represented by the tree" (Ibid. 29).

David N. Freedman addressed this question extensively in an article entitled "Yahweh of Samaria and his Asherah" published in *Biblical Archaeologist,* asking "Do you spell the word *asherah* with a capital *A* or a small *a?*" (1987:249)

Ajrud Inscrip. [4 of 9 pages]

Freedman states, "Should the inscription at Q[K]untillet Ajrud be read as referring to Yahweh's 'asherah' (perhaps a wooden pole) or to his 'Asherah' (a goddess [wife/] consort)?" (Ibid. 243)

The debate revolves around a grammatical syntax issue that combines a Hebrew pronominal suffix with a personal name.

Some Hebrew grammar experts claim this combination negates the use of a capital *A* and requires the translation as a common noun with a lower case *a* as in *asherah* (Ibid. 247).

Following the lower case *a* translation for *asherah,* several possibilities emerge:

Sacred

Tree

a "sacred tree" (Lemaire 1984b:42),
a "grove of trees" (Ibid.),
a "wooden pole" (Freedman 1987:247),
a "sacred grove" (Ibid.) or
a "holy place" (Ibid.).

These interpretation possibilities generate the following blessing translations:

"I have blessed you by Yahweh of Samaria and
his *sacred tree,*"
"I have blessed you by Yahweh of Samaria and
his *grove of trees,*"
"I have blessed you by Yahweh of Samaria and
his *wooden pole,*"
"I have blessed you by Yahweh of Samaria and
his *sacred grove*" or
"I have blessed you by Yahweh of Samaria and his *holy place.*"

In addition, some experts suggest the *asherah* lost its association with the goddess Asherah and became a "hypostasis[*] of Yahweh" (Smith 1990:87), generating the translation of:

"I have blessed you by Yahweh of Samaria and his
formerly-female-then-neutered-now-male
sacred tree/wooden pole/grove of trees/sacred grove or holy place."

It remains uncertain if this translation would accurate reflect the historical reality intended.

*A "sexually undifferentiated cultic symbol" which can then be reassigned to a male deity (Keel 1998a:234).

Returning to the Hebrew grammatical syntax problem of combining a pronominal suffix with a personal name, the *Anchor Bible Dictionary* states, "That it is the goddess Asherah herself who is denoted by 'his Asherah' [although it] is syntactically inappropriate, since personal names are not found with a pronominal suffix in biblical Hebrew" (Freedman 1992:I. 484).

Ajrud Inscrip. [5 of 9 pages]

However, the *Anchor Bible Dictionary* continues, indirectly "the allusions probably do imply that Asherah was Yahweh's [wife/] consort" (Ibid.).

Thus, although a grammatical anomaly, Ajrud's Hebrew blessing inscriptions most likely reference Asherah as Yahweh's wife.

Sacred a/Asherah

This is a curious controversy considering that over 55 years ago the Father of Biblical Archaeology, William F. Albright, conclusively demonstrated that, according to biblical sources, sacred trees were planted and named asherahs after the goddess Asherah. Albright substantiates this association writing in *From the Stone Age to Christianity*, stating that biblical documentary sources list "the planting of sacred trees called *asherahs*" (1957:310).

In addition, Albright specifically states the sacred trees were actually named "asherahs" after the goddess "Asherah," and one biblical passage explicitly refers to them as the "trees of Asherah" (Ibid.).

Almost 30 years after Albright, and over 25 years ago, the discussion continued in a *Journal of Biblical Literature* article entitled "Asherah in the Hebrew Bible and Northwest Semitic Literature," which reaffirmed Albright's conclusion, stating the evidence strongly suggests the Old Testament asherah "was a wooden pole symbolizing the goddess Asherah" (Day 1986:392).

Further analyzing the biblical evidence in conjunction with Kuntillet Ajrud's inscriptions in *Asherah and the Cult of Yahweh in Israel,* author Saul M. Olyan states, "The biblical evidence . . . suggests that the asherah was a cult symbol representing the goddess Asherah, which was an acceptable and legitimate part of Yahweh's cult in non-deuteronomistic circles. This association of the asherah and the cult of Yahweh suggests in turn that Asherah was the consort[/wife] of Yahweh in circles both in the north and the south" (1988:33).

Additional support for this assessment comes from Mark S. Smith writing in *The Early History of God: Yahweh and the Other Deities in Ancient Israel*. Smith states that the majority of experts now believe "the biblical and extrabiblical evidence support the

view that Asherah was a goddess in ancient Israel and that she was the [wife/]consort of Yahweh" (1990:88).

Ajrud Inscrip. [6 of 9 pages]

As a result, despite the grammatical anomaly in Kuntillet Ajrud's inscription, there is mounting conviction that Asherah was the wife of Yahweh throughout both the southern and northern areas of Ancient Israel.

In a *Scandinavian Journal of the Old Testament* article entitled "The Divorce of Yahweh and Asherah in Hos 2, 4-7.12 FF," author William D. Whitt reiterates this conclusion stating, "There is a growing consensus that these inscriptions reflect the belief that Asherah was the consort/wife of Yahweh" (1992:47).

Has this grammatical anomaly been overplayed and exaggerated?

Writing over 20 years ago, Whitt suggests this is the case, "Scholars have made entirely too much of the so-called grammatical problem . . . the obvious meaning of which is 'his Asherah'" (Ibid.).

Elaborating further, Whitt states, "Many scholars deny this meaning [Yahweh and his Asherah] on the ground that a PN [personal, proper noun] cannot have a pronominal suffix; . . . If a PN can appear in construct . . . as we find at Elephantine [another Hebrew religious center], I fail to see why a PN cannot appear with a pronominal suffix" (Ibid.).

Over 25 years ago, Ajrud's inscriptional controversy was analyzed in a *Biblical Archaeologist* article entitled "Yahweh of Samaria and his Asherah" by David N. Freedman.

Freedman first questioned the appropriateness of applying a rule made up thousands of years after the fact, noting it is "a strange grammatical construction . . . [to invoke] a rule that someone invented in the nineteenth century that says it is impossible" (1987:247).

Next, Freedman parallels Ajrud's asherah/Asherah anomaly to another historical association in the same genre.

Referencing William Shakespeare's play *Romeo and Juliet,* Freedman cites a grammatical parallel to the expression 'Yahweh and His Asherah:'

"For never was a story of more woe
Than that of Juliet and her Romeo" (Ibid. 249).

Romeo and Juliet's closing lines, Freedman believes, are quite specific and evoke minimal misunderstanding – it is clearly Romeo who is the object of Juliet's affection.

Grammatical anomalies aside, Freedman contends 'Yahweh and His Asherah' is an equivalent comparison to 'Juliet and her Romeo,*' and although grammatically questioned by today's standards, the message conveyed remains explicit – Asherah is the object of Yahweh's affection.

Ajrud Inscrip. [7 of 9 pages]

Freedman's assessment was affirmed in *The Hebrew Goddess* by author Raphael Patai, stating, "These inscriptions [of Kuntillet Ajrud and Khirbet el-Qom which pair 'Yahweh and his Asherah'] show that in popular religion the Goddess Asherah was associated with Yahweh, probably as his wife, and that 'Yahweh and his Asherah' were the most popular divine couple" (Patai 1990:53).

Additionally, Patai notes, "the worship of Asherah as the consort[/wife] of Yahweh ('*his* Asherah'!) was an integral element of religious life in ancient Israel prior to the reforms introduced by King Joshiah in 621 BCE" (Ibid.).

Encapsulating Kuntillet Ajrud's asherah/Asherah controversy in relation to other archaeological artifactual parallels in *Biblical Archaeology Review,* author J. Glen Taylor contends that even if her cult symbol is cited, the Ajrud inscriptions imply a wife/consort of Yahweh's, "In other words . . . the inscriptions from Kuntillet 'Ajrud imply Yahweh's association with a consort even if the inscriptions refer only to her cult symbol named "asherah" with a lower case *a*" (1994:54).

Subsequently, the majority of scholars now translate Ajrud's Inscription 1 with the capital A of the goddess Asherah, as

"I have blessed you by Yahweh of Samaria and his Asherah."

*Freedman also parallels the plot of Shakespeare's *Romeo and Juliet* (where Romeo initially had another girlfriend before Juliet) to Asherah's shift from El (and Baal according to biblical writers) to Yahweh (Freedman 1987:241-249).

Ancient Kings/Gods Before Goddesses

2. Kuntillet Ajrud Inscription 2:
"I bless you by Yahweh of Teman and by
his Asherah"

A second Hebrew blessing inscription pairing Yahweh with the goddess Asherah was discovered on another Ajrud storage jar.

Ajrud Inscrip. [8 of 9 pages]

Although subject to the same asherah-or-Asherah controversy discussed above, *Asherah Goddess Of Israel* author Richard J. Pettey translates the inscription as:

"I bless you by Yahweh of Teman and by
his Asherah" (1990:192).

3. Kuntillet Ajrud Inscription 3:
"... give YHWH of Teman and his ASHERAH
...YHWH of Teman and his ASHERAH ..."

A third Hebrew dedicatory inscription was discovered on one of Ajrud's plaster walls. This blessing inscription again pairs Yahweh with Asherah – this time not once, but twice, on two separate lines.

According to the *New Encyclopedia of Archaeological Excavations in the Holy Land,* Ajrud's excavator Ze'ev Meshel translates this fragmentary dedicatory inscription as

"... your days may be prolonged and you shall be satisfied
... give YHWH of Teman and his ASHERAH
...YHWH of Teman and his ASHERAH ..."
(Meshel 1993:1462 V.4).

4. Kuntillet Ajrud Inscription 4:
Prayer to Asherah/Asherata/Ashirta

A fourth Hebrew inscription referencing Asherah was discovered in a dedicatory prayer on one of Ajrud's plaster walls.

According to *The Cult of Asherah in Ancient Israel and Judah,* this Hebrew prayer inscription begins with the name of the goddess, Asherata or Ashirta (Hadley 2000:134, 98), an earlier rendition of Asherah's name (Ibid. 124).

---

asherah or Asherah?? – An Immaterial Question

The "inscriptions from Kuntillet 'Ajrud imply Yahweh's association with a [wife/]consort even if the inscriptions refer only to her cult symbol named "asherah" with a lower case *a*" (Taylor 1994:54).

Hebrew Worship of the Mother Goddess Asherah

According to *The Hebrew Goddess*, the "continuity of Asherah worship in Israel is a fact which must be recognized and remembered in any attempt to trace the subsequent role played by the concept of a female divinity in the popular religion of the people of Judaea and their heirs, the Jews.

 Yet whatever her origin and whatever her cult, there can be no doubt about the psychological importance that the belief in, and service of, Asherah had for the Hebrews . . . she was the great mother-goddess, giver of fertility, that greatest of all blessings" (Patai 1990:46, 52).

If There was No Wife . . .
Who was Yahweh Divorcing?

The Bible contains a speech by the prophet Hosea in which he refers to "Yahweh's wife and called her the 'mother' of his audience" (Whitt 1992:32).

Traditionally, this has been interpreted as a metaphor of marriage between the god Yahweh and Israel. Hosea, however, contradicts this interpretation by identifying Israel metaphorically as "Yahweh's children" (Ibid. 34), subsequently voiding the marriage-of-Yahweh-with-Israel misinterpretation.

Upon identifying Israel as a child of Yahweh, Hosea clearly informs us his speech is **not** intended to represent "some abstract theological mediation of Yahweh's relationship with Israel that uses the allegory of Israel as Yahweh's wife" (Ibid. 66).

Elaborating further in an article entitled "The Divorce of Yahweh and Asherah in Hos 2,4-7.12 FF" published in the *Scandinavian Journal of the Old Testament*, William D. Whitt states, "the original material in Hos[ea] 1 does not portray the relationship between Yahweh and Israel as a marriage . . . Rather, the speech is Hosea's proclamation of Yahweh's 'divorce' from Asherah" (Ibid. 33).

 "It is clear to me" Whitt explains, "that if we ask what Hosea's audience would have understood him to mean when he referred to Yahweh's wife and called her the 'mother' of his audience, the only possible answer is that an eighth century Israelite would have thought him to be speaking about the goddess Asherah" (Ibid. 32).

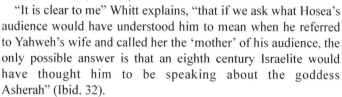 Whitt concludes stating, "The evidence . . . suggests that among the large majority of the population and in the official cults of Israel and Judah, Asherah was worshipped as Yahweh's wife/consort" (Ibid. 65).

Additional Inscriptional Considerations

Due to Ajrud's isolated location, some experts initially claimed its inscriptions were from a fringe social group. Subsequent archaeological evidence indicates this was not the case and Ajrud was actually controlled by Israelites (Keel 1998a:247).

Ajrud Inscrip. [9 of 9 pages]

Although the inscriptions came from a southern complex under Israelite control, Ajrud also had a far reaching, northern presence. Neutron-activation analysis of the storage jars reveals they were produced in the Jerusalem area (Ibid.), made from Tel Miqne or Ashdod clay (Hadley 2000:111) and manufactured by Judaeans (Ibid.).

The unexpected discovery of Hebrew goddess inscriptions within an Israelite-Judaean environment, raises unsettling questions. Some find the 4 pairings of Yahweh, with the goddess Asherah in dedicatory, Hebrew blessing formulas disconcerting.

Encapsulating the controversy in *The Forbidden Goddess*, William G. Dever states Asherah's identification as Yahweh's wife/consort was both early and late in Israel's history, "In other words, she shouldn't be here but here she is" (Rhys-Davies 1993).

Writing in *Biblical Archaeologist*, David N. Freedman questions whether this entire controversy would have arisen had the god paired with Asherah been someone other than Yahweh. Freedman states that if the divine name before Asherah's "had been 'Baal' and not 'Yahweh,' then there would have been general agreement that two gods were intended" (1987:247).

Asherah: Goddesses in Ugarit, Israel and the Old Testament affirms Freedman's conclusion stating, if Asherah had been associated with any other god, she would have been identified, without major controversy, as the god's consort/wife (Binger 1997: 109).

Ancient Hebrew Translation Challenge

Part of the interpretational challenge scholars encounter in deciphering ancient Hebrew inscriptions is this:

tfltthgrmrfdrsdnsdrwnwtbscpsrskrmnttcnpsrttlltpcslwvstnsdggnlwrbhht.

Which translates as:

The Hebrew language does not use vowels, capital letters, punctuation marks or spaces between words and is read from right to left.

IRON AGE REFERENCES

Introduction to Kuntillet Ajrud Drawings

Kuntillet Ajrud's Pithos A Drawings 1, 2 and 3

The above drawings were discovered at Kuntillet Ajrud on a pithos/storage jar, which excavators identify as Pithos A.

    Two standing figures and a seated figure are the focus of Drawing 1 (top right). Drawing 2 (below center) depicts a cow looking over her shoulder at her nursing calf. The cow's front leg overlaps the foot of one of the standing figures, securing her in the graphic landscape.

    Drawing 3 (top left) depicts a stylized tree flanked by nibbling ibexes/caprids,* all positioned above the back of a striding lion.

*Scholars have used both terms of identification; an ibex being a wild goat of the genus Capra.

Drawings after: Shanks et al 1992:135 (1 and 2); Taylor 1994:57 (3).

Kuntillet Ajrud Drawing 1: Three Figure Grouping

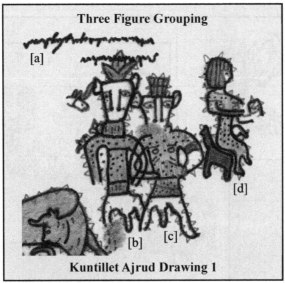

Three Figure Grouping

[a]

[d]

[b]   [c]

Kuntillet Ajrud Drawing 1

Ajrud Draw. [2 of 19 pages]

A Hebrew blessing inscription [a] is inscribed above the heads of Drawing 1's standing figures [b] and [c]. Slightly elevated and to the right, a seated figure holds a lyre [d].

These elements are drawn into an aggregate composition by the elbow of the figure [c] touching the chair of seated figure [d] and the foot of figure [b] overlapping the leg of Drawing 2's nursing cow.

▷ **[a] Hebrew Blessing Inscription of Drawing 1**

The previously discussed Hebrew blessing inscription [a] "I have blessed you by Yahweh of Samaria and his Asherah," is inscribed above the heads of the two standing figures.

Although this direct positioning suggests a relationship between the inscription and the images, as with all things Asherah, this also is subject to controversy.

Some experts contend the inscription above the figures was added after the drawings, which would, they believe, void a relationship between the two (Hadley 2000:152).

In and of itself, however, a later date for the inscription does not necessarily negate a connection with the images.

Drawing after Shanks et al 1992:135.

It is possible an individual may have seen the figures after they were drawn, identified them as possible representations of Yahweh and Asherah, then subsequently added the blessing inscription at a later date.

▷ **[b] and [c] Standing Figures of Drawing 1**

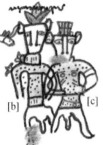

Pithos A's frontally facing, standing figures [b] and [c] have generated considerable discussion.

Their faces have been described as flat-nosed and bovine or leonine. Their protruding ears are elevated; both figures wear headdresses.

It is unclear whether the figures have beards or collared garments. Their elbows point outward; their legs are bowed with a tail or penis* depicted between them. Female breasts are depicted on figure [c].

[b]   [c]

The two standing figures have been variously identified as depictions of the Egyptian god Bes, or, as a bovine couple personifying Yahweh and Asherah.

The merits of each possibility are examined below.

▷ **[b] and [c] Standing Figures of Drawing 1**
 •Egyptian Dwarf-God Bes, Description and Iconography

Some experts identify Ajrud's two standing figures as depictions of the Egyptian dwarf-god Bes.

According to *The Gods of the Egyptians,* Bes is usually depicted "in the form of a dwarf with a huge bearded head, protruding tongue, flat nose, shaggy eyebrows and hair, large projecting ears, long but thick arms, and bowed legs; around his body he wears the skin of an animal of the panther tribe, and its tail hangs down and usually touches the ground behind him; on his head he wears a tiara of feathers" (Budge 1969: 284).   Drawing after Ibid. 286.

*Questions arise over the existence of the tail or penis of figure [c] on the original drawing (Keel 1998a:219). Lacking a penis and depicted with female breasts, figure [c] becomes female (more on this following).

The similarities between Egypt's dwarf-god Bes and Ajrud's standing figures [b] and [c] are compared on the table below:

Egyptian God Bes	Ajrud's Figures [b] and [c]
dwarf form	possible
huge head	possible: long heads
bearded	possible
protruding tongue	no
flat nose	yes
shaggy eyebrows and hair	no
large, protruding ears	possible
long, thick arms	possible: long arms, not thick
bowed legs	yes
animal skin	possible, a dotted garment
tail	tail or penis
tail touching ground	no
tiara of feathers	possible

Noting that Ajrud's standing figures [b] and [c] share 2 (of 13), and another possible 8 (of 13), of Bes' attributes led some experts to conclude both figures depict the Egyptian god Bes.

▷ [b] and [c] Standing Figures of Drawing 1
• Breasts and Tail or Penis of Figure [c]

If figure [c] does depict the dwarf-god Bes, however, there remains the question of his female breasts. According to some experts, figure [c]'s female breasts are to be understood as a "bisexual-feminized," variant form of Bes (Keel 1998a:219).

Assessing figure [c] as a bisexualized figure raises the tail or penis question.

Although figure [c] has been traditionally depicted with female breasts and a tail or penis, an article in *Biblical Archaeology Review* by Uzi Avner questions this portrayal.

In an article entitled "Sacred Stones in the Desert," Avner states, "In my opinion, this portrayal results from an inaccurate restoration that has led many scholars to identify the figures as two male deities" (2001:36).

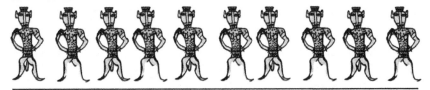

"In fact," Avner continues, "nothing in the [original] painting itself indicates the presence of a tail or penis on this figure" (Ibid.).

Following Avner's observation, the representations below depict Ajrud's standing figure [c] with and without the attached tail or penis:

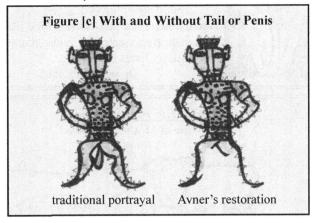

Figure [c] With and Without Tail or Penis

traditional portrayal   Avner's restoration

Upon the removal of figure [c]'s tail or penis, and with the inclusion of female breasts, figure [c] becomes female, thus forming a male and female duo with figure [b].

This male-and-female couple now parallels symbolism found at all neighboring religious sites across the area (Ibid.), increasing the likelihood that the two standing figures are to be understood as a male and female couple.

▷ **[b] and [c] Standing Figures of Drawing 1**
 ▪**Bovine Representation of Yahweh and Asherah**

Divine

Bovines?

Faces of Ajrud's Standing Figures

[b]

[c]

Additionally, Avner states, the Ajrud standing "figures represent Yahweh and the goddess Asherah, the former wearing a bull mask and the latter that of a cow" (Ibid.).

Avner is one of a group of experts suggesting the faces of figures [b] and [c] are bovine, not leonine, and depict Yahweh as the Bull of Heaven and Asherah as the Heavenly Cow Goddess.

Drawings after Avner 2001:37.

Bovinely

Female

Similar Iconographic Associations:
Bovine/Bison and Female
~33,000 BCE

A digital camera mounted on a telescopic pole captured this image from France's Chauvet Cave.

This Paleolithic/Old Stone Age configuration depicts a part-bison/bovine figure and a female (represented by pubic triangle, legs and hips) (Clottes 2001:120).
Drawing after Ibid.

Divine

Bovine

Similar Historic Associations:
Bovine of Mother Goddess
~2475 BCE

Once displayed on the temple facade at Tel al-Ubaid, this copper relief is one of two "bulls of the mother-goddess Ninhursag" and is believed to be "the oldest known bulls in relief" (Bogdanos 2005: 32). Drawing after Ibid.

Bovine

Female

Similar Historic Associations:
Bovine-Headed Goddess
~2004 BCE

This cylinder seal impression depicts an enthroned and winged Cow-Headed Goddess surrounded by serpentine symbols, a crescent moon, a fish, two kneeling figures, one standing and one seated figure.
Drawing after Collon 1987:38 Fig 134.

Divine

Bovine

To fully understand this divine bovine interpretation, one must travel back in history.

Ajrud Draw. [6 of 19 pages]

• Bovine Representation of Yahweh and Asherah
Divine Bovine Historic Symbology

Spanning thousands of years, bovine symbolism per-meates across Paleolithic caves and Neolithic shrines into Cretan reliefs and Grecian mythology:

Lascaux Cave Painting
~15,000 BCE

Catal Hoyuk Neolithic Shrine
~5950 BCE

Knossos Palace Wall Relief
~1400 BCE

Dominating the Ancient Near East religious landscape for over 5,000 years, the artifactual evidence indicates the divine bovine religio-tradition moved from Syria (south of the Taurus/Bull Mountains of Anatolia) into Egypt (Campbell 1969:142). Drawings after: Burenhult 2003:116 (Lascaux); Mellart 1967:Fig. 37 (Catal Hoyuk); Vasilakis 2002:192 (Knossos, reversed image).

Divine Bovine Historic Symbology
-Mesopotamian Bovine Traditions
Goddess-as-Cow and God-as-Bull

Bovine Mother

Goddess

Traditionally, the bovine symbolism of Goddess-as-Cow was one "of the earliest historical objects of worship, occurring among the Mesopotamian population." This representation personified the "Goddess as [a] cow, ruling over the food-giving herd" (Neumann 1963:124).

At the dawn of writing, the religious prose of the earliest cuneiform tablets used bovine imagery to characterize their Great Goddess Inanna.

Divine

Bovine

History's first known author and daughter of Akkadian King Sargon the Great, the high priestess Enheduanna, described the Great Goddess Inanna as

a "wild bull Queen,"

a "Great Mother Cow" and

a "divine ecstatic wild cow" (Meador 2000:119, 131, 176).

The Goddess-as-Heavenly-Cow representations personified "the embodiment or symbol of vital [life] force" (James 1994:88).

Birth of

Sun-God

Celestial

Goddess

~ Female Imagery and the Bountiful Earth ~
Similar Historic Associations:
Virgin Birth of the Sun
~2000 BCE/100-400 CE

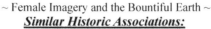

This configuration depicts the celestial, Egyptian Sky-Goddess Nut as she daily gives birth to the sun.

Sacred trees and a horned altar form a shrine around the Goddess of Life and Love, Hathor, on whom the sun's rays descend.

This motif is identified as a Solar Virgin Birth, whereby the sun is swallowed by the goddess and born daily (Campbell:1949 Fig. 16).

Although dating to the 1st-4th centuries CE, this composition represents Egyptian legends dating back thousands of years earlier. Drawing after Ibid.

Celestial

Goddess

Similar Historic Associations:
Celestial Goddess on Bovine
~1000-850BCE

Discovered on the island of Samos, this cylinder seal impression depicts a goddess standing on the back of a bovine. A king and a second goddess stand before her.

Both goddesses carry weapons and are framed by astral symbols representative of Queens of Heaven.
Drawing after Collon 1987:136 Fig. 573.

Ancient Goddess and Bovine Associations

The divine bovine imagery included male deities, as depicted on this Mesopotamian plaque at left.

In addition, Enlil, the head of the Sumerian pantheon, was described on ancient tablets as "a big bull, [who] set his foot on the earth" (Kramer 1981:304). Drawing after Spycket 2000:98 Fig. 77.

Ajrud Draw. [7 of 19 pages]

Divine Bovine Historic Symbology
-Mesopotamian Bovine Traditions
Goddess-as-Cow and King-as-Bull/Calf

Early Mesopotamian kings used bovine symbolism/epithets, in conjunction with the goddess, to establish their claim to divinity and the throne.

To achieve their bovine association, the kings defined the goddess as the Heavenly Cow-Goddess and themselves as "a calf of an all-white cow," "a king born of a wild cow, nourished (?) on cream and milk," "a calf born in a stall of plenty," and "a young bull born in a year of plenty" (Kramer 1981:278).

Through this bovine association, early Sumerian kings sanctified their claim to kingship and divinity.

Divine Bovine Historic Symbology
-Egyptian Bovine Traditions
Goddess-as-Cow and God-as-Bull/Calf

Divine

Bovine

Cow-
Headed

At the other geographical end of the Syro-Palestinian corridor, Egyptian bovine tradition defined "the Great Goddess" as a "celestial cow" nourishing "the earth with her milky rain"* (Neumann 1963:128).

The Egyptians incorporated two Celestial Cow Goddesses into their mythology: "Hathor, the great, cow-headed mother goddess, and Nut, the heavenly cow goddess who waters the earth with her rain-milk[*] and carries the sun god on her back" (Ibid. 218).

Mother
Goddess

As heaven personified, the goddess Nut was described "as 'the cow who bore the bull,'" daily giving birth to the sun as "'the Bull of Heaven'" (James 1994:58).

Birth of

Sun-God

While Nut was birthing the sun, the "cosmic cow-goddess Hathor" gave birth to the god Horus, who was also identified as "'the bull of his mother'" (Campbell 1964:59).

*Greek mythology would later define the Milky Way as the breast milk of their Mother Goddess Hera.

Female
&

Bovine

Similar Historic Associations:
Goddess Europa and Bovine
~700-550 BCE

Grecian mythology identifies Zeus as a great white bull who abducts Europa (for whom the continent of Europe is named).
Drawing after Vassilakis 1995:16.

Bovine

Goddess

Similar Historic Associations:
Goddess and Birthing Bovine
~2000-1000 BCE

A Naked Goddess stands above a birthing cow* as a god approaches. Behind her stands a second goddess with upraised arms in a posture of benediction.

Crescent moons, a rosette star, a bird, a lion and smaller figures flank the primary scene on this intricate cylinder seal discovered in Syro-Palestine.
*At first glance, a cow with horns giving birth appears curious until one recalls horns were intentionally bred out.
Drawing after Collon 1987:166 Fig 777.

Goddess
&

Bovine

Similar Historic Associations:
Minoan Bovine Jumpers
~1500-1250 BCE/1917 CE

This modern portrayal of a ceremonial bull jumper was inspired by Minoan frescoes of religious bull-jumping exhibitions.
Drawing after Hare 2006.

Divine Bovine Historic Symbology
-Egyptian Bovine Traditions
Goddess-as-Cow and King-as-Bull/Calf

Ajrud
Draw.
[8 of 19
pages]

Bovine
Divine

Mother
Goddess

Paralleling Mesopotamian kings, Egyptian rulers also established their connection with the divine by identifying themselves with, and under the protection of, the Heavenly Cow Goddess Hathor, who was regarded "as the divine mother of the reigning king" (Morris 2000:51):

Bovine-
Headed

Mother
Goddess

Cow Goddess Hathor,
Mother of Egyptian Rulers
~1473-526 BCE

Hathshepsut
~1473 BCE

Amenhotep II*
~1427 BCE

Ramses I
~1279 BCE

Psamtik III
~526 BCE

*also identified as Thutmose III ~1479 BCE (Pritchard 1954:136)
Drawings after: Pritchard 1954:136 (Amenhotep); Tyldesley 1994:226 Fig. 36 (Hathshepsut); Zivie 2002:30 (Ramses); Morris 2000:51(Psamtik).

Divine Bovine Goddesses of Antiquity

Similar Historic Associations:
Grecian Bovine Coupling
~700-550 BCE

The divine bovine couple motif permeates into Grecian mythology in a patriarchally corrupted form.

According to the Greeks, Cretan King Minos sacrifices a bull to the god Poseidon, who considers the bull to be inferior to another bull which Minos owns. In retaliation for the inferior sacrificial offering, Poseidon causes Minos' wife, Queen Pasiphae, to fall in love with the unsacrificed bull.

In order to physically "satisfy her desire" (Cotterell 1999:64), the bovinely infatuated Queen hides inside a hollow cow form and has it placed in the bull's pasture. Queen Pasiphae becomes pregnant and gives birth to an infant son with a human body and the head of a bull – the minotaur. Minos orders the construction of an elaborate labyrinth within his Knossos palace as a place to hide his infant half-bovine son.

Young Athenians, according to Grecian legend, are sent into Minos' labyrinth to appease the minotaur. In an attempt to slay the half-bovine beast, the Grecian prince/hero Theseus volunteers to be sacrificed.

Through the aid of Minos' daughter, the Princess Ariadne,* Theseus slays the minotaur. After saving Theseus' life and assisting in the murder of her half-

The complexity of Crete's Knossos east palace wing reinforces the labyrinth-minotaur myth.

brother, Ariadne* flees with Theseus who promptly abandons her on a nearby island.

Through their patriarchal mythologizing, the Greeks created their own bovine couple/coupling, transforming the once great Celestial, Nutritive-Cow Mother Goddess into a bovinely-nymphomaniac queen.

*In another hidden mythological dimension to this narrative, Ariadne was a pre-Grecian Vegetation Goddess prior to her patriarchal degradation.
Drawings after photos by Kathy Yasich, Herakleion Museum, Crete and Athens National Museum.

Divine Bovine Historic Symbology
-Syro-Palestinian Evidentiary Considerations
Ras Shamra Bovine Literature References (~1440 BCE)

Written "in a language closely resembling Hebrew" (Patai 1990:60), Ras Shamra's mythological traditions greatly influenced the developing religion in neighboring Syro-Palestine.

Although El, the Canaanite head male god, was identified as a "Bull" (Pritchard 1973:93), it was the younger god Baal whose love interest bordered on the bovine (Ibid. 92).

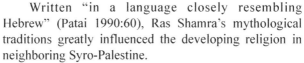

Bovine as

Infatuated by the warrior-goddess Anat/Anath, Baal's love for her was bovinely expressed by his love for a "heifer" which "was merely a mythological expression of his union with Anat" (James 1994:75).

Their divine bovine union was described and enumerated mythologically:

> ". . . Puissant Baal complies.
> He desires a cow-calf in Dubr,
> A heifer in Shihlmemat-field . . .
> Lies with her times seventy-seven,
> ([. . .]). . . times eighty-eight.[*]

Divine
Goddess

> She ([conc])eives and gives birth to Math."
> (Pritchard 1973:109).

*for a total of 6,776 times (no ancient erectile dysfunction here)

-Syro-Palestinian Evidentiary Considerations
Palestinian Bovine Artifacts
Israelite Cult Site Bull (~1200 BCE)

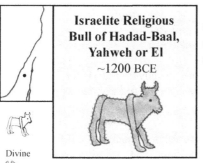

Israelite Religious Bull of Hadad-Baal, Yahweh or El
~1200 BCE

Divine

This bronze, bull figurine was discovered at the only early 12th century BCE Israelite religious site/shrine (Shanks et al 1992:iii).

The significant location of this discovery attests to the use of bovine imagery during the formative years of Israel's cultural and religious development.

According to *Gods, Goddesses and Images of God in Ancient Israel*, this bronze, bull figurine likely represents the deities "Hadad-Baal, Yahweh" or "El" (Keel 1998a:118). Drawing after Shanks et al 1992:cover.

Bovine

Goddess
&

Mother
Bovines

Similar Historic Associations:
Warrior Goddess Anat and
Nursing Bovine
~1000-925 BCE

Discovered at southern Tel el-Far'-ah, this seal impression depicts an archer above a nursing cow.

This composition, according to *Gods, Goddesses, and Images of God In Ancient Israel,* is a "paratactic combination of two pictorial themes" (Keel 1998a:126).

Recalling that the Warrior Goddess Anat is described in Egyptian texts as "a suckling cow" and in Ugaritic literature as "a suckling mother animal," and that previous archaeological artifacts identify Anat as "a warrior goddess and patroness of the soldiers" (Ibid.), this configuration "could be linked to the warrior class known as the Ben-Anat [meaning "Son of the Goddess 'Anat" (Dever 2005:128)]" (Keel 1998a:126).

Drawing after Ibid. 129 Fig. 155b.

Ancient Palestinian Warrior Goddesses

Goddess
&

Bovines

Similar Historic Associations:
Goddess and Bovine
~1200-1000 BCE

These fragments, discovered at Hazor, are the remains "of a deity [a goddess] standing on a bull" (Pritchard 1975:65).

The goddess wears a necklace culminating in spirals and framing a circular pendant with an embedded cross.   Drawing after Ibid. Pl. 66.

-Syro-Palestinian Evidentiary Considerations
  Palestinian Bovine Artifacts
    Cow Goddess Depictions (~1000-925 BCE)

Palestinian bovine representations in the form of a nursing cow, have been discovered at Jerusalem, Shechem and Megiddo. According to *Gods, Goddesses and Images of God In Ancient Israel*, the following three nursing cow configurations are Palestinian personifications of a goddess (Keel 1998a:143).

Ajrud Draw. [10 of 19 pages]

Goddess &

Nursing Bovine

Bovine Nursing

Mother Goddess

Jerusalem Goddess with Nursing Bovines
~1000-925 BCE

Discovered at Jerusalem, the above configuration depicts a goddess (Ibid.) holding the horns of nursing cows. Fluttering doves (epiphanies of the goddess) rest on the bovines' backs and face the goddess.

The following Palestinian examples also depict nursing cows as personifications of the life-sustaining, nutritive Mother Goddess.

Bovine Nursing

Mother Goddess

Palestinian Nursing Goddesses
~1000-925 BCE

Discovered at Shechem, the left image depicts a dove/bird above the back of a nursing cow, while a lion rests on the back of a nursing bovine on the right image from Megiddo (Ibid.).

Nursing animals, doves/birds and lions are attributes of Ancient Near East goddesses. When displayed in conjunction with bovine images (as above), these Palestinian artifacts are understood as representations of the goddess. Drawings after Keel 1998a:142: Fig. 165a (top); Fig. 165b, 165c (bottom).

Divine

Bovine

Similar Historic Associations:
Bovine Goddess Nintu
~3000-2340 BCE

Once displayed on an altar pedestal within a temple dedicated to the goddess Nintu, this Mesopotamian bearded,* cow figurine likely represents the "Lady of Birth," the goddess Nintu (Frankfort 1996:59).

*Nintu's beard indicates she embodied superhuman power (Ibid.). Drawing after Ibid. Il. 62.

Divine

Bovine

Similar Iconographic Associations:
Bovine Goddess Hathor
~1570-1070 BCE

Identified as the "Nurturing Cow of Heaven," the "Celestial Cow" and "the Great Goddess [who] nourishes the earth with her milky rain" (Neumann 1963:128-130), the goddess Hathor is pictured here reclining on the edge of a papyri marsh.

Drawing after photo by Lindy Ruttmann, Kelsey Museum, Ann Arbor.

Bovine
Mother

Goddess

Similar Historic Associations:
Bovine Mother Goddess
~800 BCE

Discovered at Arslan Tash, this ivory inlay depicts a cow nursing her infant calf.

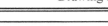

According to *The Art and Architecture of the Ancient Orient*, this motif is "understood throughout the near East" to personify/represent "any mother goddess" (Frankfort 1996:317). Drawing after Ibid. 322 Il. 376.

Goddess and Bovine Associations of Antiquity

-Syro-Palestinian Evidentiary Considerations
Palestinian Bovine Artifacts
Bovine-Headed Stela (~1000-900 BCE)

Excavations near the Sea of Galilee at Bethsaida uncovered a three-foot stela that depicts an armed, bull-headed figure "symbolically protecting the city" (Arav 2000:50).

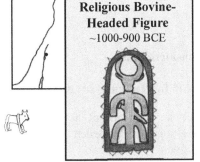

Religious Bovine-Headed Figure
~1000-900 BCE

Representing one of Bethsaida's chief deities, this stela is further evidence of early Israelite bovine imagery and "the influence of this [bovine] tradition on early Israelite religion" (Ibid.).

Recalling that historically Yahweh was "worshipped as Baal in the guise of a young bull" (James 1994:79), this stela may represent Yahweh.

-Syro-Palestinian Evidentiary Considerations
Palestinian Bovine Artifacts
Tanaach Cult Stand (~1000 BCE)

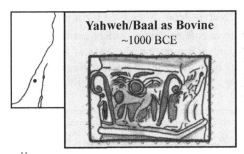

Yahweh/Baal as Bovine
~1000 BCE

Reflective of the Egyptian and Mesopotamian influences on Syro-Palestine, another bovine example comes from the previously discussed religious/cult stand of Taanach.

The upper register of Tanaach's 4-tiered religious/cult stand depicts

Bovine as

Deity

a young bull flanked by stylistic, sacred trees. This bull, according to *The Early History of God: Yahweh and the Other Deities in Ancient Israel*, likely personifies either Yahweh or Baal (Smith 1990:51).

Drawings after: Arav 2000:50 (top); Taylor 1994:56 (bottom).

Ancient Goddess and Bovine Associations

-Syro-Palestinian Evidentiary Considerations
Palestinian Bovine Artifacts
Judahite and Jerusalem Bovines (~970 BCE)

Ajrud
Draw.
[12 of 19
pages]

Continuing the Palestinian bovine tradition, 143 bovine figurines have been unearthed in southern Judah/ Palestine, of which 32 were discovered within Jerusalem (Keel 1998a:194).

-Syro-Palestinian Evidentiary Considerations
Palestinian Bovine Artifacts
"Young bull is Yaw [Yahweh]" Inscription (~800 BCE)

Any lingering doubts about the influence of neighboring bovine beliefs upon Syro-Palestine was dispelled with the discovery of an 8th century BCE pottery inscription.

Discovered at Israel's ancient capital of Samaria, the inscription specifically identifies Yahweh in bovine terms, as "Young bull is Yaw [/Yahweh]" (Smith 1990:51).

Israelite Religion Evolves from Near East Religion

Israel from Canaan

According to a *Biblical Archaeology Review* article entitled "The History of Israelite Religion: A Secular or Theological Subject?" "The religion of Israel was born the child of ancient Near Eastern religion, and especially the religious culture of ancient Canaan" (Cross 2005:45).

Similar Historic Association of the Gods
Yahweh Evolves from the god El
(which ultimately led to the pairing of the goddess
Asherah with Yahweh)

Yahweh from El

The Origins of Biblical Monotheism: Israel's Polytheistic Background and the Ugaritic Texts declares that "By some point in the late monarchy, it is evident that the god El was identified with Yahweh, and as a result, Yahweh-El is the husband of the goddess, Asherah" (Smith 2001).

Ancient Female Divine Bovines

-Syro-Palestinian Evidentiary Considerations
Palestinian Bovine Artifacts
Samarian Bovine Vessels (~800 BCE)

Ajrud
Draw.
[13 of 18
pages]

Also dating to the eighth century BCE, an additional 83 bovine vessels were discovered at a religious installation within Israelite's capital city of Samaria (Keel 1998a:194).

-Syro-Palestinian Evidentiary Considerations
Biblical Bovine References

Although written years after the fact and not a contemporary primary source, biblical texts describe Israel's early religious practices and include references indicating ancient Israel embraced bovine imagery:

-Hosea 8:6 likens Yahweh to a bull/calf of Samaria,

Divine

-1 Kings 12:28 describes Israel's King Jeroboam setting up two golden bull/calf shrines for worship at Dan and Bethel and

-the analogy in Numbers 24:8 "derived from the bovine imagery of El. [which presents] The image of Yahweh having horns 'like the horns of the wild ox'" (Smith 1990:51).

Bovine

Israel
from
Canaan

According to *The Early History of God: Yahweh and the Other Deities in Ancient Israel*, the personification of Yahweh-as-bull/bovine was a natural progression from the El-as-bull/bovine Canaanite bull iconography tradition (Ibid.).

Yahweh
from
El

These biblical references, combined with archaeological evidence, provide testament to the existence of bovine iconography, and, specifically, to Yahweh's identification as a bull/bovine.

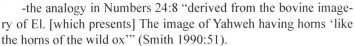
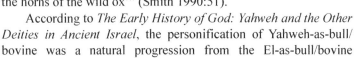

Similar Historic Association of the Gods
Asherah and Yahweh Evolves from Asherah and El
(which ultimately led to the pairing of the goddess Asherah with Yahweh)

Yahweh
from
El

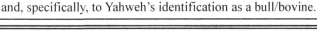

Almost 30 years ago, *Biblical Archaeology Review* stated "It is well-known that in Israelite religion Yahweh replaced the great god El as Israel's god. If Yahweh replaced El, it would seem logical . . . that, at least in the popular religion of ancient Israel . . . Asherah functioned as the wife of Yahweh" (Lemaire 1984b:46).

In summary, a multitude of archaeological artifacts provide evidence that bovine traditions were an integral religious component of Palestine's and Israel's early religious formation and developmental years.

Under the weight of this evidence, the possibility of Ajrud's standing figures representing the bovine pair of Yahweh and his Asherah remains likely.

Ajrud
Draw.
[14 of 19 pages]

-Syro-Palestinian Evidentiary Considerations
Similar Palestinian Headdress Iconography
Palestinian Scarabs (~1800-1550 BCE)

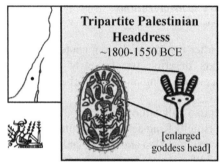

Tripartite Palestinian Headdress
~1800-1550 BCE

[enlarged goddess head]

Similar Palestinian Headdresses
~1800-1550 BCE

Bovine

Goddess

Headdresses similar to Ajrud's standing figure [b] appear on earlier Palestinian artifacts.

fig. [b]

Discovered at Shechem, this configuration depicts the head of a "Branch Goddess" (Keel 1998a: 29) wearing a tripartite headdress stylistically similar to Ajrud's standing figure [b].

Although of unknown Palestinian provenience, each of these three images (at left) depicts a goddess head (Ibid. 28).

Their ear positioning is a bovine reference, indicating the images are local Palestinian adaptations of Egypt's Cow-Goddess Hathor.

Each of the goddess heads are crowned with a

fig. [b]

headdress of feathers(?) or palm leaves(?), stylistically similar to Ajrud's standing figure [b].

Drawings after Ibid. 30 Fig. 14a (top); 27 Fig. 13a, b, c (bottom).

Bovine

Goddess

Similar Iconographic Associations:
Hathor as Bovine Goddess of Life
~1648-1530 BCE
Bovine ears and reversed ankhs define Hathor as a bovine Goddess of Life on this Egyptian seal.
Drawing after Freeman 1999:22.

-Syro-Palestinian Evidentiary Considerations
Similar Palestinian Headdress Iconography
Palestinian Figurines (~1600-1450 BCE)

Ajrud Draw. [15 of 19 pages]

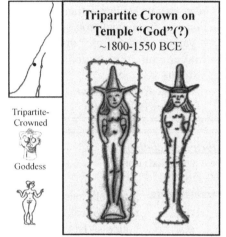

Tripartite Crown on Temple "God"(?)
~1800-1550 BCE

Tripartite-Crowned Goddess

This ancient mold (far left) was discovered in the temple worship area of a religious installation at Nahariyah. The cast statue (right) depicts a naked goddess wearing a tripartite crown stylistically similar to Ajrud's standing figure [b].

Despite the obvious female characteristics of this figurine, it is identified as a "god" in *The World of the Bible* (Van Der Woude 1986:372). Drawings after Mazar 1990:220.

fig. [b]

Similar Striated Headdresses
~1600-1450 BCE

These Palestinian figurines (left) share a stylistic similarity to the vertical, striated headdress of Ajrud's standing figure [c].

fig. [c]

The (left) female figurine was discovered at an unknown Palestinian provenience. The figurine (at right) was discovered at Megiddo, although similar fragments were also recovered at Gezer, Taanach, Shechem and Tel Abu Hawam (Keel 1998a:54). Drawings after Pritchard 1954: 162 Fig. 469.4 (left); 161 Fig. 467 (right).

Figurine with

Pubic Triangle

Similar Historic Associations:
Triangular Female Representation
~3000 BCE

From the dawn of writing through biblical times, this inverted triangle has symbolized the "Female pubic part: 'woman,' 'female'" (VanDer Woude 1986:52 Fig. 6.3).

Sacred

Sistrum

Isis

Sistrum

Similar Historic Associations:
Egyptian Queens with Sistrums
~1279-13 BCE

Two Egyptian queens, wives of Ramses the Great, elevate Hathor sistrums in this depiction of a ceremonial procession.

Variant designs are displayed on the queens' sistrums.

Image from *Egyptian Designs* 1999 Fig. 065.

Sacred

Sistrum

Egyptian

Sistrum

Similar Historic Associations:
Isis Priestess with Sistrum
~700-450 BCE

This religious procession, dedicated to the goddess Isis, depicts Grecian priests and priestesses carrying ceremonial objects.

The priestess (far left) shakes a sistrum in her upraised hand, making a gentle, melodic noise believed to drive away bad spirits and negative influences.

Drawing after Witt 1971:Pl. 30.

Sacred

Sistrum

Sistrum → Ceremonial Church Bells → Motorcycle Folklore
Legend of the Motorcycle Bell

The Egyptian sistrum evolves into Christianity's ceremonial church bells then into motorcycle folklore.

According to the Legend of the Motorcycle Bell, evil spirits will attach themselves to motorcycles that are not protected by a melodic bell (which must have been received as a gift).

-Syro-Palestinian Evidentiary Considerations
Similar Palestinian Headdress Iconography
Palestinian Hathor Sistrums (~1300-1050 BCE)

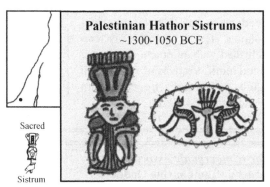

Palestinian Hathor Sistrums
~1300-1050 BCE

Sacred

Sistrum

Discovered in Palestine at Tel el-Ajjul, these bovine Hathor sistrums* display striated linear attributes similar to the headdress of Ajrud's figure [c]. Flanking the god-desses' heads are

Ajrud Draw. [16 of 19 pages]

fig. [c]

uraei/rearing cobras (left) and striped felines (right).

Palestinian Hathor Sistrums
~1300-1050 BCE

Sacred

Sistrum

These Lachish examples of Pal-estinian sistrums (at left) depict the goddess Hathor flanked by rearing cobras.

Hathor, as the Cow Goddess displays elevated-cow ears with str-

fig. [c]

ated headdresses similar to Ajrud's figure [c]. The left representation displays distinctive leonine/bovine facial features.
Drawings after Keel 1998a:69 Fig. 74, 75d (top); 75a, b (bottom).

*The sistrum is an Egyptian religious, cere-monial, musical instrument used almost exclusively by queens (right) and/or priestesses (left).

A long standing, religious tradition, a Gre-cian sistrum-carrying priestess is depicted (left) in a ceremonial procession dating several hundred years after the queens' depiction.

Musical

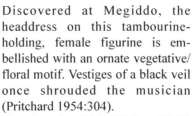

Goddess

Similar Iconographic Associations:
Palestinian Tambouine Figurine
~1000-750 BCE

Discovered at Megiddo, the headdress on this tambourine-holding, female figurine is embellished with an ornate vegetative/ floral motif. Vestiges of a black veil once shrouded the musician (Pritchard 1954:304).
Drawing after Ibid. 162 Fig. 469.12.

Musical

Goddess

Similar Iconographic Associations:
Dead Sea Shrine Tambourine Goddesses
~840 BCE

These female figurines, clutching tambourines, were discovered at a shrine near the Dead Sea.

The *Archaeology of the Land of the Bible Vol. II* states these figurines may depict the goddess Astarte (Stern 2001a:206), who coalesced with the goddess Asherah.
Drawings after Daviau 2002:48.

Israelite Culture Evolves from Canaanite Culture

Israel from Canaan

A *Biblical Archaeology Review* article entitled "How a People Forms," states that although Israel claimed to be distinct from the Canaanites, in actuality, such was not the case.

Although "Israel defined itself as 'not Canaanite' . . . the archaeological and textual record reveals that, in its formative centuries, Israel . . . was a lot more what it claimed *not* to be than otherwise" (Leith 2006:22).

Israelite Goddess from Canaanite Goddess

"In other words, Israel was essentially Canaanite . . . [and] we now know that the religious landscape of Israel included one or more Canaanite goddesses" (Ibid.).

-Syro-Palestinian Evidentiary Considerations
Similar Palestinian Headdress Iconography
Hazor Tambourine Figurine (~1000-925 BCE)

Ajrud
Draw.
[17 of 19
pages]

Striated Headdress on Tambourine Goddess
~1000-925 BCE

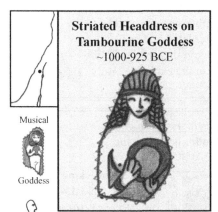

Musical

Goddess

fig. [c]

This fragmentary, Palestinian, female figurine, discovered at Hazor, displays a striated headdress (a modified form of, and stylistically similar to, Ajrud's figure [c]). Holding a tambourine next to a bare breast, she wears bracelets and an elongated headdress.

According to an article entitled "Pagan Yawehism: The Folk Religion of Ancient Israel" published in *Biblical Archaeology Review,* this depiction likely represents a goddess "playing a tambourine or holding a dove – [both] a traditional emblem of goddesses in all periods throughout the ancient Near East" (Stern 2001b:27).

Drawing after Keel 1998a:165 Fig. 190a.

[d]

[c]

Kuntillet Ajrud Drawing 1: Three Figure Grouping
▷|d| Seated Figure with Lyre

Returning to Drawing 1's Three Figure Grouping, the seated figure [d] is depicted slightly elevated and to the right of Ajrud's two standing figures. Figure [c]'s bent elbow touches figure [d]'s throne, securing her within the image's landscape.

Seated Ajrud Figure

[d]

Wearing an ornate coiffure and dotted garment, female figure [d] holds a lyre while seated on a decorative throne. Female breasts and a penis or appendage are depicted on her image.

This female figure was extensively analyzed in a *Hebrew Studies* article entitled "Recent Archaeological Confirmation of the Cult of Asherah in Ancient Israel" by William G. Dever.

Comparing the stylistic similarity of figure [d]'s distinctive garment, coiffure

Drawing after Avner 2001:37.

Vestiges of the Great Mother as Heavenly Bovine Goddess

As the Divine Mother of Humanity and Divinity, vestiges of the Great Mother Goddess as the Heavenly, Celestial Cow Goddess extend into present-day.

In antiquity, a Roman symbol for the goddess, the cornucopia/horn of plenty, represented the heavenly cow spilling out earth's abundant harvest; her "image is still advertently invoked today in the expletive 'Holy Cow'" (Walker 1983:181).

Goddess & Bovine

Similar Historic Associations:
Heavenly Goddess on Bovine
~1500 BCE

A shepherd king stands before a Naked Goddess on this cylinder seal impression. Standing on the back of a bovine and framed with a leafy garland, this is a representation of a Heavenly, Vegetative Prosperity Goddess.

Behind the king, a seated couple flank a sacred stylized tree (top register), while four worshippers approach (bottom register). An epiphany of the goddess Inanna/Ishtar, the eight-rayed Venus star, assimilates the goddess into the configuration.

Drawing after Neumann 1963:Pl. 54d.

Animal Mother

Goddess

Similar Historic Associations:
Heavenly Bovine Goddess Hathor
~712-657 BCE

This Egyptian image depicts Hathor as the Heavenly Cow Goddess, emerging from a papyrus swamp. Any person wearing this amulet would be under the protection of the goddess. Drawing after Freeman 1999:30.

Nursing Animal Mother Goddesses of Antiquity

and embellished throne with other archaeological discoveries, Dever concluded the seated figure may represent the enthroned goddess Asherah (1982:38).

Once again, as with all things Asherah, not all experts agree. Believing Dever's conclusion to be an over-statement, some experts identify figure [d] as a mere musician with breasts and a penis or appendage.

Ajrud
Draw.
[18 of 19
pages]

Kuntillet Ajrud Drawing 2: Nursing Cow and Calf

Religious Blessing of the Goddess

Kuntillet Ajrud Drawing 2

Animal
Mother

Goddess

Divine

Bovine

Drawing 2 of Kuntillet Ajrud's Pithos A pictures a cow tenderly watching over her nursing calf.

Historically throughout the Ancient Near East, the nursing cow-animal mother motif was regarded as a personification of the Goddess as Animal Mother (Hawkes 1968:101).

In Palestine, this configuration was understood as a "specific-ally religious" depiction "of blessing . . . connected . . . with the goddess" (Keel 1998a:215). Drawing after Shanks et al 1992:135.

Animal
Mother

Goddess

Similar Historic Associations:
Goddess as Animal Mother

Arslan Tash ~1600 BCE
~8th c BCE

Crete
~1600 BCE

Discovered within Crete's Knossos palace temple repositories, this ivory plaque represents the Goddess as Animal Mother (Hawkes 1968:101).

The Nursing Animal Mother Goddess motif personified the symbolic association of a timeless, universal configuration, which was understood throughout the Ancient Near East as any Mother Goddess (Frankfort 1996:317).

Drawing after Hawkes 1968:101.

Tree of
Life

Goddess

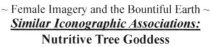

~ Female Imagery and the Bountiful Earth ~
Similar Iconographic Associations:
Nutritive Tree Goddess
~1552-1306 BCE

This Egyptian representation depicts "The Date-Palm Goddess, Dispensing Nourishment" (Neumann 1963:242). Drawing after Ibid. Fig. 52.

Vegetative
Tree

Goddess

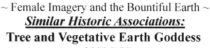

~ Female Imagery and the Bountiful Earth ~
Similar Historic Associations:
Tree and Vegetative Earth Goddess
~2000 BCE

The female personification of nature is symbolically represented on this Indus Valley configuration depicting a supine "Earth Goddess with a plant growing from her womb" (Campbell 1962:166). Drawing after Ibid. Fig. 16.

Sacred

Tree

Similar Historic Associations:
Sacred Tree of Asherah Evolves Into Maypole
The sacred tree tradition continues into the Semitic asherah of the goddess Asherah – precursor of the British maypole (Lockyer 1906).

Israelite Mythology Connects YHWH with Asherah
According to *The Religions of Ancient Israel: A Synthesis of Parallactic Approaches,* the Kuntillet Ajrud "data affirm that the link between YHWH and Asherah was part of Israelite mythology" (Zevit 2001:651).

Kuntillet Ajrud Drawing 3:
Sacred Tree/Asherah Flanked by Nibbling Ibexes

Sacred Tree

Flanked by Ibexes

Symbolic

Lion

Lachish

Vase

Tanaach

Sacred Tree/Asherah Flanked by Nibbling Ibexes

Kuntillet Ajrud Drawing 3

Stand

Drawing 3, also on Pithos A, depicts nibbling ibexes flanking a lotus-blossomed Sacred Tree.

Ajrud Draw. [19 of 19 pages]

The stylized, Sacred Tree is positioned above the back of a striding lion.

The ibexes-nibbling-on-a-sacred-tree motif continues an established Asherah tradition, previously noted on the Lachish Fosse Temple vase, the Tanaach cult stand and numerous other archaeological artifacts.

According to *The Cult of Asherah in Ancient Israel and Judah*, this representation personifies the goddess Asherah "in the form of the sacred tree flanked by two ibexes" (Hadley 2000:153).

This assessment is congruent with that of the majority of scholars and additionally confirmed in *Biblical Archaeology Review*, "Here the ibexes nibble from a stylized tree that represents the goddess Asherah, who stands, like [the goddess] Qudshu, on a lion's back" (Avner 2001:33). Drawing after Ibid. 37.

Sacred Tree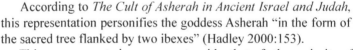

Flanked by Ibexes

Similar Iconographic Associations:
Sacred Tree/Asherah Flanked by Nibbling Ibexes
~1350-1150 BCE

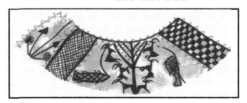

Pairs of ibexes flank a stylized Tree of Life on this pottery fragment discovered at Megiddo. Holy water cascades from the sacred tree and connects to the fish, symbolizing fertility and life (Keel 1978:138). Drawing after Ibid. Fig. 181.

Author's Note: Kuntillet Ajrud has one more distinctive iconographic element which deserves mention.

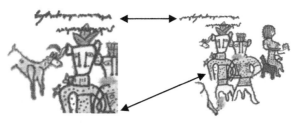

Upon making a 90 degree rotation of Ajrud's Pithos A, an ibex becomes visible nibbling on lotus blossoms above the shoulder of the larger, standing figure (Keel 1998a:212).

Recalling that a nibbling ibex is a common motif within Asherah's constellation, this configuration affirms that Asherah allusions are likely embedded within this iconography.

IRON AGE REFERENCES

V. Kuntillet Ajrud   ~830-760 BCE

Introduction
Inscriptions
Drawings
Conclusion
  Summary of Kuntillet Ajrud Inscriptions
  Summary of Kuntillet Ajrud Drawings
  Final Conclusion

Kuntillet Ajrud Conclusion
Summary of Kuntillet Ajrud Inscriptions

The Hebrew term *'srth,* translated asherah-or-Asherah, appears 5 times in Kuntillet Ajrud's dedicatory, blessing inscriptions. It is paired with the god Yahweh 4 times.

Scholars are divided in their interpretation of the term. Some translate it as Asherah (a goddess); others interpret it as asherah (a cult symbol representing the goddess).

 Over 25 years ago, in an attempt to circumvent analysis paralysis, *Asherah and the Cult of Yahweh in Israel* encapsulated the controversy stating, "The cult symbol represents the goddess, and the cult symbol is clearly tied to Yahweh" (Olyan 1988:34).

In addition, evaluation of ancient texts in conjunction with archaeological discoveries of recent decades affirms, "A place for Asherah and her cult symbol in Israelite religion seems assured by recent discoveries and research on other extant texts" (Ibid. 74).

 Extrapolating further, inscriptions pairing Asherah with Yahweh make it clear that "Asherah and her cult symbol were legitimate not only in popular Yahwism, but in the official cult as well" (Ibid.).

Summary of Kuntillet Ajrud Drawings

Kuntillet Ajrud's drawings contain distinctive goddess motifs and references.

Historically, scholars have identified goddesses by specific configurations, such as the representation of Asherah as the sacred tree, flanked by ibexes and positioned above her signature lion (Drawing 3).

Three additional goddess references (Drawing 1, the bovine figure [c]; Drawing 1, the seated musician figure [d]; and Drawing 2, the nursing cow) remain likely, but uncertain, Asherah identifications.

In summary, Ajrud's drawings contain 1 definite Asherah representation and 3 additional goddess references, which are likely Asherah identifications (recalling Asherah was Palestine's primary goddess).

Drawing 3	Drawing 1, figure [c]	Drawing 1, figure [d]	Drawing 2
Asherah reference	likely goddess Asherah reference	likely goddess Asherah reference	likely goddess Asherah reference

Final Conclusion

Ajrud
Concl.
[2 of 3
pages]

The profound implications of Kuntillet Ajrud's archaeological discoveries give rise to a provocative question about the marital status of Israel's god,

"Is the God of Israel really a bachelor god or not?"
(Shanks et al 1992:137)

Over 20 years ago, addressing a symposium at the Smithsonian Institute, a panel of biblical experts reported that both Israelite and Judahite religious practices included the worship of a goddess,

 "One of the things we learn from the Kuntillet Ajrud inscriptions is that there was a tradition of Israelite piety (and probably Judahite piety as well, since both the southern and northern kingdoms are represented at the site) that included the worship of a goddess alongside Yahweh" (Ibid.).

Elaborating further, the panel next addressed the question,

"Did God Have A Wife?"*

and the ". . . short answer is:

Yes,

 some Israelites in some historical periods believed that Yahweh had a consort."
(Ibid.)

Commenting upon the academic and social situation, the Smithsonian panel stated that although "the idea of an Israelite goddess seems alien to us . . . in the Iron Age it was a fixed feature of the religion – at least in some circles" (Ibid. 138).

Author Sandra Scham summarized the debate surrounding the implications of Ajrud's archaeological discoveries in an *Archaeology* article entitled "The Lost Goddess of Ancient Israel," stating "Biblical scholars were at first reluctant to accept the pairing of Yahweh and Asherah" (2005:38).

Although archaeological artifacts are primary, contemporary evidence, the response to questioning long held social beliefs was to negate the evidence.

 "Those who were wont to take the biblical narrative at face value," Scham explained, "were incensed by the image of a polytheistic Israel that worshiped a divine couple" (Ibid.).

*A question addressed in William G. Dever's 2005 book entitled: *Did God Have a Wife? Archaeology and Folk Religion in Ancient Israel.*

The result has been a series of legitimate, and suspect, claims whereby any "number of people disputed the find, the translation, and the interpretation of the translation" (Scham 2005:38).

Scham parallels the Ajrud controversy with a similar, previously debated notion in biblical academia – the dispute over whether Israelite-religion-was-the-same-as-Canaanite-religion.

Ajrud Concl. [3 of 3 pages]

Israelite Religion from Canaanite Religion   Although academically accepted now, when archaeologists initially began to suspect that Israelite-religion-was-the-same-as-Canaanite-religion, their thesis was vehemently rejected by biblical scholars.

Scham states that the transition to the factual redefinition of Israelite-religion-was-the-same-as-Canaanite-religion was due to the persistence of archaeologists after extensive analysis of the artifactual, forensic evidence (Ibid. 40). Thus, although initially met with resistance, knowledge gained through factual, archaeological analysis subsequently brought forward a more accurate historical record.

Scham believes a similar shift in the was-Asherah-the-wife-of-Yahweh debate, to a more factual history of Asherah-was-the-wife-of-Yahweh, will eventually be furthered by archaeologists (Ibid.).

Why is the notion of an Israelite goddess such an uncomfortable concept to so many? Perhaps because she has been buried for thousands of years.

Addressing this dilemma, Scham states, "Ultimately, the campaign to eliminate the goddess has failed. 'Asherah was buried long ago by the Establishment,' declares archaeologist and author William G. Dever. 'Now, archaeology has excavated her'" (Ibid. 36).

According to *Archeology of the Land of the Bible*, "The discoveries at Kuntillet Ajrud open a window onto the world of contemporary Israelite religion in a period prior to the Deuteronomic theology of Jerusalem which inspired our Masoretic old Testament" (Mazar 1990:449).

. . . and through that window the vanquished goddess Asherah has re-emerged.

Likely Goddess Asherah Representations

VI. Iron Age IIC ~800-586 BCE

In spite of condemnation by prophets and reforming kings, worship of a companion goddess with Yahweh "was deeply rooted in both Israel and Judah in preexilic times."

Biblical Archaeologist
(Freedman 1987:249)

Asherah references in this section include:

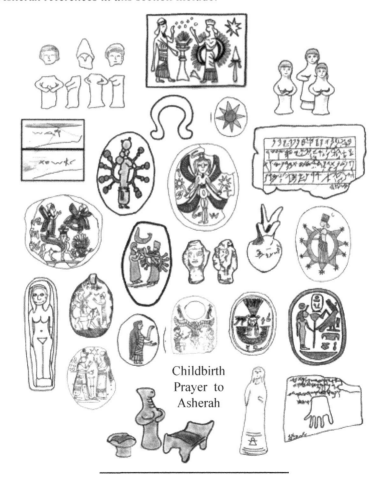

Childbirth
Prayer to
Asherah

Jerusalem Mother Goddesses
~800-650 BCE

front side front side

Over 400 fragmentary pillar figurines, similar to those at left, have been discovered in Jerusalem.

According to *Jerusalem: Excavating 3000 Years of History*, these figurines were unearthed in the only Jerusalem rooms that can be securely dated

[1 of 2 pages]

to Old Testament times (Kenyon 1967:84).

Discovered throughout all of Judah, many of these figurines were originally painted red, black and white, some with painted necklaces (Stern 2001a:207).

The pillar figurines were formed by adding arms, breasts and heads to tubular, tree-pillar bases. Their arms encircle exaggerated breasts, placing emphasis upon the nurturing aspect of "the elemental mother-goddess" (Kenyon 1967:101).

Mother Goddess

Asherah

Biblical Archaeology Review identifies the pillar figurines as the Mother Goddess Asherah with her generative and life-sustaining powers (Hestrin 1991:51).

Drawings after Kenyon 1967:102 Fig. 9.3, 9.4, 9.8; 103 Fig. 10.5, 10.6.

Mother Goddess

Asherah

Similar Historic Associations:
Palestinian Mother Goddesses
~539-332 BCE

Mother Goddesses are depicted on these seals discovered at 'Atlit and Tel Megadim.

Although some of the Isis-motif seals were imported, archaeological evidence indicates others were produced locally in Palestine (Stern 2001a:539).

Drawings after Ibid.

Tree

Goddess

Reconstructed Tree-Pillar Figurines

Although hundreds of pillar figurines have been unearthed, no pillar figurines have been found intact, nor are there enough fragmentary pieces to reassemble even one complete figurine.

[2 of 2 pages]

Commenting on this phenomenon, excavator Kathleen Kenyon states it is "remarkable" that despite the hundreds of fragmentary pieces not even one complete figurine can be restored (1967:101).

Kenyon concludes the severity of this damage is attributed to deliberate destruction and intentional breakage (Ibid.).

Adding to the discussion, *The Cult of Asherah in Ancient Israel and Judah* suggests the pillar figurines may be miniature replicas of the larger "asherah poles" that once stood in the Jerusalem temple and throughout Palestine (Hadley 2000:209).

Drawing after Stern 2001a:206 I.87.

Tree
Pillar

Goddess

Similar Iconographic Associations:
Tree Goddess Nut
~600 BCE

The "Tree Goddess Nut" (Neumann 1963:Pl. 103) emerges from the tubular base of a tree trunk on this bronze, Egyptian vessel. Branches sprout from her body.

Crowned with a solar disk, the goddess offers sustenance to a kneeling worshipper; an offering table is depicted between them.

Drawing after Ibid.

Religious
Goddess

Womb
Symbol

**Jerusalem Goddess Asherah
Tomb Headrests**
~800-700 BCE

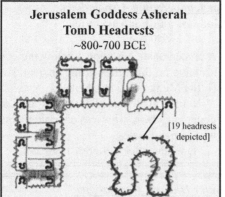

[19 headrests
depicted]

A multiple tomb burial site, discovered at Jerusalem's Dominican Ecole Biblique, displays Ω/womb-shaped headrests cut into rock.

Throughout the Ancient Near East, this distinctive hairstyle is identified as an epiphany of the Egyptian Goddess Hathor.

According to *What Did the Biblical Writers Know and When Did They Know It?* this Hathor Goddess identification extends to include the goddess called "the Holy One," "Qudshu," who coalesces with the Canaanite goddess Asherah (Dever 2001:180).

This discovery indicates devout Judaeans were buried within the Ω-shaped headrests of the goddess Asherah, securing her eternal blessing and protection, at their spiritual epicenter, Jerusalem (Ibid.).   Drawings after Keel 1998a:368 Fig. 357a, 357b.

Mother
Goddess

Womb
Symbol

Similar Iconographic Associations:
Priestess in Religious Ceremony
~1300 BCE

Discovered at Tyre, this cylinder seal impression depicts a religious, presentation scene with a priestess. An omega womb-shaped, Ω-symbol, a crescent moon, the Pleiades and the 8-rayed star of Inanna/Ishtar are also depicted. Drawing after Collon 1987:174 Fig. 811.

Stylistically Similar Iconography of Antiquity

Fruitful

Symbol

Similar Iconographic Associations:
Goddess and Pomegranate
~900 BCE

A pomegranate is sculpted below the goddess' neckline on this relief of the ancient, Hurrian/ Hittite Mother Goddess Kubaba.

Kubaba coalesces with the Phrygian mother goddess Cybele, who was also often portrayed with pomegranates.

Drawing after Cotterell 1999:292.

Fruitful

Symbol

Similar Historic Associations:
Goddess Fate Sealed by Pomegranate
~700-600 BCE

Grecian mythology explains the dormant winter season and spring's rejuvenation in terms of betrayal, abduction, rape, grief, resurrection and a pomegranate.

The myth begins with the head god Zeus giving his brother Hades (the underworld god) permission to abduct Zeus' daughter Persephone and carry her off to the underworld.

Persephone's mother, Demeter, is grief stricken and inconsolable. As the Earth Goddess, Demeter's sorrow turns the land barren – winter has arrived.

The gods exert divine peer pressure upon Zeus to rescind his sanction of Persephone's abduction and kidnapping. Zeus concedes, allowing Persephone to return.

Upon Persephone's resurrection, Demeter's joy is so great that earth's landscape is rejuvenated – spring has arrived.

During her time below, however, Persephone was tricked into eating a pomegranate seed and is now required to spend part of the year in the underworld. When Persephone returns to Hades, Demeter's grief returns and a period of dormancy again blankets the earth – signaling the return of winter once again.

Fruitful

Symbol

Similar Iconographic Associations:
Goddess and Pomegranate
~600 BCE

A pomegranate necklace, associated with the goddesses Kore and Persephone (duBois 1988: 53), is depicted on this crowned, Boeotian figurine.
Drawing after Ibid. Fig. 3.

Fruitful

Symbol

From the Temple of Yahweh . . . or Asherah . . . or Baalah/Baalath . . . or Not

~800 BCE

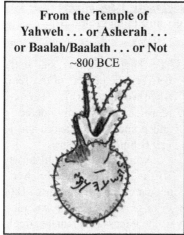

[1 of 2 pages]

Once prominently displayed in the Israel Museum, this ivory pomegranate was claimed to have been the sole surviving relic from King Solomon's Temple (Shanks 1992:42). The museum's certainty masks the uncertainty of the situation.

This ivory pomegranate surfaced in France after allegedly being smuggled out of Israel.

Nothing is known about the circumstances or original location of the pomegranate's discovery. Undeterred, the Israel Museum purchased the pomegranate in 1988 for $550,000 through an anonymous donor using a Swiss bank account (Ibid.).

Measuring just over 1.5 inches, this tiny artifact generated seismic headlines:

"Probable Head of Priestly Scepter from Solomon's Temple Surfaces in Jerusalem" (Lemaire 1984a:24), and

"Pomegranate: Sole Relic from Solomon's Temple, Smuggled Out of Israel, Now Recovered" (Shanks 1988:36).

Concurring with these claims, a recent *History Channel* presentation entitled "Digging for the Truth: Archaeology and the Bible" claimed the pomegranate to be the only artifact ever recovered from Solomon's Temple (Kent 2001).

Considering the uncertain circumstances and unknown discovery location of the pomegranate, claims that the pomegranate comes from King Solomon's Temple remain problematic.

Responding to the Solomonic Temple claims, Tel Aviv archaeologist Aharon Kempinski stated, in a *Biblical Archaeology Review* article entitled "The Pomegranate Scepter Head – From the Temple of the Lord or from a Temple of Asherah?" that it is highly "unlikely" the pomegranate comes from the Jerusalem Temple of Solomon (Shanks 1992:43).

Drawing after Stern 2001b:27.

Fruitful

Symbol

Similar Iconographic Associations:
High Priestess and Pomegranates
1910 CE

The High Priestess sits enthroned between the pillars* of the Temple of Solomon on this Tarot card representation. Embroidered palms and pomegranates adorn the temple veil behind the priestess.

According to Tarot historians, the High Priestess made her first appearance on Tarot cards ~1800 CE. Prior to that date she was identified as the Papess (the female pope).

Drawing after Waite 1910.

*These pillars are stylistically similar to the asherahs, the temple shrine columns of the 10-9th centuries BCE, which some scholars correlate to the Solomonic pillars.

Fruitful

Symbol

Similar Iconographic Associations:
Goddess and Pomegranates
~700 BCE

Flanked by rosettes, this gold, electrum plaque is one of seven forming an ancient, elaborate necklace.

Discovered at Rhodes, the plaques depict winged goddesses flanked by, and holding the tails of, pairs of companion lions.

The intricate designs were impressed, filigreed and granulated (Ogden 1992: 44). Attached, bronze pomegranate pods dangle from the plaques (Willis 1993: 127). Drawing after Ogden 1992:44.

Fruitful

Symbol

Similar Historic Associations:
Biblical Vulva is a Pomegranate

In the biblical text *Song of Songs 8:2,* the pomegranate is used as a euphemism symbolizing the female vulva.

In the same article Baruch Halpern of York University considers the relic-from-King-Solomon's-Temple claim to be suspect, stating the only certain thing is that it is "com-

pletely uncertain" that the ivory pomegranate actually came from the Jerusalem Temple of Solomon (Ibid. 45).

Adding to the complexity of the problem, a section of the inscription encircling the pomegranate's shoulder, is broken and several of the original letters are missing.

Scholars translate the pomegranate's remaining inscription as:

"Belonging to the Temp[le of _____]h,
holy to the priests" (Shanks 1992:42-45).

Proponents claiming the relic came from Solomon's temple translate the inscription as:

"Belonging to the Temp[le of Yahwe]h,
holy to the priests" (Ibid.).

The untold part of this story, however, is that the names of two goddesses,* Asherah and Baalah/Baalath, could also "fit" within the missing section (Shanks 2005b:63). These would generate the translation as:

"Belonging to the Temp[le of Ashera]h,
holy to the priests," or
"Belonging to the Temp[le of Baala]h[/Baalath],
holy to the priests."

Additional controversy has recently been added to the pomegranate debate. All of this hype and publicity may have been all for naught and much ado about nothing.

In 2004, the Israel Antiquities Authority and an investigating committee of the Israel Museum declared the ivory pomegranate a

forgery (Shanks 2005b:62-3).

Despite being introduced to the world as the "Probable Head of Priestly Scepter from Solomon's Temple" (Lemaire 1984a:24) over 25 years ago, and being prominently displayed at the Israel Museum "as the only relic from the Solomonic Temple" (Shanks 2005b:62-3), the ivory pomegranate is not, and likely never was, the only relic from the Solomonic temple.

Fruitful

Symbol

*Throughout antiquity pomegranates have symbolized Mother Goddesses. The association of a pomegranate with a goddess would be a natural, seamless transition.

Drawing after Avigad 1990:160.

Sacred

Tree

~ *Ancient Symbology* ~

Tree of Great Mother Goddess, Asherah   **Menorah**

[1 of 2 pages]

Analyzing the history and symbolism of the menorah in *A Study of the Menorah: The Seven-Branched Lampstand,* author L. Yarden concluded the menorah evolved from a stylization of Israel's sacred almond tree (1971:40).

Used both medicinally and cosmetically, the fruit of the almond tree fruit was an area delicacy. The almond tree's seed and its edible part "are identical," thus considered to be "both 'a beginning and an end; a beginning in that it springs from no other power than itself'" (Ibid.) and an end in natural accordance with nature.

The first tree of the year to blossom and the last to lose its leaves, the almond tree personified "an ideal image of life, resurrection and [the] 'White Goddess'." (Ibid.)

The almond tree's archaically Semitic etymology, *Amygdala,* is retained in its botanical name, *Amygdalus communis,* conceivably meaning "Great Mother . . . image of All Living

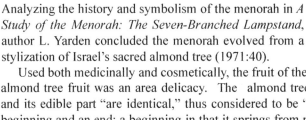 . . . identified in Phrygia with Cybele and known at Rome . . . as *Mater Magna*[/the Great Mother]" (Ibid. 41).

Born of the White Goddess and Great Mother Goddess, the menorah retains its symbolic association with her.

Contemporary with the earliest, temple menorah image (Taylor 1995:46), Philo of Alexandria (~30 BCE-50 CE) described "the light of the menorah . . . like [biblical] Sarah . . . a sort of spiritualized Great Mother or 'Virgin Mother' of Nations, embodying the cosmic 'female principle'." (Ibid. 47)

Over 1,000 years after Philo, the Jewish *Zohar* (~1300 CE) continues the symbolic association. Describing the lighting of the menorahic lampstand, the *Zohar* instructs rabbis that "the community of Israel receives the light whilst the supernal Mother is crowned, and all the lamps are illumined from Her" (Ibid. 50).

Ancient
Hand

Symbol

Paleo-Hebrew Inscription and Blessing Symbol
~750-700 BCE

Brought to light by illegal excavations, this bench tomb inscription was discovered in Jerusalem's antiquities market by William G. Dever.

Formerly with Hebrew University, Dever was able to trace the artifact to the Judaean site of Khirbet el-Qom.

[1 of 3 pages]

Although the incised hand is readily identifiable as a protective, "good luck" symbol intended to ward off evil (Dever 2005:132), the inscription above the symbol is more problematic, remaining a source of controversy and consternation since its 1967 discovery over 45 years ago.

The undeniable, "clearly Israelite" (Ibid.) inscription is a blessing formula invoking Asherah in conjunction with the Hebrew god Yahweh not once, but 3 times.

This is a problem. Why would the Canaanite goddess *Asherah*, or her symbolic sacred tree, the *asherah*, be paired with a proclaimed bachelor god in an ancient, Israelite blessing inscription? It is a blasphemous notion.   Drawing after Ibid. 133.

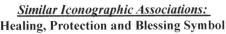

Ancient
Hand

Symbol

Similar Iconographic Associations:
Healing, Protection and Blessing Symbol
~4000-3500 BCE

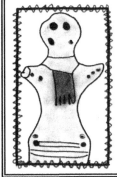

Sharing a stylistic and functional similarity to Khirbet el-Qom's incised hand, this figurine depicts the partial image of a hand incised on its torso.

Although thousands of years older, the blessing hand is an ancient symbol, still in Ukrainian use today, where it is said to promote healing and provide protection from diseases and evils (Gimbutas 1989:300).

Drawing after Ibid. 301 Fig. 481.

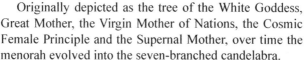

~ *Ancient Symbology* ~

Tree of Mother Goddess Asherah ⟹ **Menorah**

Originally depicted as the tree of the White Goddess, Great Mother, the Virgin Mother of Nations, the Cosmic Female Principle and the Supernal Mother, over time the menorah evolved into the seven-branched candelabra. [2 of 2 pages]

Reaffirming the menorah's stylistic religio-historicity in a *Journal for the Study of the Old Testament* article entitled "The Asherah, the Menorah and the Sacred Tree," author Joan E. Taylor states it "therefore seems likely that the iconographical concept lying behind the menorah owes much to the actual forms of asherim, images of the goddess Asherah" (1995:51).

Extensive analysis of the menorah's stylistic, iconographic and historical development led Taylor to conclude that the "menorah was designed with the usual form of an asherah – the cultic symbol of the goddess Asherah – firmly in mind" (Ibid. 29).

This menorahic-goddess association is illustrated in a medieval manuscript converging the influences of a Mesopotamian, sacred seven-branched tree and an enthroned Mother Goddess and child:

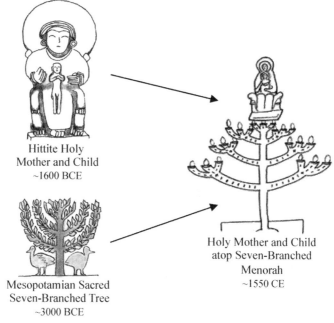

Hittite Holy
Mother and Child
~1600 BCE

Mesopotamian Sacred
Seven-Branched Tree
~3000 BCE

Holy Mother and Child
atop Seven-Branched
Menorah
~1550 CE

Drawings after: Yarden 1971:Fig. 213 (top left); Canby 1986:56 (bottom left); Yarden 1971:Fig. 40 (right).

According to a *Biblical Archaeology Review* article entitled "Who or What Was Yahweh's Asherah?" the Khirbet el-Qom inscription translates as follows:

"1. Uryahu *the wealthy man had it written:*
2. Blessed be Uryahu by Yahweh
3. and *by his asherah*; from his enemies *he saved him!*
4. *(written) by* Onyahu
5. . . . *and by his asherah*
6. . . . *(and by) his (ashe)r(ah)*" (Lemaire 1984b:44).

Once again, it is uncertain whether this Paleo-Hebrew text is to be interpreted as asherah or Asherah.

Undeniably certain, however, is the appearance of an Israelite blessing which pairs asherah-or-Asherah with Yahweh 3 times.

Encapsulating the debate, author Andre Lemaire states "Whatever an asherah is, Yahweh had one!" (Ibid.)

Historically, the term asherah-or-Asherah has been variously interpreted as "a holy place," "a sacred tree," "a pole," "a grove of trees" (Ibid. 42) or as the goddess Asherah.

As discussed previously, these translation possibilities generate the following range of diverse blessings:

"Blessed be Uryahu by Yahweh and by *his holy place,*"
"Blessed be Uryahu by Yahweh and by *his sacred tree,*"
"Blessed be Uryahu by Yahweh and by *his pole,*"
"Blessed be Uryahu by Yahweh and by *his grove of trees,*" or
"Blessed be Uryahu by Yahweh and by *his goddess, Asherah.*"

Sacred

Tree

It is a curious debate considering that over 55 years ago, the Father of Biblical Archaeology, William F. Albright, stated that the sacred trees were named asherahs after the goddess Asherah.

Tree

In *From Stone Age to Christianity: Monotheism and the Historical Process,* Albright noted that planting sacred trees, called asherahs, are so named after the goddess Asherah and are specifically referred to as the "trees of Asherah" (1957:310).

Goddess

Tree

Concurring with Albright's assessment, a chapter in *Civilizations of the Ancient Near East* entitled "Ahab of Israel and Jehoshaphat of Judah: The Syro-Palestine Corridor in the Ninth Century," states that the word a/Asherah refers to the goddess or the religious symbol of the goddess (Blenkinsopp 1995:1317).

Goddess

Sacred

Extrapolating further, author Joseph Blenkinsopp concludes that regardless of the translation rendered, each of the cult/religious symbols (a holy place, a sacred tree, a pole or a grove of trees) are to be understood as attributes of the goddess Asherah (Ibid.).

Tree

Yahweh
is his
Anat
and
Asherah

Similar Historic Associations:
Yahweh is 'his Anat and Asherah'

Archaeological discoveries have introduced a once unthinkable dynamic into the religio-historic landscape. Information gained from archaeological excavations provides new insights into previously unclear biblical translations and interpretations.

One example of a textual reevaluation and reassessment is Hosea 14:8, where God addresses Ephraim through the prophet Hosea. Traditional translations of the verse do not include the names of two goddess cited in the original text. The translation is often rendered as follows:

"O Ephraim, what more have I to do with idols?
I will answer him and care for him.
I am like a green pine tree;
your fruitfulness comes from me"
(Buursma 1989:969).

When the text is returned to its original translation, two goddess names appear:

"Ephraim, what have I to do any more with idols?
I [Yahweh] am his Anat and his Asherah.*
I am like a leafy cyprus-tree;
From me is thy fruit found"
(Patai 1990:53).

*This infers the goddesses' ability to provide "the people with the blessings of fertility" (Ibid.) is now usurped by Yahweh.

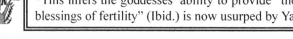

The One and Many Asherah

According to *The Asherah in the Old Testament*, "In each locality the worship of Asherah had its peculiar characteristics. For example:

in Assyria she was the consort of Amurru,
at Ugarit the consort of El,
in south Arabia the companion of the moon-god Wadd,
and among the Nabataeans of Tema she was one of a triad
of which the other two members were Salm and Shingala"
(Reed 1949:89).

Sacred

Tree

Tree

Goddess

Tree

Goddess

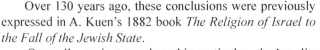

Over 130 years ago, these conclusions were previously expressed in A. Kuen's 1882 book *The Religion of Israel to the Fall of the Jewish State.* [3 of 3 pages]

Generally, ancient people and in particular, the Israelites, Kuen states, made very little distinction, if any, between the deity and its symbol or image (Reed 1949:23).

This past knowledge is gradually permeating into the current religio-historical landscape as more experts acknowledge that whether asherah-or-Asherah refers to the goddess, or her symbol as an "agent of blessing" invoked with Yahweh, it is Asherah's eminence in ancient Israel that provides the symbol's potency (Dever 2001:185-6).

Encapsulating the controversy in *Biblical Archaeology Review* Othmar Keel poses the question: "What does the cult symbol asherah represent if not the goddess Asherah?" (Keel 2007:10)

Tree
Pillar

Figurine

Goddess Tanit, Astarte and/or Asherah
~732-604 BCE

Discovered at Shavei Zion, this clay figurine depicts the goddess "Astarte" (Stern 2001a: 78).

The symbol of the goddess Tanit/Tannit, is incised on her skirt, establishing Astarte and Tanit as the same goddess (Ibid.).

In addition to the goddesses Astarte and Tanit, a third goddess, Asherah, who assimilated with Astarte (Dever 2001:195) may also be represented on this figurine.

The identification of Asherah with Tanit/Tannit is affirmed by *Asherah and the Cult of Yahweh In Israel,* stating Tanit/Tannit was Asherah's popular epithet during the first millennium in the Phoenician-Punic world (Olyan 1988:60).

Drawing after Stern 2001a:78 Il. 40.

Queen of

Heaven

Similar Iconographic Associations:
King Before Queen of Heaven
~1000-800 BCE

This seal impression depicts a Celestial Queen of Heaven standing on a pedestal and surrounded by an astral nimbus.

An Assyrian king is depicted before the goddess. A moon, the Pleiades and a galaxy of images surround the pair. Drawing after Collon 1987:184 Fig. 883.

Queen of

Heaven

Similar Iconographic Associations:
Hera as Queen of Heaven
~1885 CE

The Grecian goddess Hera, depicted here as the Queen of Heaven, directs Helios to raise the sun at dawn (Livy:1885).

Standing on a cloud, the goddess holds a bird-crowned scepter (similar to one discovered at Lascaux Cave).

Drawing after Cotterell 1999:49.

Queen of

Heaven

Similar Iconographic Associations:
Blessing Queen of Heaven
~800-700 BCE

The goddess Ishtar, in her aspect as the Queen of Heaven, is depicted on this Mesopotamian seal impression.

Flanked by winged genies, Ishtar wears a stellar crown. Standing on a canopied platform, the goddess extends her arm in a gesture of benediction toward a kneeling worshipper.

Drawing after photo by Marilyn Lindsey, Metropolitan Museum.

Queen of

Heaven

Queen of Heaven and Worshipper
~732-630 BCE

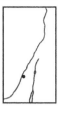

Discovered at Tel Dor, this stamp seal impression depicts a worshipper standing pointedly before a goddess.

Framed within a celestial nimbus, this is a representation of the goddess in her aspect as the Queen of Heaven.

Deeply rooted in Ancient Near East religio-socio-historicity, the goddesses Asherah, Astarte and Ishtar were often identified as Queen(s) of Heaven. This title is a vestige of the former sovereignty of the "Great Mother Goddess" as she recedes into the background and approaches "the end of her career in Israel" (Becking 2001:118-9).

Drawing after Stern 2001a:67 Fig. I.34.

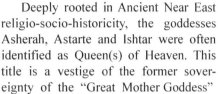

Queen

of

Heaven

Queen of Heaven and Worshipper
~724 BCE

Made from a marble scarab discovered at Shechem, this impression depicts a worshipper before the armed "Warrior Goddess Ishtar" (Younger 2003:42).

Wearing a horned crown, the goddess raises her hand in a gesture of benediction. Framed by the star of Venus and the seven stars of the Pleiades (Campbell 1998:317), this configuration depicts the goddess in her aspect as the Queen of Heaven.

Recalling that Queen of Heaven was one of Asherah's titles (Becking 2001:118-9) and Asherah coalesced with Ishtar and Astarte (Dever 2001:195), this configuration may also represent the Canaanite and Hebrew goddess Asherah.

Drawing after Campbell 1998:317.

Queens of Heaven of Antiquity

Queen of

Heaven

Similar Iconographic Associations:
Queen of Heaven on Lion Throne
~800 BCE

This cylinder seal impression depicts a celestial Queen of Heaven seated upon a lion throne, welcoming two worshipping figures. This cylinder seal is made of dark brown agate with a pink-orange center band.
Drawing after Collon 1987:129 Fig. 554.

Star of
Queen

of
Heaven

Similar Iconographic Associations:
Queen of Heaven on Lion Throne
~900 BCE

An Assyrian worshipper, priest or king, approaches an astral goddess seated upon a lion throne.

Surrounded by celestial symbols, this is a depiction of the goddess as the Queen of Heaven.
Drawing after Frankfort 1939:Pl. XXXIIIg.

Ancient Goddesses on Lion Thrones

Queen
of

Heaven

Beth Shean Queen of Heaven
~720-600 BCE

The Queen of Heaven referenced by the biblical prophet Jeremiah (7:18; 44:17-19) is depicted within an astral nimbus on this Beth Shean configuration.

Recalling that the goddess Asherah was worshipped in ancient Israel during the first millennium (Coogan 1995:42), the goddess depicted here may represent Asherah in her aspect as Queen of Heaven.

Drawing after Keel 1998a:293 Fig. 288b.

Queen
of

Heaven

Palestinian Queen of Heaven
~720-600 BCE

This seal impression depicts the Assyrian goddess Ishtar as the Queen of Heaven within a celestial radiance.

Its discovery at Ashdod confirms that inhabitants of Iron Age IIC Palestine were familiar with the goddess Ishtar (Keel 1998a:292)

Advances in scholarship expand Jeremiah's 7:18 Queen of Heaven identification beyond Ishtar and Astarte to include Asherah (Becking 2001:118-9), as "the two often coalesced in the Iron Age" (Dever 2001:195). Drawing after Keel 1998a:293 Fig. 288a.

Queen
of

Heaven

Star of Queen of Heaven
~720-600 BCE

Discovered at Megiddo, an amulet seal generated these impressions of a worshipper and the goddess' symbolic star, (Keel 1998a:292).

The goddess' star is reflective of her aspect as the Queen of Heaven, who is identified as Ishtar, Astarte and Asherah (Becking 2001:118-9). Drawings after Ibid. 297 Fig. 289.

Hebrew Queen

of Heaven

Similar Historic Associations:
Roman Queen of Heaven, Isis
~200 CE

The Roman author Apuleius invoked the goddess Isis as the Roman Queen of Heaven (Budge 1969:218).

Queen of

Heaven

Similar Iconographic Associations:
Eternal Queen of Heaven, Isis

Holding a sistrum, the Great Goddess Isis is depicted (right) as the Queen of Heaven and Eternity. Her foot rests upon her emblematic jug of the holy water of life.

Dating back almost 3,000 years, an inscription on her Sais temple reads:

"I, Isis, am the ALL,
I am the Past, the Present,
and the Future"*
(Hall 1928).

*A precursor to Christianity's *Alpha and Omega* postulate, conceptually adapted and modified through the use of the first (alpha) and last (omega) letters of the Greek alphabet.
Drawing from Hall 1928.

Ancient Goddesses of the Holy Waters of Life

Hebrew Queen of Heaven
~720-600 BCE

Although discovered at an unknown provenience, an inscription on this seal paleographically identifies it as Hebrew (Keel 1998a:338).

Holding star flowers, a multi-winged, crowned goddess is depicted on this Hebrew seal impression.

The astral flowers define her as a representation of the Queen of Heaven, possibly Astarte (Ibid.).

Recalling that Asherah coalesced with Astarte and Ishtar as the Queen of Heaven, this seal may also represent Asherah. Drawing after Ibid. 337 Fig. 331a.

Queen of Heaven

King Before Queen of Heaven
~720-600 BCE

Discovered at Shechem, this cylinder seal impression depicts the goddess Ishtar as the Queen of Heaven "*in a shining wreath* or in a nimbus of stars*" (Keel 1998a:292).

An Assyrian king, in an oath-making posture (Ibid.) stands before the astral goddess.

Recalling that the Queen of Heaven was one of Asherah's epithets (Becking 2001:118-9), this configuration may also represent the Canaanite and Hebrew goddess Asherah.

Drawing after Keel 1998a:298 Fig. 287.

Queen of Heaven

Hebrew Queen

Similar Historic Associations:
Hebrew Queen of Heaven Personifies Blessing of Food, Health and Security

of Heaven

Astral Queen

According to *Gods, Goddesses and Images of God In Ancient Israel,* the Queen of Heaven personifies the maternal transmission of blessing through food, health and security (Keel 1998a:339).

of Heaven

Asherah
as
Queen

of
Heaven

Similar Historic Associations:
Queen of Heaven before
Queen of Hades
~2100 BCE

According to the *Myths of Babylonia and Assyria,* this configuration depicts the Queen of Heaven, Inanna, emerging from the primordial holy water.* Inanna stands before the Queen of the "Great Below, Hades" (MacKenzie 1915:96)

Displeased with Inanna's appearance, the Queen of Hades hangs her upon a stake and turns her into a corpse.

After three days of death, Inanna is resurrected from the dead.

According to *History Begins at Sumer*, Inanna's rising from the dead is history's first tale of resurrection (Kramer 1981:154-167), predating the resurrection of Jesus of Nazareth by over 2,000 years.

*a reference analogous to Asherah's Proto-Sinaitic (~1450 BCE), 'Lady Asherah of the Sea' and 'the Lady who treads on the Sea (dragon)' epithets.

Drawing after MacKenzie 1915:96.

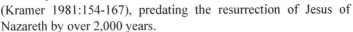

Lady
Asherah

of the
Sea

Queen
of

Heaven

Similar Historic Associations:
Goddess Night as Queen of Heaven
1891 CE

This representation, according to *The Eleusinian and Bacchic Mysteries*, depicts the "goddess night" (Taylor 1891:169) under a celestial canopy.

Although a modern composition, the iconographic tradition of a Celestial Goddess as Queen of Heaven dates back several thousand years.

Drawing after Ibid.

Asherah as Queen of Heaven
~720-600 BCE

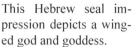

This Hebrew seal impression depicts a winged god and goddess.

According to *Gods, Goddesses, and Images of God In Ancient Israel*, this is a Judaean representation of the Hebrew god "Yahweh" (above a cherub as in Psalms 18:11) and the Canaanite/ Hebrew goddess "Asherah" (above her signature stylized, sacred tree as the Queen of Heaven) (Keel 1998a:340).

Unknown Provenience

Experts believe and "Judahite owner could have connected this constellation of images" with Yahweh and Asherah (Ibid.).
Drawing after Ibid. 337 Fig. 331b.

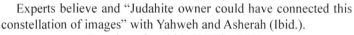

Similar Historic Associations:
Mary, Mother of Jesus as
Queen of Heaven
1954 CE

On October 11, 1954, Pope Pius XII officially invested Mary, the mother of Jesus of Nazareth, as the Catholic Queen of Heaven.

In actuality, the title was in use thousands of years before it was adopted by the Catholic Church. This is confirmed in *The Encyclopedia of Theology: The Concise Sacramentum Mundi*, which explains that although the title "Queen of Heaven" actually "comes from mythology" it is used by the church "in a non-mythological sense" (Rahner 1975:899).

Similar Iconographic Associations:
Queen of Heaven Mold
~1800 BCE

Discovered at Mari, this ancient cake/bread mold reveals that cakes or breads were baked for the Queen of Heaven over 1200 years before the biblical, baking-for-the-goddess condemnation by the prophet Jeremiah (7:16-20; 44:19) (Shanks 2003:44).   Drawing after Ibid.

Lion-
Headed

Goddess

Similar Iconographic Associations:
Lion-Headed Goddess Guide
~1165-1085 BCE

The Lion-Headed Goddess Sekhmet safely conducts the deceased to Osiris on this illustration from a mythical Egyptian New Kingdom papyri of the Book of the Dead (Keel 1978:199). Drawing after Ibid. Fig. 273.

Lion-
Headed

Goddess

Similar Iconographic Associations:
Pharaoh as Lion-Headed Goddess
~1550 BCE

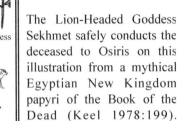

This fragmentary artifact depicts the Egyptian Pharaoh Ahmose as the Lion-Headed Warrior Goddess Sekhmet (whom he often compared himself to).

Ahmose credited his successful military recapture of the Nile Delta to the intercession of the Warrior Goddess, Sekhmet. Drawing after Harvey 2001:52.

Lion

Goddess

Similar Historic Associations:
Minoan Great Goddess and Lion
~1550-1400 BCE

Discovered within the Minoan Knossos palace, this seal impression depicts the Cretan "Great Goddess" standing alongside her emblematic lion (Alexiou 1998:73).
Drawing after author's photo, Heraklion Museum, Crete. Thank you to Susan Glassow and Carol Christ.

Lion-
Headed

Goddess

Lion-
Headed

Goddess

**Acre Lion-Headed
Goddess**
~720-587 BCE

A serpent-crowned, Lion-Headed Goddess is depicted on this Palestinian seal impression discovered at Acre.

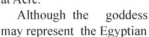

Although the goddess may represent the Egyptian Lion-Headed Sekhmet, an epithet several hundred years older than this seal identifies Asherah as "the 'One of the Lion,' or the 'Lion Lady'" (Cross 1973:33), suggesting this Acre seal configuration may represent Asherah.

Drawing after Keel 1998a:352 Fig. 338b.

**Judaean Lion-Headed
Goddess**
~700 BCE

This Hebrew, multi-cultural, inscribed seal exemplifies the fluid exchange and assimilation between ancient cultures.

Discovered in Judah, it is one of dozens of seals with "Hebrew inscriptions and Egyptian motifs" (Lubetski 2001:49).

This Lion-Headed Goddess may represent the Egyptian Sekhmet (Ibid.) or the "Lion Lady" aspect of the goddess Asherah (Cross 1973:33).

Drawing after Lubetski 2001:49.

Asherah
as
Queen

of
Heaven

Similar Historic Associations
Asherah Venerated in Palestine, Philistine and Egypt

According to *Only One God? Monotheism in Ancient Israel and the Veneration of the Goddess Asherah,* ancient inscriptions discovered in or near Judah and Israel indicate that "Asherah as a goddess and as a religious object [the asherah] was venerated in the coastal area of Palestine from Tyre to the Philistine Pentapolis, and even in Egypt" (Becking 2001:40).

**Ekron Asherat/
Asherah Dedications**
~700 BCE

Three dedicatory inscription segments were discovered within a Temple Complex at Ekron. The inscription at left reads "sacred to [the goddess] Asherat[/Asherah]" (Stern 2001a:118).

Two additional, dedicatory inscriptions were also discovered within the Ekron Temple Complex, which translate as:

"for Asherah" and

"holy according to the prescription of Qudshu(?)" (Becking et al 2001:42-3).

According to *Only One God? Monotheism in Ancient Israel and the Veneration of the Goddess Asherah*, these inscriptions attest to the worship of Asherah under the name of Qudshu at Ekron (Ibid.) (as at Ugarit 700 years earlier).

Although the last inscription remains uncertain, experts believe the combined presence of these inscriptions indicates the existence of a sanctuary for the Asherah at Ekron (Ibid.).

Drawings after Stern 2001a:119 Fig. I.57.

Archaeology is the Primary Evidentiary Source

According to *The Cambridge Companion to the Bible*, as a primary evidentiary source, the "finds at Kuntillet Ajrud [and other early settlements] are especially important because they include a large number of inscriptions from the biblical period – a time frame from which the remains of written records are scanty" (Kee 1997:87).

Goddess and Animal Associations of Antiquity

Goddesses

on Lions

Goddess Ishtar/Astarte/ Asherah on Lion
~700 BCE

Discovered at Ekron, this medallion depicts the goddess Ishtar/Astarte standing on the back of a lion before a worshipper (Stern 2001a:125). The hand of the goddess is upraised in a gesture of blessing/ benediction. The Pleiades frame the goddess' head.

Recalling that Ishtar and Astarte coalesced with Asherah (Dever 2001:195) and that "Lion Lady" was an ancient epithet of Asherah (Cross 1973:33), this medallion likely represents the Canaanite/ Hebrew goddess Asherah. Drawing after Stern 2001a:125 Fig. I.60.

Goddess

on Lion

Similar Iconographic Associations:
Goddesses on Lions
~3000-2334 BCE

Dating back over five millennia, this Iranian, partial cylinder seal impression depicts goddesses on the backs of lions.

Transcending time and geography, these iconographic elements remain within the constellation of the goddess over several thousand subsequent years.
Drawing after Collon 1987:164 Fig.758.

Ancient Goddess and Lion Associations

Tree of

Life

~ Female Imagery and the Bountiful Earth ~
Similar Iconographic Associations:
Resurrecting Tree of Life Goddess
~835 BCE

This image, from the Papyrus of Nesipakashuty, depicts the nourishing Tree of Life Goddess Nut providing bread and drink to a kneeling worshipper.

The goddess' name, Nut, is inscribed on the trunk of the tree and above the head of the goddess confirming the two are analogous. (Keel 1978:187). Drawing after Ibid. Fig. 255.

Similar Historic Associations:
Menorah Evolves from Tree of Asherah

Analysis of the iconographic and historical aspects in the stylistic development of the seven-branched menorah, according to the *Journal for the Study of the Old Testament,* reveals the "menorah was designed with the usual form of an asherah – the cultic symbol of the goddess Asherah – firmly in mind" (Taylor 1995: 29)

Nurturing

Goddess

Tree-Pillar Figurines Symbolize Nurturing, Prosperity Goddess

According to *Only One God? Monotheism in Ancient Israel and the Veneration of the Goddess Asherah,* the tree-pillar "figurines in any case may be considered as a symbol of the goddess who cares, nourishes and brings prosperity" (Becking et al 2001:66).

Similar Historic Associations:
Resurrection Through Communion* of the Asherah Tree of Life

The Asherah/Tree of Life/Tree of Knowledge or Pomegranate Tree "was sacred to the fertility goddess. It acquired its name, asherah, 'source of life,' from the resemblance of its ripe fruit . . . to the Source of All Life, the Mother's sacred asherah . . . The fruit was regarded . . . as the flesh of the Mother, so that to eat the fruit of knowledge from the tree of life was to consume the very asherah of the Asherah, and to become one with the goddess and share in her resurrection"* (Harwood 1992:68).

*A tradition continued by present day Catholics as they receive the body of Christ at communion.

Tree of

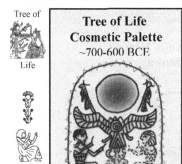

Life

Tree of Life Cosmetic Palette
~700-600 BCE

Embellished with goddess iconography, this Tel Dor cosmetic stone palette depicts a circular hollow where cosmetic powders were mixed.

Elaborating on this imagery, *Biblical Archaeology Review* identifies the kneeling figures flanking the sacred Tree of Life as priests and states the birds are symbolic of the goddess Astarte (Stern 1995:55).

Recalling that sacred trees personified the goddess Asherah (Reed 1949:23), who was identified with Astarte (Dever 2001:195), this depiction may also reference Asherah.   Drawing after Stern 1995:55.

Blessing
Mother

Goddess
Asherah

Asherah Pillar Figurine and Miniatures
~700 BCE

A miniature bed and lamp or birthing stool is pictured with a Judaean pillar figurine in this assembly.

This collection, according to *Gods, Goddesses and Images of God In Ancient Israel*, reflects peaceful and maternal attributes, bestowing protection and blessing upon a family (Keel 1998a:333).

Experts identify the pillar figurines with the goddess Asherah (Jacobs 2001:4; Dever 2005:188).
Drawing after Keel 1998a:334 Fig. 329.

Mother
Goddess

Asherah

Pillar Figurines Personify the Canaanite and Hebrew Mother Goddess Asherah

Biblical Archaeologist states that the pillar figurines which "depict the 'mother goddess' nude, en face, often with exaggerated sexual characteristics, they are undoubtedly fertility figurines – that is, talismans to aid women in conception, childbirth, and lactation. They may safely be connected with the veneration of Asherah, the principal Canaanite mother goddess, whose cult continued into the Late Bronze Age and was popular even in ancient Israel" (Dever 1987).

Goddess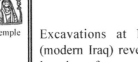

Temple

Queen of

Heaven

Similar Historic Associations:
Over 3,500 Consecutive Years of Worship at the
Temple of the Queen of Heaven,
the Goddess Inanna
~3300 BCE - 225 CE

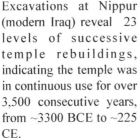 

Excavations at Nippur (modern Iraq) reveal 23 levels of successive temple rebuildings, indicating the temple was in continuous use for over 3,500 consecutive years, from ~3300 BCE to ~225 CE.

Level VII

Level X

Level XVII

Inscriptions reveal the temple was dedicated to the goddess Inanna, "Queen of Heaven" and "Goddess of Love and War" (Hansen 1962:75).

Inanna's temple of ~2600 BCE measured an amazing 275 feet by 80 feet.   Drawing after Ibid. 83 Fig. 13.

Goddess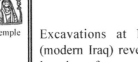

Temple

Similar Historic Associations:
Temple of Goddess Astarte
~1000 BCE

This is a depiction of the ruins of a Cyprus temple dedicated to the goddess Astarte.

Across the Mediterranean, ancient temples dedicated to Astarte and goddesses were decorated "with serpentine motifs" emblematic of the "snake priestesses" or "snake goddesses" (Wunderlich 2002:276).

Astarte is one of the goddesses identified with the Grecian Aphrodite, born of sea foam from Cyprus.

Drawing after author's photo, Cyprus.

Ancient Goddess Temple Coins

Goddess Temple Dedication
~700 BCE

Measuring 185 feet in length and 125 feet wide, the remains of an Ekron temple is "one of the largest Iron Age structures ever to be excavated in Israel or Jordan" (Demsky 1998:53).

Goddess
Temple

Dedication

A 220-pound stone, containing a dedication, was discovered within the temple's innermost sanctuary, its 'Holy of Holies.' The royal inscription was produced by King Achish of Ekron who dedicated this temple to a goddess.

According to *Biblical Archaeology Review*, the royal inscription translates as follows:

"The temple which he built, Achish,
son of Padi, son of *Ysd*, son of Ada, son of Ya'ir,
ruler of Ekron, for Ptgyh [/Potnia] his lady.
May she bless him, and protect him and
prolong his days, and bless his land" (Gitin 2005:23).

Elaborating further in a *Biblical Archaeology Review* article entitled "Discovering a Goddess: A New Look at the Ekron Inscription Identifies a Mysterious Deity," author Aaron Demsky points out *Ptgyh* is an unknown goddess term, and, the identification of one of the name's inscribed letters is uncertain.

Analyzing the unclear letter, Demsky suggests that the name of the unknown goddess *Ptgyh* could be rendered as *Potnia* – a Grecian, goddess term meaning "mistress" or "lady" (Demsky 1998:57).

Demsky further states the Ekron "inscription is, in fact, dedicated to Potnia, the generic 'divine mistress,' a title that may, in this case, refer to the Canaanite goddess Asherah" (Ibid.).

Drawing after Gitin 2005:53.

Similar Historic Associations:
'Potnia Theron' is Goddess of Nature and Animals

Known throughout the Aegean, the goddess 'Potnia Theron' personified divine influence over the forces of nature (Starr 1961:178). Her dominion over the animal kingdom earned her various epithets including Goddess/Mistress of Animals and Queen of Wild Beasts (Pritchard 1954:303).

Goddess

Head

Jerusalem Goddess and Lioness Heads
~700 BCE

A juglet discovered in the "principal remains of biblical Jerusalem," known as the "City of David" (Negev 2001:260), contains two impressed female faces and the head of a lioness (on the side between them).

According to *Archaeology of the Land of the Bible Vol. II,* the faces represent Astarte with her distinctive Judaean headdress (Stern 2001a: 210).

The lioness head between the goddess' faces, however, suggests the depicted goddess may also represent the "Lion Lady" Asherah (Cross 1973:33), who often coalesced with Astarte (Dever 2001: 195).   Drawing after Stern 2001a:210 Fig. I.90.

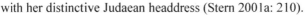

Similar Iconographic Associations:
Tel Sera Goddess Heads
~732-604 BCE

Goddess

Head

These female, figurine heads were discovered at Tel Sera.

Pressed from molds, they are identified as the goddess Astarte by the *Archaeology of the Land of the Bible Vol. II* (Stern 2001a:121). Drawing after Ibid.

Similar Iconographic Associations:
Palestinian Goddess Head
~600 BCE

Goddess

Head

Discovered within an acropolis site at Rabbath Ammon, this female head represents the goddess Astarte (Harrison 2002:14). Drawing after Ibid. 15.

Childbirth Prayer to Asherah ~700 BCE

Written in a Phoenician dialect similar to biblical Hebrew, a protective prayer to the goddess Asherah was discovered within an ancient Temple of Ishtar (Pettey 1990:195-6) at Arslan Tash.

The prayer seeks childbirth protection and assistance from the goddess Asherah (Reed 1949:80), identifying her as the "Goddess of Eternity" (Ibid. 3).

In part, the translation reads:

Childbirth
Prayer to
Asherah

"The Eternal One[*] has made a covenant oath with us,
Asherah[*] has made (a pact) with us"
(Cross 1973:17).

*Note the parallelism and formulaic juxtaposition in the equivalent exchange of 'Eternal One' and 'Asherah.' This literary technique of antiquity assisted scholars in deity identification.

Similar Historic Associations:
Asherah Deliberately Deleted from Genesis Childbirth

The above Arslan Tash, protective, childbirth prayer to Asherah spotlights a new dimension in the correct interpretation of the Genesis 30 biblical text.

According to *The Asherah in the Old Testament* author William L. Reed, a reassessment is needed in the biblical account of the birth of Asher (1949:80-81).

According to Genesis 30:9-13, Zilpah (Leah's maid) gives birth to two sons by Leah's husband. In appreciation, Leah names the babies Gad and Asher after two deities (Ibid.).

However, Reed notes, verse 13 could be translated another way, rendering an entirely different reading and interpretation:

Biblical
Childbirth
Prayer to
Asherah

"Leah cried, 'With Asherah's help! for maidens must call me happy!' so she called his name Asher" (Ibid.).

"As the text now stands," Reed continues, "the word for [Asherah is an] obvious play on words in an attempt to show the derivation of the Hebrew name 'Asher'" (Ibid.).

Affirming Reed's assessment and extrapolating further in *The Society of Biblical Archaeology Proceedings,* C. F. Ball states "the present state of the text of verse 13 is the result of an attempt by a later scribe to eliminate the reference to the pagan goddess, Asherah" (Ibid.).

POSTLIMINARY VESTIGES

VII. Babylonian Period & Beyond   ~586 BCE +

The religion of Judaism was reshaped by prophets and priests during exile,
making it "fiercely monotheistic in its denial of any other god or goddess."

"A God for Both Sexes," *The Economist*
(Armstrong 1996:66)

Asherah references in this section include:

"Lady of Byblos"
Offering
by Yahwistic King

Libation Vessels
Ordered
"for the Asherah and
her Sanctuary"

Throne of Ashtoret/
Asherah/Astarte

Temple of Asherah
Votive Offerings
Presentation

Goddess Statue and
Dedications to "Ashtorim
[/Asherah] of the Sharon"

Temple Pillared Hall
Dedication to "Astarte in the
Asherah Sanctuary"

At this point in the historical record, monotheism and a powerful male priesthood are emerging "and it appears that there was an attempt to deliberately suppress the cult of Asherah . . . There was room for only one god and it was a male deity" (Rhys-Davies 1993).

Eventually ". . . this Yahweh-alone party . . . emerged as [the] local official religion . . . [then] painstakingly redacted and revised the 'cult collection,' which we now know as the Hebrew Bible.

They convinced post-exilic Judahites to accept its teachings about the oneness of the divine, the evils of Asherah and a host of other things. . . .

Gradually, the collection came to assume the status of a sacred text of a local monotheistic official religion. Poised as such it provided the foundation for the advent of Pharisaic Judaism, Christianity and eventually Islam" (Berlinerblau 2000:11).

Symbol
of

Goddess
Tanit/
Asherah/
Eve

Asherah/
Tanit is
Eve

**Ashkelon Goddess
Symbol of Tanit/
Asherah/Eve**
~550 BCE

Discovered at Ashkelon, this goddess symbol represents Tanit/Tannit and Asherah.

Canaanite Myth and Hebrew Epic linguistically cites the parallelism between Tanit/Tannit* as "the One of the Serpent" and Asherah as "Lady of the Serpent," suggesting an association between the two (Cross 1973:32-3).

Asherah and the Cult of Yahweh In Israel additionally notes both goddesses are similarly associated with trees, which further strongly supports the identification of Tanit and Asherah (Olyan 1988:60).

Both goddesses also share the title "Eve," which "is an attested epithet of Tanit/Asherah in the first millennium BCE" (Ibid. 71).

*Tanit's name is also documented among the first Proto-Sinaitic inscriptions, incised on the side of a sphinx discovered within an ancient temple of Hathor (Cross 1973:574).

Drawing after Gore 2001:83.

Symbol
of

Goddess
Tanit/
Asherah/
Eve

**Symbol of Tanit/
Asherah/Eve**
~539-332 BCE

The symbol of the goddess Tanit*/Asherah is incised on this lead weight discovered at Ashdod-Yam.

*The assimilation of ancient religious traditions variously also identify her as Tanit-Ashtoret and Tanit-Pane-Ba'al (Stern 2001a: 575). Drawing after Ibid. 574.

Ancient Elevated Arm Iconography

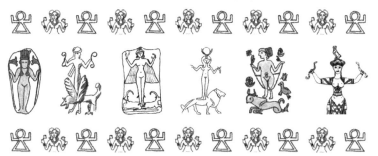

Coin of
Asherah

and
Yahweh

**Gaza Coin of Astarte/
Asherah/Anat and
Yahweh**

~538-323 BCE

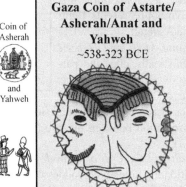

This Gaza coin is a depiction of "Ashtart [/Astarte/Asherah]-Yaw"* (Langdon 1964:44) alternately identified as "Anat-Yaw"* (Ibid. 388).

Recalling that the goddesses Astarte and Anat coalesced with Asherah (Oden 1976:31-36) renders Asherah as a third candidate for this female portrayal.

*According to Jewish sacred writings, Yaw was the original name of their deity before "it was extended into a verbal form, apparently Yahweh" (Langdon 1964:42). Drawing after Ibid. 44 Fig. 24.

Gaza
Coin of
Asherah

and
Yahweh

Similar Iconographic Associations:
**Coin of Baal/El*/Yahweh/Zeus and Atargatis/
Asherah*/Hera***

~300 CE

The symbol of the Syrian goddess** is depicted between seated deities, and within the 'Holy of Holies,' on this third century CE Hierapolis coin.

The deities are identified as Atargatis/Asherah*/Hera,** seated on a lion throne, and Baal [Adad]/El*/Yahweh/Zeus seated on a bovine throne, wearing a bovine mask (Langdon 1964:36).

*This identification is made per a similar Hierapolis coin referenced in an article from *Biblical Archaeologist* entitled "The Persistence of Canaanite Religion" (Oden 1976 Fig. 3).

**The presence of the lion and dove indicate the goddesses Atargatis, Asherah and Hera coalesce with Ishtar of Assyria, who is associated with the dove "in all Semitic mythology" (Langdon 1964:36). Drawing after Ibid. Fig. 21.

Ancient Goddess Temple Coins

| **Goddess Statue and Dedications to Ashtorim/Asherah** ~539-332 BCE | Excavation within an Eliachin shrine area in the Sharon Plain led to the discovery of inscriptions and a goddess statue. |

The inscriptions are dedications to the goddess "Ashtorim[/Asherah] of the Sharon" (Stern 2001a:506) and provide evidence of goddess worship within the Sharon Plain area.

| **Temple of Asherah Votive Offerings Presentation** ~530-522 BCE | According to *Archaeology of the Land of the Bible Vol. II,* an inscribed bowl fragment, discovered at ancient Akko/ Acco, lists votive offerings |

presented to the temple of Asherah (Stern 2001a:383).

Asherah on

`Throne

Purposely Degraded Goddess

| **Throne of Ashtoret*/ Asherah/Astarte** ~538-245 BCE | A stone throne, used as a display pedestal for religious statues, was discovered at Khirbet et-Tayibeh. |

A unique and rare find, the throne contains both graphics and an inscription. Reflective of the assimilation within ancient cultures, sphinxes/cherubim recline on the sides of the throne, while Egyptian lotus flowers and a Phoenician dedicatory inscription are inscribed on its back.

The inscription reads "To my lady, to Ashtoret[*/Asherah/] ('Astarte) . . . I am 'Abdubasti son of BodBa'al" (Stern 2001a:513). *According to the *Bulletin of the American Schools of Oriental Research*, the goddess name "Ashtoreth"/"Ashtaroth" is a deliberate degradation, a "bastardized form" of the goddess' name (Dever 1984:21).

Ancient Goddesses on Lion-Thrones

King
Before

Goddess

Similar Iconographic Associations:
King Before Goddesses
~1894-1763 BCE

A kilted king stands between goddesses on this Babylonian seal impression (Collon 1987:2).

This ancient Near East presentation scene depicts a king, surrounded by minor goddesses, approaching a primary goddess.

It is through this ceremonial religious tradition, of sanction by the goddess, that the king establishes his sovereignty and becomes "deified" (Ibid. 39). Drawing after Ibid. 2 Fig. 1.

Kings Before Goddesses of Antiquity

Ashtoreth is Deliberately Shamed Goddess

Deliberate
Shamed
Goddess

Fundamentally, the goddess name Ashtoreth is a deliberate combination of a goddess name and the Hebrew word for shame.

According to *The Interpreter's Dictionary of the Bible*, Ashtoreth is a "deliberate Hebrew misvocalization of the name of the Canaanite fertility-goddess [Astarte]," created when "Hebrew scribes . . . substituted the vowels of . . . 'shame,' in the last two syllables" (Buttrick 1962:255).

Confusion Between Asherah and Astarte

Asherah
and/or
Astarte

According to *The Hebrew Goddess*, "In the 14th century B.C.E. Amarna letters written by Canaanite petty chieftains to their overlords, the king of Egypt, the names Asherah and Astarte interchange, which may indicate a lack of clear distinction between the functions and personalities of these two goddesses. . . the same confusion between Asherah and Astarte is found in the Bible and persisted even among scholars down to our days" (Patai 1990:37).

King Before

Goddess

Crown of Goddess

Isis

King Yahumelekh Before His Goddess, Ba'alat-Gebal/Asherah
~500-400 BCE

As he approaches an enthroned goddess, King Yahumelekh* presents an offering inscriptually dedicated to "his goddess, the 'Lady of Byblos'" (Pritchard 1973: 345).

The seated, local goddess Ba'alat-Gebal, is depicted "in the shape and with the attributes of the Egyptian goddess Hathor" (Stern 2001a:489).

The interjection of Egyptian deity attributes into the local cult demonstrates the fluid level of ancient, religio-cultural assimilation.

Inscriptions convey the synthesis of deity names, as in the case of this local goddess Ba'alat-Gebal, who is also identified with Astarte/Ashtoret[/Asherah] and Tanit-Pane-Ba'al (Ibid. 505).

Strikingly, the inclusion of *Yahu-* (an early rendering of Yahweh) as a component in King *Yahu*melekh's name, suggests this stela depicts an early Yahwistic king presenting offerings to a goddess.

*Variously translated as Yehawmilk, Yehumelek and/or Jehawmelek.　　　Drawing after Pritchard 1973 Fig. 130.

Isis-Crowned

Goddess

Similar Iconographic Associations:
Goddess Baalath-Gebal/Astarte[/Asherah]-Isis
~100-200 CE

Astarte (Hill 1910:lxiv) stands on this Byblos coin holding a small cross.

The *Catalogue of the Greek Coins of Phoenicia*, states this goddess is depicted "Like Baalath-Gebal on the [above] stele of Jehawmelek, she wears the head-dress of Isis, and is best called Astarte[/Asherah]-Isis" (Ibid. lxiv). The reverse side of this coin depicts the crown of Isis.

Drawings after Ibid. Pl. XII7.

Clay
Ashoreth/
Astarte/
Asherah

**Little Clay Ashtoreth/
Astarte/Asherah**
~500-375 BCE

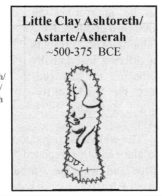

The *Archaeological Encyclopedia of the Holy Land* states this Achzib, clay, figurine represents the "Pregnant Ashtoreth[/Astarte/Asherah]" (Negev 2001:17).

Standing upon a pedestal base, this female figure rests her hand upon her extended abdomen. Her head tilts in a pensive posture.

Drawing after Ibid.

Clay
Ashtoreth/

Astarte/
Asherah

Similar Historic Associations:
"Little Clay [Ashtoreth/]Astarte[/Asherah]"
~600 BCE & 1894 CE

"The little guardian Astarte which protects Mnasidika,
modeled at Camiros by a very clever potter.
She is as large as your thumb, of fine-ground yellow clay.
Her tresses fall and circle about her narrow shoulders.
Her eyes are cut quite widely and her mouth is very small.
For she is the All-Beautiful.
Her right hand indicates her delta, which is peppered with tiny
holes about her lower belly and along her groins.
For she is the All-Lovable.
Her left hand supports her round and heavy breasts.
Between her spreading hips swings a large and fertile belly.
For she is the Mother-of-All" (Louys 1864).

This hymnal prayer to the goddess Astarte was written by the-writer-who-really-wasn't, Bilitis, an alleged associate of the-lesbian-who-really-wasn't, Sappho.

"The Bilitis hoax (which, although purely a male fantasy, has literary merits in its own right) took Europe by storm" (Hare 2006). Due to its explicit sexual nature, English publication was restricted until the 1960s.

Claiming himself to be the translator of ancient texts and a student of the classics, Pierre Louys assured the historical, literary value of these works by salting "*Bilitis* with a number of quotations from real poets, including Sappho, to make it even more convincing" (Ibid.).

Libation Vessels Ordered for Asherah and Her Sanctuary
~400 BCE

According to *Only One God? Monothe-ism in Ancient Israel and the Veneration of*

 *the Goddess Asherah*, an ancient decree orders religious utensils made "for the Asherah and her sanctuary" near Akko/Acco (Becking 2001:41).

Libation Vessels

The mandate reads:

"Decree to the smiths, who shall give a magnificent treasure(?) to SLT, who is over the Asherah(-sanctuary):
10 chalices; 25 decanters;
70 large pixi-jars; 60 jars;
60 ewers; 57 blown vases and
30 small bowls" (Ibid.).

This decree attests to the worship of Asherah, and a temple/sanctuary dedicated to her, at Akko/Acco.

Libation Vessels

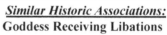
Similar Historic Associations:
Goddess Receiving Libations
~1800 BCE

Seated upon a quadruped throne, a Crowned Goddess holds a chalice bowl while a priest pours libations on this Anatolian seal impression.
Drawing after Canby 1986:51.

Libation Vessels

Similar Historic Associations:
Goddess Receiving Libations
~1500 BCE

This Mycenaean, gold signet ring depicts lion-headed subjects presenting libation vessels to an enthroned goddess.

The goddess holds an up-raised chalice; her feet rest atop a footstool. A sacred bird hov-ers behind the goddess. The top of the configuration references both heaven (astrally) and earth (vegetatively).
Drawing after author's photo, National Museum, Athens.

Goddess in Temple

Similar Iconographic Associations:
Goddess Astarte in Temple
~218-29 CE

The goddess Astarte is framed within a temple archway on this coin from Caesarea (Hill 1910:109). To her right, a bird rests atop her scepter.
Drawing after Ibid. Pl. XIII7.

Goddess in Temple

Similar Iconographic Associations:
Goddess Astarte in Temple
Crowned by Alexander the Great(?)
~218-219 CE

Standing within a temple entrance, the goddess Astarte is crowned by a male figure, possibly Alexander the Great (Hill 1910:110) on this Caesarean coin.
Drawing after Ibid. Pl. XIII9.

Goddess in Temple

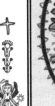

Similar Iconographic Associations:
Goddesses Astarte and Nike in Temple
~208 CE

Holding a cruciform staff, the goddess Astarte stands between stylized asherah temple pillars alongside Nike, the Victory Goddess (Hill 1910:86).

Standing on a pedestal column, the winged Nike (often depicted with Athena) crowns Astarte with a laurel wreath on this coin minted at ancient Berytus.
Drawing after Ibid. Pl. XIb.

Goddess in

Temple

Temple Pillared Hall Dedication to Astarte and Asherah ~222 BCE

A building inscription, discovered at Ma'sub (likely from a north Syrian temple at Umm el-Ahmed), dedicates a pillared hall to "Astarte in the Asherah sanctuary" (Becking 2001:41).

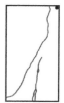

Goddess in

Temple

Initially puzzling, the statement is clarified by *Only One God? Monotheism in Ancient Israel and the Veneration of the Goddess Asherah* explaining it as a dual meaning indicating both the goddess and her sanctuary, in that the "name of Asherah originally meant the holy precinct of the mother-goddess . . . or referred to the sacred pole or tree representing the goddess"* (Ibid.).

The Symbolism of the Biblical World by author Othmar Keel provides a demonstrative interpretation of this statement. Referencing a temple model shrine (depicted left) from neighboring Cyprus, Keel believes the entrance pillars likely represent asherahs (1978:164-5).

Extrapolating further, Keel states the pillars are not structural necessities, but rather iconographic embellishments used to define the temple as a personification of life forces (Ibid.).

*This is also true for Asherah's "other name or title of Qudshu" (Becking 2001:41).

Cyprus shrine drawing after Dever 2008:58.

Asherah

Pillars

Similar Historic Associations:
Asherah Temple Pillars of Stylized Sacred Trees Personify the Source of Life

From the very earliest times, the stylized, sacred tree was deeply embedded within the religious traditions of the Ancient Near East.

According to the *Israel Exploration Journal,* "The sacred tree . . . symbolized the source of life and represented growth and regeneration" (Hestrin 1987:214).

Goddess

Tanit/
Asherah

Seal of Goddess Tanit/Asherah*
~200 BCE

The triangular body and upraised arms of the goddess Tanit/Tannit/Asherah* are depicted on this clay impression created from a seal discovered within a Kedesh archive room.

The symbol of the goddess is depicted directly above a Phoenician inscription reading "He who is over the land" (Berlin 2005:40).

According to a *Biblical Archaeology Review* article entitled "Life and Death on the Israel-Lebanon Border: Excavation Yields Thousands of Seal Impressions," this seal may have belonged to the governor of Kedesh (Ibid.).

*Recalling Tanit/Tannit was an epithet for Asherah (Olyan 1988:60).

Drawing after Berlin 2005:40.

Goddess

Tanit/
Asherah

Similar Iconographic Associations:
Goddess Tanit/Astarte/Asherah
~600 BCE

This ornate Carthage figurine depicts the goddess Tanit/Astarte/Asherah (Soren 2000:27). The goddess faces frontally, holding a tambourine. Rosette stars cascade down the front of her elaborately decorated garment; she wears an elaborate crown and a necklace.   Drawing after Ibid.

Goddesses of Antiquity with Tambourines

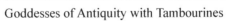

Witch Trial Contract Signed by Asherah, Satan, Demons and a Priest
1632-34 CE

Almost 2,000 years would pass before the vanquished goddess Asherah resurfaces as a trial witness in the witch burning years.

During the 1632-34 witchcraft trial of French Roman Catholic priest Urban Grandier, the court's evidence included this contract* signed by the goddess Asherah, Satan, demons and the accused priest.

Accused by Carmelite nuns of bewitching them into imprudent acts, the priest's fate was sealed when the Cardinal overseeing his trial presented this contract* as prosecution evidence.

Grandier was subsequently tortured, convicted and burned alive at the stake.

*Written backwards in abbreviated Latin, the document's validity had to be verified before it was admissible as trial evidence. Trial records state its authenticity was "vouched for by Baalbraith, the Secretary of his Satanic majesty" (Carus 1996:364).   Drawing after Ibid.

CONCLUSION

Popular among the Hebrew tribes for over 300 years, worship of the goddess Asherah was introduced into the Jerusalem Temple by Solomon's son, King Rehoboam, around 928 BCE.

For at least 236 of the 370 years the Solomonic Temple stood in Jerusalem, "the statue of Asherah was present in the Temple, and her worship was a part of the legitimate religion approved and led by the king, the court, and the priesthood."

The Hebrew Goddess
(Patai 1990:50)

Previous Historic Association:
Hebrew Seal of Asherah and Yahweh
~720-600 BCE

As discussed previously, a winged god and goddess are depicted on this Hebrew seal impression.

According to *Gods, Goddesses, and Images of God In Ancient Israel*, this is a depiction of the Hebrew god "Yahweh" (above a cherub as Psalms 18:11) and the Canaanite/Hebrew goddess "Asherah," (above a stylized tree as the Queen of Heaven) and any "Judahite owner could have connected this constellation of images" with Yahweh and Asherah (Keel 1998a:340). Drawing after Ibid. 337 Fig. 331b.

Unknown Provenience

Similar Historic Associations:
Yahweh's Wives

Although the notion of Asherah as Yahweh's wife may be disconcerting to some, in actuality Asherah was but one of Yahweh's wives.

According to a presentation by the *Biblical Archaeological Society* entitled "The Goddess in the Hebrew Bible," **"Not only does Yahweh have a consort, but he's got one in every town"** (Freedman 1999).

Gaza Coin of Yahweh and Astarte/Anat/Asherah

-Yahweh and Asherah in Samaria. The previously discussed Hebrew, blessing inscriptions of Kuntillet Ajrud and Khirbet el-Qom explicitly pair Yahweh with Asherah at Samaria.

-Yahweh and Astarte in Jerusalem. Referencing Jeremiah's speech denouncing worship of the Queen of Heaven (an epithet of Ishtar/Astarte), experts conclude Astarte is Yahweh's counterpart at Jerusalem (Ibid.).

-Yahweh and Anat in Bethel. Papyri correspondence from a Jewish garrison at Elephantine list an offering to the goddess Anat-Yaho (Anat belonging to Yahweh), who is analogous to Anatbethel (Anat of Bethel associated with Yahweh) (Ibid.).

Conclusion

In today's information age, the black hole of Women's History
remains disconcerting. Filling this void, the shovels of
archaeology are resurrecting what the pens of history forgot and [1 of 2 pages]
forcing a reassessment of history's narrative.

Archaeology's unearthed artifacts are windows into the past and
thoughts frozen in time, transmitting the socio-religious reality of their
day. Through this prism of rediscovery, the thousands of discovered Syro-
Palestinian female figurines and artifacts* are resurrecting a lost
dimension of history – the forgotten worship of goddesses.

Goddess worship, however, conflicted with the rise of monotheism and
the formation of the Old Testament. Posing a threat to the monotheistic
definition of god, the feminine component of religion had to be eradicated.
By the end of the 7th and 6th centuries BCE, the only major goddess surviving in Palestine was Asherah (Keel 1998b:38), but Asherah's days
were numbered also and she was soon eliminated.

Reflecting upon Asherah's vanquishment, *The Forbidden Goddess*
asks: "How could a goddess so loved by the people be so hated by the Old
Testament writers?" (Rhys-Davies 1993).

The answer lies with the Old Testament authors who "represented the
orthodox right-wing, nationalist parties who edited the Bible," explains
archaeologist and biblical scholar Professor Dever. "They were all male.
They represented the establishment. They didn't like the idea of a consort
– a female consort of Yahweh's. Asherah was at the very least a nuisance,
at the very worst, she was a real threat to their idea of what god was like
and therefore she had to disappear" (Ibid.).

---

*The historically dismissive attitude toward these archaeological
discoveries is unfounded. As pristine historical representations, the
significance of these artifacts can not be overstated.

The Art of the Ancient Near East defines the art/artifacts of ancient
cultures as religious reflections, declaring "in the whole of the ancient
Near East, art was inseparable from religion" (Lloyd 1961:12).

The Cambridge Illustrated History of Prehistoric Art states art/artifacts
reflect what is important within a society not just "for their own sake, but
as vehicles of feelings and meanings whose origins are personal, social
and religious" (Raphael 1998:83).

~ Attributes of the Goddess Asherah ~

Snake/Serpent   Sacred Tree

The earliest written records indicate the snake/serpent and sacred tree were epiphanies of the Canaanite and Hebrew Mother Goddess Asherah.

Similar Iconographic Associations:

From time immortal, the snake/serpent and sacred tree were essential components of ancient religious traditions:

Stone Snake/Serpent:
"Earliest Religious Evidence" (Minkel 2006)
~70,000 BCE

Snake/Serpent & Sacred Tree at
"World's First Temple" (Scham 2008:22)
~11,000 BCE

Snake/Serpent & Sacred Tree   **Snake/Serpent & Female**
~2,000 BCE   ~2,000 BCE

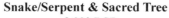

Drawings after: Minkel 2006 (top); Scham 2008:26 (center);
Langdon 1964:177-8 Fig. 68, 69 (bottom).

The sands of time provide the key in deciphering the past and understanding Asherah's demise. Silent witness to a time long ago, the Lucian coin (below) metaphorically depicts Asherah's vanquishment:

Metamorphic Vanquishment of the Hebrew Mother Goddess Asherah
~225-44 CE

Guardian serpents/snakes attempt to protect the Hebrew Mother Goddess as figures with upraised axes prepare to destroy Asherah and her signature sacred tree.
Drawing after d'Alviella 1894.

Almost a thousand more years would pass before Asherah reemerges as the Shekinah (Patai 1990:96) – a transfigured female divinity in Kabbalistic tradition.

Identified as the "Bride of Yahweh" (Rhys-Davies 1993), Jewish Gnostic mythology also defines Shekinah as the Creatress of the world and the first man (Husain 1997:90).

Shekinah's legacy is manifest yet today as Jewish wedding services memorialize the union of God and his Sabbath bride, begging the question:
"Who else could it be – but Asherah?"

Once submerged in our historical consciousness, Asherah's rediscovery is now a recovered dimension of Women's History, as archaeology provides a historical bridge, enabling the past, to educate the present and empower the future.

APPENDIX A

Pre-Late Bronze Age
Additional Syro-Palestinian Considerations

"The dawn of history in all parts of Western Asia discloses the established worship of a nature-goddess in whom the productive powers of the earth were personified. She is our Mother Earth, known otherwise as the Mother Goddess or Great Mother. Among the Babylonians and northern Semites she was called Ishtar: she is the Ashtoreth[/Asherah] of the Bible, and the Astarte of Phoenicia."

The Syrian Goddess
(Strong 1913)

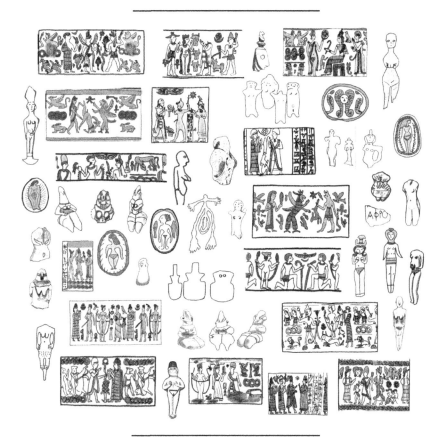

A. Pre-Late Bronze Age Additional Syro-Palestinian Considerations

This section introduces Pre-Late Bronze Age figurines discovered within the Syro-Palestinian corridor.

History's Oldest Known Artwork/Sculpted Figurine
~250,000 BCE

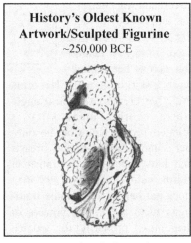

This two-inch figurine, discovered at Berekhat Ram in the Golan Heights, is history's oldest known art object and sculpted figurine. Discovered between two basalt layers respectively dated at 800,000 BCE and 233,000 BCE, experts place the figurine's age closer to the lower end at ~250,000 BCE (Bahn 1998:87).

Inspecting the figurine, some suggested the formation resembled the female form and had been deliberately shaped, others disagreed claiming it was a natural rock formation.

The controversy was resolved when Harvard University's expert in prehistoric art, Alexander Marshack, microscopically examined the figurine and concluded flint implements had deliberately formed a head, breasts and buttocks (Rochman 1997:23).

Elaborating further upon the deliberate shaping of the Berekhat Ram figurine, *The Cambridge Illustrated History of Prehistoric Art* stated it was an "intentionally enhanced object and indisputably an 'art object'" (Bahn 1998:87), making it history's oldest known sculpted figurine.   Drawing after Rochman 1997:23; Bahn 1998:87.

Primal Goddess Represents Oldest Worship

According to *The Hebrew Goddess*, "the oldest cosmogonies, like the oldest worship of concretely represented deities, typically start with a primal goddess" (Patai 1990:24).

Worship of Mother Earth as Bountiful Goddess

In "the neolithic village stage," *The Masks of God: Occidental Mythology* states, "the focal figure of all mythology and worship was the bountiful goddess Earth, as the mother and nourisher of life and receiver of the dead for rebirth" (Campbell 1964:7).

Decorated

Female
Figurine

Decorated Protective Female Figurine
~6700-6500 BCE

This headless, female figurine is one of several discovered at Ain Ghazal.

Her ample body is decorated with notched incised lines. A demarcation across her hipline suggests a skirt or garment. Her arms encircle her breasts; a pubic triangle (with a center linear slit) is positioned directly below her bosom.

Her rounded abdomen and breasts suggest these types of figurines may have been protective talismans for women during pregnancy and birth cycles (Rollefson 1998:56).

Although the site excavator does not believe the female figurines represent divinities, he assigns them the divine powers of protecting life and promoting happiness, primarily for women (Ibid. 57). Drawing after Ibid. 56.

Similar Iconographic Associations:
Decorated Neolithic Female Figurines
~5,000 BCE

Decorated

Female
Figurine

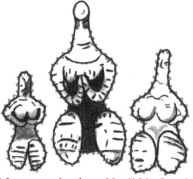

Discovered in Mesopotamia, these Neolithic female figurines are stylistically similar to those found in neighboring Palestine. Drawing after Spycket 2000:44.

Village's Religious Mother Goddess ~6700-6500 BCE

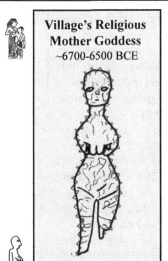

Discovered at Ain Ghazal, this female figurine "may have been a village's 'mother goddess'" (Rollefson 2003:249).

Ancient Civilizations describes Ain Ghazal as the place where "some of the earliest people of the Holy Land were . . . producing items of beauty for religious purposes" (James 1998:22).

Site excavator Gary O. Rollefson concurs, describing the Neolithic statues as portraying "rich expressions of religious belief" (2003:248).

According to *The Bulletin of the American School of Oriental Research*, the "figures of women exhibiting their breasts can therefore be viewed as metaphors using the everyday life experience of a tender mother nursing her child to express the bounty of nature" (Schmandt-Besserat 1998:13).

Drawings after: Rollefson 2003:249 (top); Schmandt-Besserat 1998:3.2 (right).

Ain Ghazal female torso with genitalia

Jericho's Religious Mother Goddess ~6700-6500 BCE

This clay figurine is one of two discovered within a Neolithic shrine area at Jericho.

Site excavator and author of *Digging Up Jericho*, Kathleen Kenyon, states these small figurines served a religious purpose, likely as Mother Goddesses of a fertility or prosperity cult (1957:59).

Although not depicted, the second figurine wears a long robe and has her hands positioned beneath her breasts, a posture Kenyon considers be an "attitude . . . typical of the conventional Mother Goddess figurines" discovered throughout a multitude of Near Eastern cultures (Ibid.). Drawing after Ibid.

Birthing

Goddess

Temple Birthing Goddess
~6,000 BCE

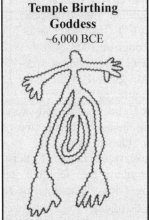

Discovered within a cave (which served as an ancient goddess temple) in Timna Valley, Israel, this rock carving depicts a woman giving birth (Ben-Ari 2009:8).

Located near ancient copper mines, the cave was later incorporated into a larger ~1318 BCE temple complex dedicated to the patron deity of the site, Hathor, the Goddess of Mining, Fertility and Prosperity.

Drawing after Ibid.

Birthing

Goddess

Similar Iconographic Associations:
Bohemian Birthing Goddess
~6,000 BCE

Dating back almost eight millennia, this "Birth-Giving Goddess" (Gimbutas 1982:177) is depicted on a pottery dish discovered at Kolesovice, Bohemia. Her elevated hands hold branches and a chalice.

Drawing after Ibid.

Mothers of Antiquity

Yarmukian Religious Goddesses
~5600-5100 BCE

Yarmukian Settlements

[1 of 2 pages]

One mile south of the Sea of Galilee, archaeologists discovered the Neolithic village of Sha'ar Hagolan. Nestled in the Jordan Valley on the banks of the Yarmuk River, the ancient inhabitants of Sha'ar Hagolan and its neighboring settlements became known as the Yarmukians.

Neolithic

Goddess

Almost 8,000 years ago, these resourceful people designed a planned village with paved streets, alleys and courtyard homes. Among the Yarmukian ruins, 2 male and 63 female figurines have been discovered. They display (the familiar Stone Age) exaggerated, rotund bodies, bird-beaked/pinched noses and coffee-bean shaped eyes. Some exhibit minute, unusual details such as earrings, headdresses, and cloaks or scarves (Garfinkel 1993:124).

Yosef Garfinkel of Jerusalem's Hebrew University Institute of Archaeology "assumes – as do most archaeologists who study figurines from Near Eastern sites – that they served some sort of religious purpose" (Balter 2000:35).

Yarmukian

Goddess

One of the scarf-wearing Yarmukian figurines (left and above far left) has a deep hole in the bottom of her base, likely used to position her atop a pedestal, a standard or a lower body base. Experts conclude this "figurine . . . [may] have been a fertility statue or, possibly, a divine image" (Shanks 1999:64).

Drawings after: (top left to right) Spycket 2000:41, Garfinkel 2002:29, Garfinkel 2000:24; (far left) Shanks 1999:64 by Jennifer Johnson; (bottom left to right) Garfinkel 2002:29, Garfinkel 1993:124 Fig. 3, Pritchard 1975:822 Pl. 53.

Although decades have passed since the discovery of the Yarmukian female figurines, controversy and debate continue to surround them.

Some scholars suggest the female figurines represent goddess or divine figures and humanity's first form of religious expression. Other experts disagree.

[2 of 2 pages]

Irrespective of the ongoing academic dissent, Yosef Garfinkel of Hebrew University's Institute of Archaeology and co-director of the Sha'ar Hagolan excavations stands firm in his own convictions. Garfinkel recently published a book detailing the archaeological excavations entitled *The Goddess at Sha'ar Hagolan: Excavations at a Neolithic Site in Israel.*

Similar Iconographic Associations:
Neolithic Religious Goddesses
~4800-4600 BCE

Yarmukian

Goddess

Hundreds of years younger than the Yarmukians, these Neolithic female figurines display stylistically similar characteristics – rotund bodies, exaggerated hips and bird-beak/pinched noses.

Observing "snakes coiling around the abdomen" on some of the figurines, archaeologist Maria Gimbutas identified them as "Snake Goddesses" ready "to be placed on an altar and used for the reenactment of [religious, ceremonial] rites" (1989 Pl. 9).

Drawing after Ibid.

Breasted

God

Female Breasted Religious Figurine
~4500 BCE

Discovered in the Beersheba Valley, this ivory female figurine stands naked with large eyes gazing out over exaggerated breasts. Her rounded abdomen suggests pregnancy. Bald as a ping pong ball, her head covering has been lost in time.

According to a *National Geographic* article entitled "Journey To The Copper Age," this figurine may have been a symbol of "fertility" or prosperity and "likely used in rituals" (Ozment 1999:74), making her an object of veneration.   Drawing after Ibid.

Breasted

God

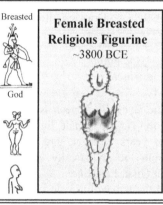

Female Breasted Religious Figurine
~3800 BCE

This naked, ivory female figurine was also discovered in the Beersheba Valley of Ancient Palestine.

The Oxford History of the Biblical World, states this figurine was used in fertility domestic or communal rituals (Coogan 1998:2) as an object of veneration.

Drawing after Mazar 1990:77; Coogan 1998:2.

Breasted

Figurine

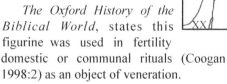

Similar Iconographic Associations:
Female Breasted Religious Figure/God
~3500-3150 BCE

Responsible for sending "forth the waters . . . that they might produce grain for the king," the Egyptian Nile River God, Hep/Hap* is always depicted with female breasts (Budge 1969:43).

The female breasts personify generative life forces "*intended to indicate the powers of fertility and of nourishment possessed by the god*" (Ibid.).

*Hep/Hap is the ancient name of the Nile River (Ibid. 42).   Drawing after Ibid. Pl. 10.

Violin

Females

Violin-Shaped Goddesses
~4500 BCE

These figurines are part of a group of 60 discovered at the ancient settlement of Gilat.

According to *The Oxford History of the Biblical World*, these "carefully executed" figurines represent "what seems to be a woman in an abstract violin-like shape" (Coogan 1998:18).

An article in *National Geographic* entitled "Journey to the Copper Age" extrapolates further, describing these figurines as "violin shaped figurines . . . [that] *may represent goddesses of a fertility[/prosperity] cult*" (Ozment 1999:74).   Drawing after Ibid.

Violin

Goddesses

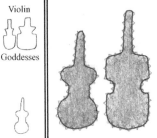

Similar Iconographic Associations:
Violin-Shaped Figurines
~2500 BCE

Discovered on the Cycladic Aegean islands, these marble, violin-shaped female figurines are thousands of years younger, and a sea voyage away from the stylistically similar figurines found at Gilat, Palestine.

Suggestive of the female form, according to *The Great Mother: An Analysis of the Archetype,* the figurines personify stylized female figures (Neumann 1963:Pl. 24).   Drawing after Ibid.

Animal-
Crowned

Cretan
Goddess

Palestinian Ivory Head
~3000 BCE

This ivory goddess or priestess head, discovered at Beersheba, is crowned with an animal seated atop a pedestal.

Although difficult to discern, *Archaeological Discoveries in the Holy Land* describes the hair on this figurine as "gathered on the top of the head" and falling "down the back in a 'pony tail'" (Perrot 1967:6).
                    Drawing after Ibid.

Goddess

Figurine

Goddess Figurines
~2000-1550 BCE

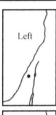

Left

Center

Right

Cast from a double mold, the naked (far left) female figurine was discovered at Megiddo. *The Ancient Near East in Pictures Relating to the Old Testament* states this figurine "may have served as an emblem of the goddess of fecundity" (Pritchard 1954:303).

Made of lead and discovered at Tel el-Ajjul, the center female figurine depicts "the goddess with her hands on her breasts" (Keel 1998a:35), a stance conferring the blessings of nature.

The gold goddess figurine (far right) was discovered with 19 others in a vessel under the platform of an ancient religious site at Nahariyah (Ibid. 29-31).

Drawings after: Pritchard 1954:161 Fig. 467 (left); Keel 1998a:34 Fig. 25b (center); Ibid. 32 Fig. 18b (right).

Goddess

Figurine

Female Figurine
~3000 BCE

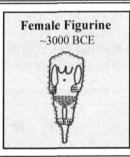

Deliberately shaped into a female figure, this bone pin was discovered at Beersheba.

Naked, with breasts exposed, this figurine has notched indentations emphasizing her pubic triangle. A post provides for secure positioning below her shortened legs. Drawing after Perrot 1967:6.

Female

Figurine

Similar Iconographic Associations:
Goddess Figurine
~4,000 BCE

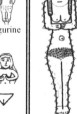

Lapis inlaid eyes create the appearance of sunglasses on this Egyptian figurine.

According to *The Atlas of Ancient Egypt*, this naked figurine "was probably a cult[/religious] figure or a mother goddess" (Morris 2000:8).

Drawing after Ibid.

Stone Age

Figurine

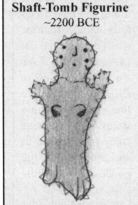

Shaft-Tomb Figurine
~2200 BCE

This unbaked, clay figurine was discovered embedded in a bone pile within a Palestinian shaft-tomb.

Discovered in a Dead Sea Bab edh-Dhra cemetery, this naked female exhibits double-pierced ears, breasts, a bird-beaked, pinched nose and an upraised arm. The circular incisions may have been used to offer seeds.

Drawing after Lapp 1967:40.

Tomb

Figurine

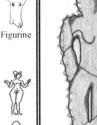

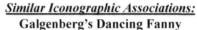

Similar Iconographic Associations:
Galgenberg's Dancing Fanny
~30,000 BCE

Made of green, serpentine stone and dating back to the Paleolithic Stone Age, this dancing(?) female figurine (left) was discovered at Galgenberg, Austria.

Due to her unique stance she has become known as Fanny after a famous Viennese dancer (left).

Drawings after Hitchcock 2005.

Early Female Imagery Represents Vegetative Mother Goddess

Some experts suggest that the early female figurines represent the "same mother-goddess who was to become so conspicuous in the later agricultural civilizations of the Near East and has been everywhere celebrated as the magna mater and mother earth" (Campbell 1969:314).

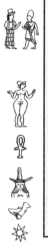

Gods, Kings and Worshippers Before Goddesses
~2000-1550 BCE

Top two and Bottom Right

Unknown Provenances

Bottom Left

Kings, deities and worshippers appear before goddesses on these ceremonial seal impressions discovered in Syro-Palestine.

The top left composition pictures a king approaching a major Syrian goddess, the owner of the seal and a suppliant goddess (Collon 1987:128). A rosette star is depicted between the king and the goddess. Although initially an epiphany of the goddess Inanna/Ishtar, her emblematic rosette star transferred to other goddesses as they became popular in Syro-Palestine.

The top right impression depicts a king approaching a goddess and a Hathor head. Behind the king stands a priest(?) with up-raised chalice.

The bottom left configuration pictures a king before a goddess holding a ceremonial object. A Naked Goddess (far left) reveals herself, bequeathing fecundity upon the king and his land.

A Naked Goddess is depicted on the bottom right impression made from a cylinder seal discovered at Tel el-Far'ah. According to *Gods, Goddesses and Images of God In Ancient Israel*, the two kneeling figures are worshippers of the revealing goddess (Keel 1998a:39), who conveys blessings and vital life forces.

Drawings after: Collon 1987:127 Fig. 544 (top left); Ibid. 166 Fig. 770 (top right); Sehesput 1993:43 (bottom left); Keel 1998a:40 Fig. 31b (bottom right).

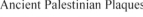

Ancient Palestinian Plaques

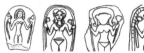

Gods, Kings and Worshippers Before Goddesses
~2000-1550 BCE

Unknown Proveniences

These expressive impressions were created from cylinder seals discovered at unknown proveniences in Syro-Palestine.

The top right configuration depicts a Naked Goddess standing before a king and lifting her skirt* to convey generative life forces. Flanked by four goddesses, the king is depicted twice on this presentation scene (Collon 1987:167). Egyptian ankhs, a rosette, a monkey and a bird complete the imagery.

A Naked Generative Goddess stands above a birthing bovine on the bottom right composition. A god approaches before her; a second goddess stands behind her with a bird, a lion and smaller figures.

The left impression depicts a king presenting an ankh to a crowned goddess. Drawings after Collon 1987: 166 Fig. 776 (top right); Fig. 777 (bottom); 127 Fig. 543 (left).

*Misidentified on forgeries as if jumping rope (Collon 1987:167).

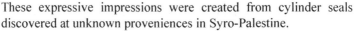

Naked Goddesses Personify Emanating Power

According to *Gods, Goddesses and Images of God In Ancient Israel,* "The nakedness of the goddess is indicative of her emanating power, on the basis of which she is sought out as one who can bring a blessing to those who worship her in private" (Keel 1998a:106).

264

Kings Before Goddesses
~2000-1550 BCE

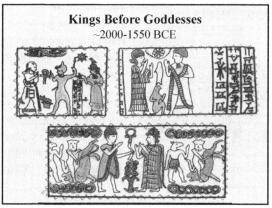

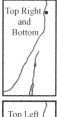

Top Right and Bottom

Top Left

A king stands before a goddess on seal impressions discovered at Minet el-Beida (top right and bottom) and Ebla (top left).

The top left impression pictures a king before a god and goddess (Collon 1987:128) with an ankh, a bull/bovine and the star of Inanna; a bird sits atop the goddess' crown.

Inanna's rosette star, a fish and a monkey are depicted in the top right configuration, while the bottom seal impression depicts a stylized tree of life, an ankh and composite animals.

Drawings after Collon 1987:49 Fig. 189 (top right); 127 Fig. 545 (top left); 54 Fig. 218 (bottom).

Gods and Kings Before Goddesses
~1700-1550 BCE

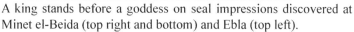

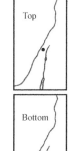

Top

Bottom

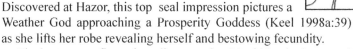

Discovered at Hazor, this top seal impression pictures a Weather God approaching a Prosperity Goddess (Keel 1998a:39) as she lifts her robe revealing herself and bestowing fecundity.

The bottom configuration, discovered at Megiddo, depicts a god (far right) approaching a Naked Goddess (Ibid.) with a robed king/worshipper standing between them.

Drawings after Keel 1998a:40: Fig. 31a (top); Fig. 30 (bottom).

Goddess Head Flanked by Uraeai
~1600 BCE

The head of the cow-eared, Egyptian goddess Hathor is pictured on this Tel Nagila configuration.

The goddess head is flanked by uraeai* (rearing cobras with dilated hoods), an ancient Egyptian symbol of royalty.

*The uraeai symbolism was emblematic of royalty and Egypt's cobra-goddess, Wadjyt/Uto, who symbolized Lower Egypt.

Drawing after Amiran 1967:45.

Pontifical

Goddess

Naked

Goddess

Pontifical Goddess
~1800-1550 BCE

A pontifical-style headdress crowns this naked female figurine discovered at Gezer (with 6 others).

One arm extends by her side while the other encircles a rounded abdomen suggestive of pregnancy. A semi-circular base allows for ease of positioning in the ground.

Drawing after Keel 1998a:34 Fig. 25a.

Pontifical

Goddess

Similar Historic Associations:
Pontifical Goddess

Seated upon a lion throne, the Syrian Mother Goddess Cybele wears a pontifical mitre and ceremonial vestments.
Drawing after Hall 1928.

Palestinian Plaques of Antiquity

Naked

Goddess

Beth Shemesh Naked Goddess ~1800-1550 BCE 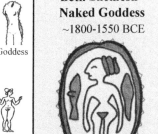	Discovered at Beth Shemesh, this seal impression depicts the Bronze Age Naked Goddess (Keel 1998a:27). Her hair is rolled in a circular, layered head covering. She is flanked by fish symbolizing the primordial holy water of creation. Her pubic triangle is accentuated. Drawing after Ibid. Fig. 10. 

Naked

Goddess

Similar Iconographic Associations:
Galilee Naked Goddesses
~100 BCE & 400CE

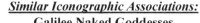

 Dating to the first century BCE, a life-size, naked statue of Aphrodite (top left), with an inscription bearing her name, was discovered at the Upper Galilee site of Omrit, where Herod had a temple built in honor of the Roman emperor Augustus.

Augustus considered himself to be a "Son of the Gods" and a direct descendent of the goddess Aphrodite's son (Overman 2003:45).

This Aphrodite figurine (at left) is one of several discovered north of the Sea of Galilee, at the mountain top village of Hippos-Sussita. Dating to the fourth century CE, it demonstrates "the cult of the goddess lingered on into the Christian period" (Shanks 2010:22).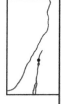

Drawings after: Overton 2003:45 (top); Shanks 2010:22 (bottom).

Naked Goddess Personifies Source of Life
The Naked Goddess personifies "the source of the power of life in plants and animals" (Keel 1998a:20), also identified as the Earth Goddess and Vegetative Prosperity Goddess.

APPENDIX B

Textual Asherah Evidence,
Biblical Emendations & Allusions

In ancient Israel and Judah, worship of the goddess Asherah was as integral a part of popular religion as "the worship of Yahweh."

Biblical Archaeology Review
(Hurowitz 2005:58)

B. Textual Asherah Evidence, Biblical Emendations & Allusions

This section lists primary Asherah textual references/inscriptions:

BCE Dates	Primary Asherah Textual References	page
~700	Arslan Tash Childbirth Prayer	229
~600-400	Grecian Rewriting of Babylonian Hymn	5
~549	Praised 4 times in Nabataean Holy Trinity	71
~539-332	Goddess Statue and Shrine Dedications to "Ashtorim/Asherah of the Sharon"	235
~538-522	Inscribed Throne Inscription "to Ashtoret/ Asherah/Astarte"	235
~530-522	Temple of Asherah Votive Offerings Presentation	235
~500	"Lady of Byblos" Offering by Yahwistic King	237
~400	Libation Vessels Ordered "for the Asherah and her Sanctuary"	239
~222	Temple Pillared Hall Dedication to "Astarte in the Asherah Sanctuary"	241

This section lists Asherah biblical emendations and recently acknowledged allusions:

Asherah Biblical Emendations:
Genesis 30:13
Deuteronomy 33:2-3
Isaiah 6:13
Jeremiah 2:27
Ezekiel 8:3
Hosea 14:8-9
Amos 8:14

Recently Acknowledged Additional Asherah Biblical Allusions:
Genesis 49:25	("Breasts and Womb")
2 Kings 18:4	(removal of Asherah poles and Nehushtan)
Proverbs 3:18	("Tree of Life")
Proverbs 8:22-31	(Wisdom as Asherah transfigured)
Isaiah 27:9	(Asherah poles)

This section lists archaeological Asherah artifacts experts attribute directly to the Israelites:

Israelite Referenced Archaeological Asherah Artifacts	page
~3200 BCE Asherah-image at Ai	4
~1220 BCE Lachish Vase & Goblet as Israel Emerging	41-45
~1000 BCE Arad 'Holy of Holies' & Lion	109,111
~1000 BCE Lachish 'Earliest Israelite Remains' an asherah?	109
~1000 BCE Rehov emerging as Israelite city	115
~1000 BCE Double-Throned Temple Shrine	131

EUROPEAN-STYLE BIBLIOGRAPHY

Aharoni, Yohanan (1967) "Arad: An Early Bronze Age City and a Biblical Fortress,"*Archaeological Discoveries in the Holy Land.* NY: Crowell, 94-99.

Ahlstrom, Gosta W. (1995) "Administration of the State in Canaan and Ancient Israel," Sasson, ed., *Civilizations of the Ancient Near East.* 587-603.

Albright, William F. (1918) "Historical and Mythical Elements in the Story of Joseph," *Journal of Biblical Literature.* 37/3-4:111-14.

_____ (1920) "The Goddess of Life and Wisdom," *The American Journal of Semitic Languages and Literatures.* 36/4:258-294.

_____(1944) "A Prince of Taanach in the Fifteenth Century B. C.," *Bulletin of the American Schools of Oriental Research.* 94:12-27.

_____ (1948) "The Early Alphabetic Inscriptions from Sinai and Their Decipherment," *Bulletin of the American Schools of Oriental Research.* 110:6-22.

_____ (1957) *From the Stone Age to Christianity: Monotheism and the Historical Process.* NY: Anchor.

_____ (1963) *The Biblical Period from Abraham to Ezra.* NY: Harper Row.

_____ (1969) *Archaeology and the Religion of Israel.* NY: Anchor.

Amiran, R. (1967) = R. A. - A. Eitan, "A Canaanite-Hyksos City at Tell Nagila," *Archaeological Discoveries in the Holy Land.* NY: Crowell, 41-48.

Arav, Rami (2000) = R. A. - R. Freund - John Shroder Jr., "Bethsaida Rediscovered," *Biblical Archaeology Review.* 26/1:44-56.

Armstrong, Karen (1996) "A God for Both Sexes," *The Economist.* 341/7997:65-70.

Avigad, Nahman (1990) "The Inscribed Pomegranate from the 'House of the Lord,'" *Biblical Archaeologist.* 53/3:157-166.

Avner, Uzi (2001) "Sacred Stones in the Desert," *Biblical Archaeology Review.* 27/3:30-41.

Bahn, Paul (1998) *The Cambridge Illustrated History Of Prehistoric Art.* NY: Cambridge University Press.

Bachofen, J. J. (1967) *Myth, Religion & Mother Right.* NJ: Princeton University Press.

Balter, Michael (2000) "Unearthing Monuments of The Yarmukians," *Science.* 287/5450:35.

Baring, A. (1991) = A. B. - J. Cashford, *The Myth of the Goddess: Evolution of an Image.* NY: Arkana Penguin.

Barnes, Craig S. (2006) *In Search of the Lost Feminine.* CO: Fulcrum.

Beck, Pirhiya (1994) "The Cult-Stands from Taanach: Aspects of the Iconographic Tradition of Early Iron Age Cult Objects in Palestine," Finkelstein - Na'aman, eds., *From Nomadism to Monarchy: Archaeological & Historical Aspects of Early Israel.* 352-381.

Becking, Bob (2001) = B. B. - Meindert Dijkstra - Marjo Korpel – Karel Vriezen, *Only One God? Monotheism in Ancient Israel and the Veneration of the Goddess Asherah.* NY: Sheffield Academic Press.

Ben-Ami, Doron (2006) "Mysterious Standing Stones, " *Biblical Archaeology Review.* 32/2:38-45.

Ben-Ari, Rafael (2009) "From an Ancient Art Gallery," *Discover.* J/A:8.

Ben-Tor, Ammon (1999) = A. B. - Maria T. Rubiato, "Excavating Hazor, Part Two," *Biblical Archaeology Review.* 25/3:22-39.

Berlin, Andrea (2005) = A. B. - Sharon Herbert, "Life and Death on the Israel-Lebanon Border: Excavation Yields Thousands of Seal Impressions," *Biblical Archaeology Review.* 31/5:34-43.

Berlinerblau, Jacques (2000) "Official Religion and Popular Religion in Pre-Exilic Ancient Israel," *The Bible and Interpretation.* <www.bible interp.com>

Biblical Archaeologist CD Archive (2005) DC: American Schools of Oriental Research.

Biblical Archaeology Review CD Archive (2005) DC: Biblical Archaeology Society.

Bierbrier, Morris L. (2001) "The Tomb of Pashedu," Weeks, ed., *Valley of the Kings.* 358-363.

Binger, Tilde (1997) *Asherah: Goddesses in Ugarit, Israel and the Old Testament.* NY: Sheffield Academic Press.

Blenkinsopp, Joseph (1995) "Ahab of Israel and Jehoshaphat of Judah: The Syro-Palestine Corridor in the Ninth Century," Sasson, ed., *Civilizations of the Ancient Near East.* 1309-1319.

Boardman, John (2000) *Persia And The West.* NY: Thames and Hudson.

Bogdanos, Matthew (2005) "Tracking Down the Looted Treasures of Iraq," *Biblical Archaeology Review.* 31/6:26-39.

Bonanno, Anthony (1990) *Malta: An Archaeological Paradise.* Malta: MJ.

Borowski, Oded (2005) "In the Path of Sennacherib," *Biblical Archaeology Review.* 31/3:24-35.

Boulanger, Robert (1965) *Egyptian and Near Eastern Painting.* NY: Funk and Wagnalls.

Bradshaw Foundation Online Learning Resource (1992) <www.bradshaw foundation.com>

Briffault, Robert (1963) *The Mothers: The Matriarchal Theory of Social Origins.* NY: Grosset and Dunlap.

Brock, Edwin C. (2001) "The Tomb of Rameses III," Weeks, ed., *Valley of the Kings.* 232-239.

Bryan, Betsy M. (2001) "Temples Of Millions of Years in Western Thebes," "The Temple of Hathshepsut," Weeks, ed., *Valley of the Kings.* 54-61, 66-75.

Budge, E. A. Wallis (1901) "Egyptian Magic," Hare, ed., *The Internet Sacred Text Archive DVD-ROM V. 6.* <www.sacred-texts.com>

_____ (1969) *The Gods of the Egyptians or Studies in Egyptian Mythology.* NY: Dover.

_____ (1973) *Osiris & The Egyptian Resurrection V. 1-II.* NY: Dover.

Burenhult, Goran, ed., (2003) *People of the Past: The Epic Story of Human Origins and Development.* CA: Fog City.

Buttrick, George A., ed., (1962) *The Interpreter's Dictionary of the Bible.* NY: Abingdon.

Buursma, Dirk R., ed., (1989) *The NIV TOPICAL Study Bible.* MI: Zondervan.

Cahill, Jane (2004) "Jerusalem in David and Solomon's Time," *Biblical Archaeology Review.* 30/6:20-31, 62-63.

Campbell, Edward F. Jr. (1998) "A Land Divided: Judah and Israel from the Death of Solomon to the Fall of Samaria," Coogan, ed., *The Oxford History of the Biblical World.* 273-319.

Campbell, Joseph (1949) *The Hero With A Thousand Faces.* NY: MJF.

_____ (1962) *The Masks of God: Oriental Mythology.* NY: Penguin.

_____ (1964) *The Masks of God: Occidental Mythology.* NY: Penguin.

_____ (1968) *The Masks of God: Creative Mythology.* NY: Penguin.

_____ (1969) *The Masks of God: Primitive Mythology.* NY: Penguin.

_____ (1974) *The Mythic Image.* NJ: Princeton University Press.

Camphausen, Rufus C. (1996) *The Yoni: Sacred Symbol of Female Creative Power.* VT: Inner Traditions.

Canby, J. V. (1986) *Ancient Anatolia.* University of Wisconsin Press.

Carus, Paul (1996) *The History of the Devil and the Idea of Evil.* NJ: Gramercy.

Caubet, Annie (1995) "Art and Architecture in Canaan and Ancient Israel," Sasson, ed., *Civilizations of the Ancient Near East.* 2671-2691.

Clotts, Jean (2001) "Chauvet Cave," *National Geographic.* 200/2:104-121.

Collon, Dominique (1987) *First Impressions Cylinder Seals in the Ancient Near East.* University of Chicago Press.

Coogan, Michael D. (1995) "10 Great Finds," *Biblical Archaeology Review.* 21/3:36-47.

_____ ed., (1998) "In the Beginning: The Earliest History," *The Oxford History of the Biblical World.* NY: Oxford University Press. 3-31.

Cornelius, Izak (1999) "No Other Gods: Emergent Monotheism in Israel (Review)," *Journal of the American Oriental Society.* 119/4:695.

Cornelius, Izak (2004) *The Many Faces of the Goddess: The Iconography of the Syro-Palestinian Goddesses Anat, Astarte, Qedeshet, and Asherah c. 1500-1000 BCE.* Fribourg: Academic Press.

Corrigan, Robert W., ed., (1967) *Euripides.* NY: Dell.

Cotterell, Arthur (1999) = A. C. - Rachel Storm, *The Ultimate Encyclopedia of Mythology.* NY: Hermes.

Cross, Frank Moore (1973) *Canaanite Myth and Hebrew Epic.* MA: Harvard University Press.

_____ (2005) "The History of Israelite Religion: A Secular or Theological Subject?" *Biblical Archaeological Review.* 31/3:42-45.

Curtis, Adrian (1985) *Ugarit (Ras Shamra).* MA: Lutterworth.

d' Alviella, Goblet (1894) "The Migration of Symbols," Hare, ed., *The Internet Sacred Text Archive DVD-ROM V. 6.* <www.sacred-texts.com>

Davidson, Hilda E. (1994) *The Lost Beliefs of Northern Europe.* NY: Routledge.

Davis-Kimball, Jeannine (2002) *Warrior Women: An Archaeologist's Search for History's Hidden Heroines.* NY: Warner.

Day, John (1986) "Asherah in the Hebrew Bible and Northwest Semitic Literature," *Journal of Biblical Literature.* 105/3:385-408.

Day, Peggy L. (1992) "Anat: Ugarit's 'Mistress of Animals,'" *Journal of Near Eastern Studies.* 51/3:181-190.

DeGrummond, Nancy (2001) "Cult of the Kiln," *Archaeology.* 54/1:60.

Demsky, Aaron (1998) "Discovering a Goddess," *Biblical Archaeology Review.* 24/5:53-58.

Deutsch, Robert (2002) "Lasting Impressions," *Biblical Archaeology Review.* 28/4:42-51, 60.

Dever, William G. (1982) "Recent Archaeological Confirmation of the Cult of Asherah in Ancient Israel," *Hebrew Studies.* 23:37-44.

_____ (1984) "Asherah, Consort of Yahweh? New Evidence from Kuntillet Ajrud," *Bulletin of the American Schools of Oriental Research.* 255:21-37.

_____ (1987) "Archaeological Sources for the History of Palestine in the Middle Bronze Age: The Zenith of the Urban Canaanite Era," *Biblical Archaeologist.* 50/3:148-177.

_____ (1995a) "Palaces and Temples in Canaan and Ancient Israel," Sasson, ed., *Civilizations of the Ancient Near East.* 605-614.

_____ (1995b) "Will the Real Israel Please Stand Up?" Part II: Archaeology and the Religions of Ancient Israel," *Bulletin of the American Schools of Oriental Research.* 298:37-58.

_____ (2001) *What Did the Biblical Writers Know and When Did They Know It? What Archaeology Can Tell Us about the Reality of Ancient Israel.* MI: Eerdmans.

Dever, William G. (2005) *Did God Have a Wife? Archaeology and Folk Religion in Ancient Israel.* MI: Eerdmans.

_____ (2008) "A Temple Built for Two: Did Yahweh Share a Throne with His Consort Asherah?" *Biblical Archaeology Review.* 34/2:54-62.

Dion, Paul E. (1995) "Aramaean Tribes and Nations of First-Millennium Western Asia," Sasson, ed., *Civilizations of the Ancient Near East.* 1281-1294.

Dostal, June (1990) *Teacher's Almanac 1990.* ME: Weston Walch.

Douglas, James D., ed., (1980) *The Illustrated Bible Dictionary.* IL: Tyndale.

duBois, Page (1988) *Sowing The Body: Psychoanalysis and Ancient Representations of Women.* University of Chicago Press.

Edwards, I. E. S. (1955) "A Relief of Qudshu-Astarte-Anat in the Winchester College Collection," *Journal of Near Eastern Studies.* 14:49-51.

Egyptian Designs. (1999) NY: Dover.

Encyclopedia Britannica. "Asherah." <www.britannica.com/eb/art-4304>

Epstein, Claire (1995) "Before History," *Biblical Archaeology Review.* 21/6: 62.

Evans, Arthur J. (1901) "Mycenaean Tree and Pillar Cult and Its Mediterranean Relations," *Journal of Hellenic Studies.* 21:99-204.

Fiema, Zbigniew T. (2003) "The Byzantine Church at Petra," Markoe, ed., *Petra Rediscovered: Lost City of the Nabataeans.* 238-249.

Finegan, Jack (1979) *Archaeological History of the Ancient Middle East.* NY: Barnes and Noble.

Finkelstein, Israel (1994) = I. F. - Nadav Na'aman, eds., *From Nomadism to Monarchy: Archaeological & Historical Aspects of Early Israel.* DC: Biblical Archaeology Society.

_____ (2001) = I. F. - N. Silberman, *The Bible Unearthed.* NY: Free Press.

Flammarion, C. (1888) "L'atmosphère: météorologie populaire (The Atmosphere: Popular Meteorology)," Hare, ed., *The Internet Sacred Text Archive DVD-ROM V. 6.* <www.sacred-texts.com>

Frankfort, H. (1939) *Cylinder Seals: A Documentary Essay on the Art and Religion of the Ancient Near East.* London: Gregg.

Frankfort, Henri (1996) *The Art and Architecture of the Ancient Orient.* CT: Yale University Press.

Freedman, David N. (1987) "Yahweh of Samaria and His Asherah," *Biblical Archaeologist.* 50/4:241-249.

_____ ed., (1992) *Anchor Bible Dictionary.* NY: Doubleday.

_____ (1999) *The Goddess in the Hebrew Bible.* DC: Biblical Archaeological Society. (vhs).

Freeman, Jill, ed., (1999) *Women of the Nile.* CA: AMORC.

Frothingham, A. L. (1911) "Medusa, Apollo, and the Great Mother," *American Journal of Archaeology.* 15/3:349-377.

Frymer-Kensky, Tikva (1992) *In the Wake of the Goddesses: Women Culture and the Culture, and the Biblical Transformation of Pagan Myth.* NY: Macmillan.

Gardiner, Sir Alan H. (1916) "The Egyptian Origin of the Semitic Alphabet," *Journal of Egyptian Archaeology.* 3:1-16.

Garfinkel, Yosef (1993) "The Yarmukian Culture in Israel," *Paleorient.* 19/1:115-134.

_____ (2000) = Y. G. - M. Miller, "The Yarwhosians," *Archaeology Odyssey.* 3/3:24.

_____ (2002) "Prize Find," *Biblical Archaeology Review.* 28/1: 29.

Gimbutas, Marija (1982) *The Goddesses and Gods of Old Europe.* University of California Press.

_____ (1989) *The Language of the Goddess.* CA: Harper.

Gitin, Seymour (2005) "Excavating Ekron," *Biblical Archaeology Review.* 31/6:40-56.

Gore, Rick (2001) "Ashkelon: Ancient City of the Sea," *National Geographic.* 199/1:66-90.

Graves, Robert (1990) *The White Goddess.* MA: Faber and Faber.

Green, Anthony (1995) "Ancient Mesopotamian Religious Iconography," Sasson, ed., *Civilizations of the Ancient Near East.* 1837-1855.

Green, Miranda (1996) *Celtic Goddesses.* NY: Braziller.

Greenstein, Edward L. (2010) "Texts from Ugarit Solve Biblical Puzzles," *Biblical Archaeology Review.* 36/6:48-53.

Hackett, Jo Ann (1998) " 'There Was No King in Israel': The Era of the Judges," Coogan, ed., *The Oxford History of the Biblical World.* 177-218.

Hadley, Judith M. (2000) *The Cult of Asherah in Ancient Israel and Judah: Evidence for a Hebrew Goddess.* NY: Cambridge University Press.

Hall, Manly P. (1928) "The Secret Teaching of All Ages: An Encyclopedic Outline of Masonic, Hermetic, Qabbalistic and Rosicrucian Symbolical Philosophy," Hare, ed., *The Internet Sacred Text Archive DVD-ROM V. 6.* <www.sacred-texts.com>

Hammond, Philip C. (2003) "The Temple of the Winged Lions," Markoe, ed., *Petra Rediscovered: Lost City of the Nabataeans.* 223-237.

Hansen, Donald P. (1962) = D. P. H. - George F. Dales, "The Temple of Inanna Queen of Heaven At Nippur," *Archaeology.* 15/2:75-84.

Hare, J. B., ed., (2006) *The Internet Sacred Text Archive DVD-ROM V. 6.* <www.sacred-texts.com>

Harley, Timothy (1885) "Moon Lore," Hare, ed., *The Internet Sacred Text Archive DVD-ROM V. 6.* <www.sacred-texts.com>

Harmon, N. B., ed., (1954) *The Interpreter's Bible.* NY: Abingdon.

Harrison, Timothy P. (2002) "Rabbath of the Ammonites," *Archaeology Odyssey.* 5/2:12-17.

Harvey, Stephen P. (2001) "Tribute to a Conquering King," *Archaeology.* 54/4:52-55.

Harwood, William (1992) *Mythology's Last Gods: Yahweh and Jesus.* NY: Prometheus.

Hawkes, Jacquette (1968) *Dawn of the Gods: Minoan and Mycenaean Origins of Greece.* NY: Random House.

Hentum, Bengt (1999) *Echoscopy CD-ROM.* Mellerud, Sweden. <www. catshaman.com>

Hestrin, Ruth (1987) "The Lachish Ewer and the Asherah," *Israel Exploration Journal.* 37:212-223.

_____ (1991) "Understanding Asherah: Exploring Semitic Iconography," *Biblical Archaeology Review.* 17/5:50-59.

HHF/Hebrew History Federation (2005) "Jews in Africa Part I – The Berbers and the Jews." <www.hebrewhistory.info/factpapers/ fp0191_ africa.htm>

Hill, George F. (1910) *Catalogue of the Greek Coins of Phoenicia.* UK: Horace Hart.

Hitchcock, Don (2005) "The Galenberg Venus - Fanny," *Venus Figures from Western Europe.* <www.donsmaps.com >

Hodder, Ian (2004) "Women and Men at Catalhoyuk," *Scientific American* 290/1:76-83.

Hollis F. J. (1952) "Philistine and Hebrew in the Land of Promise," *The Story of the Bible Told by Living Writers of Authority.* NY: Wise, 367-377.

Hornblower, Simon (1998) = S. H. - A. Spawforth, eds., (1998) *The Oxford Companion to Classical Civilization.* NY: Oxford University Press.

Hornung, Erik (1995) "Ancient Egyptian Religious Iconography," Sasson, ed., *Civilizations of the Ancient Near East.* 1711-1730.

_____ (2001) "The Tomb of Thutmosis III; The Tomb of Amenhotep II," Weeks, ed., *Valley of the Kings.* 136-145.

Horsley, Carter B. (2001) "The Surena Collection of Ancient Near Eastern Cylinder Seals," *The City Review.* <www.thecityreview.com>

Hurowitz, Victor A. (1994) "Did King Solomon Violate the Second Commandment?" *Bible Review.* 10/5:24-33, 57.

_____ (2005) "Idols of the People: Miniature Images of Clay in the Ancient Near East (Review)," *Biblical Archaeology Review.* 31/1:58-59.

Husain, Shahrukh (1997) *The Goddesses.* NY: Little, Brown.

Iakovidis, S. E. (2002) *Mycenae-Epidaurus-Argos-Tiryns-Nauplion.* Athens: Ekdotike Athenon.

Jacobs, Paul (2001) "Reading Religious Artifacts: The Shrine Room at Judahite Tell Halif," *Journal of Biblical Studies.* <www.journal ofbiblical studies.org>

James, E. O. (1994) *The Cult of the Mother-Goddess.* NY:Barnes and Noble.

James, Simon (1998) = S. J. - Anne Pearson - Jonathan N. Tubb, eds., *Ancient Civilizations.* London: Dorling Kindersley.

Johnston, Sarah I. (2004) *Religions of the Ancient World.* MA: Harvard University Press.

Kantor, Helen J. (1962) "A Bronze Plaque with Relief Decoration from Tell Tainat," *Journal of Near Eastern Studies.* 21:93-117.

Kee, Howard C. (1997) = H. C. K - E. M. Meyers - J. Rogerson - J. Anthony, *The Cambridge Companion to the Bible.* NY: Cambridge University Press.

Keel, Othmar (1978) *The Symbolism of the Biblical World: Ancient Near Eastern Iconography and the Book of Psalms.* NY: Seabury.

_____ (1998a) = O. K. - Christoph Uehlinger, *Gods, Goddesses and Images of God in Ancient Israel.* MN: Fortress.

_____ (1998b) *Goddesses and Trees, New Moon and Yahweh: Ancient Near Eastern Art and the Hebrew Bible.* London: Sheffield Academic Press.

_____ (2007) "Elite vs. Popular Religion," *Biblical Archaeology Review.* 33/3:10.

Kent, Arthur (Narrator) (2001) *Digging for the Truth: Archaeology and the Bible.* CA: MPH Entertainment for the History Channel. (dvd).

Kenyon, Kathleen (1957) *Digging Up Jericho.* NY: Praeger.

_____ (1960) *Archaeology in the Holy Land.* NY: Praeger.

_____ (1967) *Jerusalem: Excavating 3000 Years of History.* NY: McGraw.

Kikawada, Isaac M. (1972) "Two Notes on Eve," *Journal of Biblical Literature.* 91/1:33-37.

King, Philip J. (1989) "The Great Eighth Century," *Bible Review.* 5/4:22-44.

Kofou, Anna (2000) *Crete.* Athens: Ekdotike Athenon.

Kramer, Samuel N. (1981) *History Begins at Sumer: Thirty-Nine Firsts in Recorded History.* University of Pennsylvania Press.

Langdon, Stephen Herbert (1964) *Mythology of All Races-Semitic, V.5.* NY: Cooper Square.

Lapp, Paul (1967) "The Cemetery at Beb-edh-Dhara' Jordan," *Archaeological Discoveries in the Holy Land.* 35-40.

Leith, Mary Joan Winn (2006) "How a People Forms," *Biblical Archaeology Review.* 32/3:22-23.

Lemaire, Andre (1984a) "Probable Head of Priestly Scepter from Solomon's Temple Surfaces in Jerusalem," *Biblical Archaeology Review.* 10/1:24-29.

Lemaire, Andre (1984b) "Who or What Was Yahweh's Asherah?" *Biblical Archaeology Review.* 10/6:42-51.

_____ (2004) "Another Temple to the Israelite God," *Biblical Archaeology Review.* 30/4:38-44, 60.

Lemche, Niels Peter (1995) "The History of Ancient Syria and Palestine: An Overview," Sasson, ed., *Civilizations of the Ancient Near East.* 1195-1218.

Lewis, Theodore J. (1996) "The Disappearance of the Goddess Anat: The 1995 West Semitic Research Project on Ugaritic Epigraphy," *Biblical Archaeologist.* 59/2:115-119.

_____ (1998) "Divine Images and Aniconism in Ancient Israel," *Journal of the American Oriental Society.* 118/1:36-54.

Lipinski, Edward (1986) "The Syro-Palestinian Iconography of Woman and Goddess," (Review) *Israel Exploration Journal.* 36:87-96.

Lloyd, Seton (1961) *The Art of the Ancient Near East.* NY: Praeger.

Lockyer, Norman (1906) "Stonehenge and Other British Stone Monuments Astronomically Considered," Hare, ed., *The Internet Sacred Text Archive DVD-ROM V. 6.* <www.sacred-texts.com>

Louÿs, Pierre (1864) "The Songs of Bilitis," Hare, ed., *The Internet Sacred Text Archive DVD-ROM V. 6.* <www.sacred-texts.com>

Mackenzie, Donald A. (1915) "Myths of Babylonia & Assyria," Hare, ed., *Internet Sacred Text Archive DVD-ROM V. 6.* <www.sacred-texts. com>

_____ (1917) "Myths of Crete & Pre-Hellenic Europe," Hare, ed., *The Internet Sacred Text Archive DVD-ROM V. 6.* <www.sacred-texts.com>

Maidman, Maynard (1995) "Nuzi: Portrait of an Ancient Mesopotamian Provincial Town," Sasson, ed., *Civilizations of the Ancient Near East.* 931-947.

Markoe, Glenn, ed., (2003) *Petra Rediscovered: Lost City of the Nabataeans.* NY: Abrams.

Matthews, Caitlin (1992) *Sophia Goddess of Wisdom.* NY: Aquarian.

May, Herbert G. (1939) "The Sacred Tree on Palestine Painted Pottery," *Journal of the American Oriental Society.* 59/2:251-259.

_____ ed., (1984) *Oxford Bible Atlas.* NY: Oxford Press.

Mazar, Amihai (1990) *Archaeology of the Land of the Bible.* NY: Doubleday.

_____ (1998) "The Goddess of Rehov," *Biblical Archaeology Review.* 24/1:48.

_____ (2000) = A. M. - John Camp, "Will Tel Rehov Save the United Monarchy?" *Biblical Archaeology Review.* 26/2:2, 38-51.

McCarter, P. Kyle, Jr. (1992) "The Origins of Israelite Religion," Shanks et al., *The Rise of Ancient Israel.* 121-141.

McKenzie, Judith S. (2003) "Carvings in the Desert: The Sculpture of Petra and Khirbet et-Tannur," Markoe, ed., *Petra Discovered*. 165-193.

Mead, G. R. S. (1955) *Pistis Sophia*. London: Watkins.

Meador, Betty DeShong (2000*) Inanna Lady of Largest Heart: Poems of the Sumerian High Priestess Enheduanna*. University of Texas Press.

Mellart, James (1967) *Catal Huyuk: A Neolithic Town in Anatolia*. NY: McGraw Hill.

Meshel, Ze' ev (1979) "Did Yahweh Have a Consort? The New Religious Inscriptions from the Sinai," *Biblical Archaeology Review*. 5/2: 24-35.

_____ (1993) "Teman, Horvat," Stern, ed., *New Encyclopedia of Archaeological Excavations in the Holy Land, V. 4*. 1458-64.

Miller, Max (1997) "Ancient Moab," *Biblical Archaeologist*. 60/4:194-204.

Minkel, J. R. (2006) "Offerings to a Stone Snake Provide the Earliest Evidence of Religion," *Scientific America*. 12/1. <www.sciam.com>

Moorey, P. R. S. (1991) *The Biblical Lands*. NY: Bedrick.

Morris, Neil (2000) *The Atlas of Ancient Egypt*. NY: Bedrick.

Moshe, Dothan (1967) "Ashdod: A City of the Philistine Pentapolis," *Archaeological Discoveries in the Holy Land*. NY: Crowell, 129-137.

Muhly, James D. (2005) "Mycenaeans Were There Before the Israelites: Excavating the Dan Tomb," *Biblical Archaeology Review*. 31/5:44-51.

Muilenburg, James (1954) "The Meaning and Significance of the Old Testament: The History of the Religion of Israel," Harmon, ed., *The Interpreter's Bible, V. 1*. 292-348.

Nakhai, Beth A. (1994) "What's A Bamah?" *Biblical Archaeology Review*. 20/3:18-29.

Negev, Avraham (2001) = A. N. - Shimon Gibson, eds., *Archaeological Encyclopedia of the Holy Land*. NY: Continuum.

Neumann, Erich (1963) *The Great Mother: An Analysis of the Archetype*. NJ: Princeton University Press.

Oden, R. A. Jr. (1976) "The Persistence of Canaanite Religion," *Biblical Archaeologist*. 39/1:31-36.

Ogden, Jack (1992) *Interpreting The Past: Ancient Jewelry*. University of California Press.

Olyan, Saul M. (1988) *Asherah and the Cult of Yahweh in Israel*. GA: Scholars Press.

Overton, J. Andrew (2003) = J. A. O. - Jack Olive - Michael Nelson, "Discovering Herod's Shrine to Augustus," *Biblical Archaeology Review*. 29/ 2:40-49, 67.

Ozment, Katherine (1999) "Journey To The Copper Age," *National Geographic*. 195/4:74.

Packer, J. I. (1980) = J. I. P. - M. C. Tenney - W. White, *Nelson's Illustrated Encyclopedia of Bible Facts*. GA: Thomas Nelson.

Parpola, Simo (1999) "Sons of God: The Ideology of Assyrian Kingship," *Archaeology Odyssey*. 2/05:16-27, 61.

Patai, Raphael (1990*)* *The Hebrew Goddess*. MI: Wayne State University Press.

Pettey, Richard J. (1990) *Asherah: Goddess of Israel*. NY: Lang Publishing.

Perrot, Jean (1967) "The Dawn of History in Southern Palestine," *Archaeological Discoveries in the Holy Land*. NY: Crowell, 2-8.

Pritchard, James B. (1943) *Palestinian Figurines in Relation to Certain Goddesses Known Through Literature*. NY: Periodicals Service.

_____ ed., (1954) *The Ancient Near East in Pictures Relating to the Old Testament*. NJ: Princeton University Press.

_____ ed., (1969) *Ancient Near Eastern Texts Relating to the Old Testament*. NJ: Princeton University Press.

_____ ed., (1973) *The Ancient Near East: A New Anthology of Texts and Pictures, V. I.* NJ: Princeton University Press.

_____ ed., (1975) *The Ancient Near East: A New Anthology of Texts and Pictures, V. II.* NJ: Princeton University Press.

Putman, John (1988) "The Search For Modern Humans," *National Geographic*. 174/4:438-477.

Quennell, C. & M. (1959) *Everyday Life In Prehistoric Times*. NY: Putnam.

Rahner, Karl, ed., (1975) *Encyclopedia of Theology: The Concise Sacramentum Mundi*. NY: Seabury.

Raphael, Max (1998) "Objets d'Art," Bahn, ed., *The Cambridge Illustrated History Of Prehistoric Art*. 83.

Reade, Julian (1991) *Mesopotamia*. MA: Harvard University Press.

Reed, William L. (1949) *The Asherah in the Old Testament*. Texas Christian University Press.

Rethemiotakis, George (2001) *Minoan Clay Figures and Figurines*. Athens: Archaeological Society.

Rhys-Davies, John (Narrator) (1993) *The Forbidden Goddess*. Films for the Humanities and Sciences. NJ: Princeton. (vhs).

Rochman, Bonnie (1997) "On Exhibit: The First Artists," *Biblical Archaeology Review*. 23/5:23.

Rollefson, Gary O. (1998) "Invoking the Spirit: Prehistoric Religion at 'Ain Ghazal," *Archaeology Odyssey*. 1/1:54-59.

_____ (2003) "'Ain Ghazal: The Largest Known Neolithic Site," Burenhult, ed., *People of the Past: The Epic Story of Human Origins and Development*. 248-249.

Sasson, Jack, ed., (1995) *Civilizations of the Ancient Near East*. NY: Scribner.

Scham, Sandra (2005) "The Lost Goddess of Israel," *Archaeology*. 58/2:36-40.

_____ (2008) "The World's First Temple," *Archaeology*. 61/6:22-27.

Schmandt-Besserat, Denise (1998) "'Ain Ghazal Monumental Figures: A Statistical Analysis," *Bulletin of the American Schools of Oriental Research.* 310:1-17.

Shanks, Hershel (1988) "Pomegranate: Sole Relic from Solomon's Temple, Smuggled Out of Israel, Now Recovered," *Biblical Archaeology Review.* 13:36-43.

_____ (1992) "The Pomegranate Scepter Head – From the Temple of the Lord or from a Temple of Asherah?" *Biblical Archaeology Review.* 18/3:42-45.

_____ et al., (1992) = H. S. - William G. Dever - Baruch Halpern - P. Kyle McCarter Jr., *The Rise of Ancient Israel.* DC: Biblical Archaeology Society.

_____ (1995) "Scholars Speak Out," *Biblical Archaeology Review.* 21/3:24-35.

_____ (1999) "Worldwide," *Biblical Archeology Review.* 25/3:64.

_____ (2005a) "Scholars Fear to Publish Ancient House Shrine," *Biblical Archaeology Review.* 31/6:20-25.

_____ (2005b) "Update: Finds or Fakes? Ivory Pomegranate," *Biblical Archaeology Review.* 31/2:62-63.

_____ (2010) "Aphrodite Uncovered in Christian City," *Biblical Archeology Review.* 36/1:22.

Shaw, Jonathan (2003) "Who Built the Pyramids?" *Harvard Magazine.* 105/6. <http://harvardmagazine.com/2003/07>

Shearer, Ann (1996) *Athene: Image and Energy.* NY: Arkana.

Sheler, Jeffery L. (1995) "Mysteries of the Bible," *U.S. News & World Report.* 118/15:60-68.

Shone, Russell, ed., (2007) *Archaeological Reports for 2006-2007.* Athens: Council of the Society for the Promotion of Hellenic Studies.

Shepsut, Asia (1993) *Journey of the Priestess.* London: Aquarian.

Smith, Mark (1990) *The Early History of God: Yahweh and the Other Deities in Ancient Israel.* CA: Harper.

_____ (1995) "Myth and Mythmaking in Canaan and Ancient Israel," Sasson, ed., *Civilizations of the Ancient Near East.* 2031-2041.

_____ (2001) "The Origins of Biblical Monotheism: Israel's Polytheistic Background and the Ugaritic Texts," *The Bible and Interpretation.* <www.bibleinterp.com >

Soren, David (2000) "Carthage Must Be Destroyed," *Archaeology Odyssey.* 3/6:16-27.

Spycket, Agnes (2000) *The Human Form Divine.* Jerusalem: Bible Lands Museum.

Stager, Lawrence E. (1998) "Forging an Identity: The Emergence of Ancient Israel," Coogan, ed., *The Oxford History of the Biblical World.* 123-175.

Starr, Chester G. (1961) *The Origins of Greek Civilization 1100-650 B.C.* NY: Knopf.

Stern, Ephraim (1989) "What Happened to the Cult Figurines? Israelite Religion Purified After the Exile," *Biblical Archaeological Review.* 15/04:22-29.

_____ ed., (1993) *New Encyclopedia of Archaeological Excavations in the Holy Land.* NY: Carta.

_____ (1995) "Priestly Blessing of a Voyage," *Biblical Archaeology Review.* 21/1:50-55.

_____ (2001a) *Archaeology of the Land of the Bible V. II.* NY: Doubleday.

_____ (2001b) "Pagan Yahwehism: The Folk Religion of Ancient Israel," *Biblical Archaeology Review.* 27/3:21-29.

Stewart, James (1952) "The Promised Land as It Was in the Days of Joshua," *The Story of the Bible, V. I.* NY: Wise, 251-279.

Strong, Herbert A. (1913) = H. A. S. - John Garstang, "The Syrian Goddess" (translation of Lucian's "De Dea Syria"), Hare, ed., *The Internet Sacred Text Archive DVD-ROM V. 6.* <www.sacred-texts.com>

Tappy, Ron E. (2003) "Recent Interpretations of Ancient Israelite Religion," *Journal of the American Oriental Society.* 123/1:159-168.

Taylor, J. Glen (1994) "Was Yahweh Worshiped as the Sun?" *Biblical Archaeology Review.* 20/3:52-61, 90-91.

Taylor, Joan E. (1995) "The Asherah, The Menorah and The Sacred Tree," *Journal for the Study of the Old Testament.* 66:29-54.

Taylor, Thomas (1891) "The Eleusinian and Bacchic Mysteries," Hare, ed., *The Internet Sacred Text Archive DVD-ROM V.6.* <www.sacred-texts.com>

Taylour, Wm. (1983) *The Mycenaeans.* London: Thames and Hudson.

The Biblical World in Pictures CD Archive. (2002) DC: Biblical Archaeology Society.

The Comprehensive Bible Containing the Old and New Testaments According to The Authorized Version. (1866) PA: J. B. Lippincott.

Thompson, Thomas L. (1999) *The Mythic Past: Biblical Archaeology and the Myth of Israel.* NY: Basic.

Tubb, J. N. (1998) *Canaanites.* London: British Museum Press.

Urrutia, Benjamin (1973) "About El, Asherah, Yahweh and Anath," *American Anthropologist.* 75/4:1180-1181.

Van Der Woude, A. S., ed., (1986) *The World of the Bible: Bible Handbook, V. I.* MI: Eerdmans.

Vasilakis, Andonia (2002) *Herakleion Archaeological Museum.* Athens: Adam Editions.

Vassilakis, Antonis (1995) *Knossos: Mythology-History-Guide to Archaeological Site.* Athens: Adam Editions.

Waite, Arthur E. (1910) "Pictorial Key to the Tarot," Hare, ed., *The Internet Sacred Text Archive DVD-ROM V. 6.* <www.sacred-texts.com>

Walker, Barbara G. (1983) *The Woman's Encyclopedia of Myths and Secrets.* CA: Harper.

_____ (1988) *The Woman's Dictionary of Symbols & Sacred Objects.* NY: HarperCollins.

Walls, N. H. (1992) *The Goddess Anat in Ugaritic Myth.* GA: Scholars Press.

Watzman, Haim (2000) "Phoenician Resilience," *Archaeology.* 53/6:27.

Weeks, Kent R. (2001) *Valley of the Kings.* NY: Friedman.

Weinfeld, Moshe (1996) "Feminine Features in The Imagery of God in Israel: The Sacred Marriage and The Sacred Tree," *Vetus Testamentum.* 46/4:515-529.

Whitt, William D. (1992) "The Divorce of Yahweh and Asherah in Hos 2,4-7.12 FF," *Scandinavian Journal of the Old Testament.* 6/1:31-67.

_____ (1995) "The Story of the Semitic Alphabet," Sasson, ed., *Civilizations of the Ancient Near East.* 2379-2397.

Wiggermann, F. A. M. (1995) "Theologies, Priests, and Worship in Ancient Mesopotamia," Sasson, ed., *Civilizations of the Ancient Near East.* 1857-1870.

Willet, Elizabeth (2000) "Women and Israelite House Religion," *The Bible and Interpretation.* <www.bibleinterp.com>

Willis, Roy (1993) *World Mythology.* NY: Holt.

Witt, R. E. (1971) *Isis in the Ancient World.* MD: John Hopkins University Press.

Wolkstein, Diane (1983) = D. W. - Samuel N. Kramer, *Inanna, Queen of Heaven and Earth: Her Stories and Hymns from Sumer.* NY: Harper Row.

Woolley, Leonard (1961) *The Art of the Middle East.* NY: Crown.

Wunderlich, Hans G. (2002) *The Secret of Crete.* Athens: Efstathiadis.

Yadin, Yigael (1967) "The Rise and Fall of Hazor," *Archaeological Discoveries in the Holy Land.* NY: Crowell, 56-66.

Yarden, L. (1971) *A Study of the Menorah.* NY: Cornell University.

Younger, K. Lawson Jr. (2003) "Israelites in Exile," *Biblical Archaeology Review.* 29/6:36-42.

Zehren, Erich (1962) *The Crescent And The Bull.* NY: Hawthorn.

Zertal, Adam (2002) "Philistine Kin Found in Early Israel," *Biblical Archaeology Review.* 28/3:18-31, 60-61.

Zevit, Ziony (2001) *The Religions of Ancient Israel: A Synthesis of Parallactic Approaches.* NY: Continuum.

Zivie, Alan (2002) "A Pharaoh's Peacemaker," *National Geographic.* 202/4:26-31.

Index

Index

Index

Index

Index

Index

Made in United States
North Haven, CT
31 January 2024

48137274R00173